CW01249930

Children, Research and Policy

Children, Research and Policy

Edited by

**Basil Bernstein
and
Julia Brannen**

Taylor & Francis
Publishers since 1798

UK	Taylor & Francis Ltd, 1 Gunpowder Square, London EC4A 3DE
USA	Taylor & Francis Inc., 1900 Frost Road, Suite 101, Bristol, PA 19007

© Selection and editorial material
Copyright Basil Bernstein and Julia Brannen, 1996

All rights reserved. No part of this publication may be reproduced, stored in a retrieval system, or transmitted, in any form or by any means, electronic, mechanical, photocopying, recording, or otherwise, without permission in writing from the Publisher.

First published 1996

A Catalogue Record for this book is available from the British Library

ISBN 0 7484 0405 8
ISBN 0 7484 0406 6 pbk

Library of Congress Cataloging-in-Publication Data are available on request

Typeset in 10/12pt Times
by Best-set Typesetter Ltd, Hong Kong.

Printed in Great Britain by SRP Ltd, Exeter.

Essays for Barbara Tizard

Contents

Acknowledgments		ix
Introduction Basil Bernstein and Julia Brannen		1
Interview with Barbara Tizard Basil Bernstein and Julia Brannen		9
PART I	**RESEARCH**	27
Chapter 1	Specificity of Brain-Behavioural Relationships Revisited: From Epileptic Personality to Behavioural Phenotypes Michael Rutter and William Yule	29
Chapter 2	Varied Destinies: A Study of Unfulfilled Predictions Alan Clarke and Ann Clarke	47
Chapter 3	The Natural History of Early Non-attachment Jill Hodges	63
Chapter 4	Family Conversations and the Development of Social Understanding Judy Dunn	81
Chapter 5	Parents, Teachers and Schools Martin Hughes	96
Chapter 6	From Miscegenation to Hybridity: Mixed Relationships and Mixed-parentage in Profile Ann Phoenix and Charlie Owen	111
Chapter 7	Young Children at School: Inequalities and the National Curriculum Ian Plewis	136
PART II	**RESEARCH AND POLICY**	149
Chapter 8	Staffing Innovations in City Technology Colleges: Policy into Practice Jo Mortimore and Peter Mortimore	151

Contents

Chapter 9	The Thirty Year Contribution of Research in Child Mental Health to Clinical Practice and Public Policy in the UK *Philip Graham*	169
Chapter 10	The Socio-Legal Support for Divorcing Parents and their Children *Martin Richards*	185
Chapter 11	The Institute of Public Policy Research: A Case Study of a Think Tank *Tessa Blackstone*	207
Chapter 12	School-age Childcare and the School: Recent European Developments *Pat Petrie*	220
Chapter 13	Early Childhood Services in Europe: Qualities and Quality *Peter Moss*	242

List of Contributors   261

Index   264

Acknowledgments

We would like to record our gratitude to Maria Harrison, Administrative Secretary (and Barbara Tizard's ex-secretary) of the Thomas Coram Research Unit, who was responsible for the production of the manuscript. Its form underwent a number of revisions and we would like to acknowledge here both the time which Maria gave so generously and her many suggestions.

Introduction

Barbara Tizard retired from her chair and Directorship of the Thomas Coram Research Unit in 1990, but continued with her contract research until 1995. It is now fitting that her contribution to research and policy be celebrated and honoured. Barbara Tizard's research focused on the ways in which children were disadvantaged: educationally, emotionally and racially. Her research led to a reform of institutional care, to a revision of teachers' notions of the competence of children, to a disturbance of the orthodoxies of the placement of children, and created greater understanding of the complexities of the identities of children of mixed parentage. Barbara Tizard's engagement in research stemmed from a passionate but disciplined concern to provide a sounder basis for judgments, decisions, practice and agencies as these shaped children's lives and their development, often for the worse.

Barbara Tizard rarely engaged in theoretical debates of 'ivory-towered psychology'. To her the discipline was essentially a means of diagnosing social pathologies and providing a rational basis for their removal. From this perspective Barbara Tizard often found herself in conflict with dogmatic orthodoxies held either by practitioners or researchers. Indeed, it would be possible to plot her career in terms of the disturbances created by her research for both of these groups. To disturb is an important consequence of research; to point the way to more effective practice is equally and perhaps a more important consequence. Barbara Tizard accomplished both.

The editors were faced with the problem of who to invite to contribute to this volume and their decision no doubt has led to many undeserving absences. It is also possible that the decision has unduly narrowed the range of Barbara Tizard's overall contribution. For example, we do not have papers discussing Barbara Tizard's contribution to the development, influence and management of the Thomas Coram Research Unit, the largest multidisciplinary research unit in any University Department of Education. Nor is there an assessment of her work by practitioners in the social services or education. All the papers are written by authors from within the UK, although it would certainly have been possible to draw upon the international research field.

We planned to group chapters under two broad headings: Part I Research and Part II Policy. But as will be seen, most of the chapters in Part I raise issues of policy, and those in Part II often depend upon research. However, the orientation of the chapters in Parts I and II are clearly different and make different demands on the reader. We decided to restrict contributions to individuals who were, at different times, closely associated with Barbara Tizard throughout her research career. We thought, and we hope appropriately, that it would be relevant to celebrate her career with a series of chapters which sequentially followed her research interests and which had their origin in these interests and influences. In this way the order of presentation of the chapters in Part I matches the developments of Barbara Tizard's own research. In Part II the chapters address general issues of policy arising out of Part I.

Part I Research

Our decision to invite papers which marked the different projects in Barbara Tizard's research career and to present these papers here in the same temporal order shows the reader the pioneering nature of the different projects and their influence on later research. However, following the temporal sequence of Barbara Tizard's research projects in the chapters which form Part I creates problems in its own right. There is the danger of creating the impression that the disparate research concerns have no underlying unity or motivation. Certainly, Barbara Tizard's various researches were very much a response to critical issues of practice, a desire to expose the shortcomings of practice and to show how they could be improved. In this sense the research was often prompted by contemporary problems. However, we believe that the apparently disparate projects are integrated and motivated by a common and powerful concern to understand the origins and consequences of various forms of fractured relations which sadly mark the experience of children and to find ways of changing the painful and damaging conditions which blight the lives of some children.

The chapters we now briefly present, despite the abstract nature of some and their common concern with rational procedures, share Barbara Tizard's fundamental concern.

The first two chapters of Part I, those by Rutter and Yule, and Alan and Ann Clarke, arise out of the authors' association with Barbara Tizard during her period at the Institute of Psychiatry (see 'Interview'). The starting point of Rutter and Yule's chapter is research by Barbara Tizard conducted in the early 1960s in which she challenged the concept of the 'epileptic personality'. Rutter and Yule discuss, with some cautions, contemporary advances in the linkage of behaviour patterns to brain disfunctions in children. They consider that effective research in this area will now require collaboration and integration between a range of disciplines, a growing requirement in other areas of research. The Clarkes' paper draws attention to the problem of predictability in developmental studies of children. The Clarkes review research in a range of different areas which include personality development, early attachment, the effects of sexual abuse and intelligence. The Clarkes consider that 'devel-

Introduction

opment is *potentially somewhat open-ended*' and 'probabilities are not certainties and deflection for good or ill are possible but always within the limits imposed by genetic institutional and social trajectories'.

Jill Hodges discusses the developmental consequences of early non-attachment in children: research pioneered by Barbara Tizard during the early and late 1970s. On the basis of a follow-up study of contrasting groups of children, Hodges considers there is some evidence that, irrespective of early institutionalization, the nature of the attachment of the child to the mother may, under specific conditions, have consequences for the child's peer-group relations at sixteen years of age. Jill Hodges' chapter shows the importance of closely monitored longitudinal studies of the effects of contrasting contexts on the attachment relations of children.

Earlier in 1984 Barbara Tizard with Martin Hughes published *Young Children Learning* which was an intensive study comparing child-mother talk in the home with child-teacher talk in the pre-school. Judy Dunn develops key issues raised by this pioneering research: the nature of young children's understandings and familial talk as contexts for learning. Understandings of children and familial learning contexts were the focus of three longitudinal studies of children carried out by Judy Dunn in the UK and the USA. Perhaps a crucial finding of this research is that 'the same child frequently showed very different forms of social understanding within her or his different relationship'. This highlights the selective effect of context, interaction and emotional involvement on the child's sociocognitive understanding and relationships.

With Martin Hughes we follow up Barbara Tizard's research in the late 1970s and early 1980s into parents' involvement in their children's pre-school education. This was action-based research requiring teachers to design activities involving parents. Martin Hughes reports his own research (following the Education Reform Act 1988) into the relations between parents and schools. His findings are similar to those of Barbara Tizard some ten to fifteen years earlier: teachers' involvement in their own professionalism often prevented them from recognizing what parents had to offer.

We come to the last period of Barbara Tizard's research: into issues of race, inequality and identity. The chapters by Ian Plewis, and by Ann Phoenix and Charlie Owen, address questions of inequality of achievement and mixed parentage and identity. Ian Plewis' research developed out of the findings (Tizard *et al.*, 1988) that African–Caribbean boys were doing much less well during infant years than African–Caribbean girls and also less well than the two white contrast groups. Plewis' research focused on the relatively poor performance of African–Caribbean pupils, especially boys in mathematics (following the 1988 Education Reform Act) at the end of year two in the primary school. A fascinating finding was that some of the between-classroom differences in progress in mathematics in year two can be explained by variations in the proportion of African–Caribbean children in the classroom.

Barbara Tizard's recent research with Ann Phoenix has also played an important part in documenting and analysing the emergence of 'mixed-race' identities. Ann Phoenix and Charlie Owen situate their chapter in the complex debates about the social construction of racial identities. Based on a demographic analysis, they show the distribution of mixed parentage in the UK, both in the general British population and within the minority ethnic population. They draw on the Tizard and Phoenix Social Identities Study (1993) of the way 14–18-year-olds of black/white, black and white groups of parents construct their identity and respond to the identity impositions of others. The findings challenge theoretical and policy orthodoxies and their assumptions.

Part II Research and Policy

Most of us engaged in social science research today are influenced by, and are required to make some input into, the policy context. The impetus to carry out policy-relevant research has increased as the Research Councils (in particular the Economic and Social Research Council) change their institutional structures and methods of working in order to become more responsive to the different constituencies which are the 'users' of research.

The relationship between research and policy is complex as Barbara Tizard suggests (see 'Interview' and Tizard, 1990). The process of understanding the relationship is not easily amenable to research involving in some cases long time spans and a process of 'knowledge creep' (Weiss, 1980). It entails both investigation into the processes of influence as well as assessment of the relative effects of research. The relationship between research and policy is interactive. It is further complicated by the different positions of researchers in relation to policy: both in terms of the institutional context in which research is done but also in terms of researchers' values about what the role of research should be. Moreover, it may be that most researchers themselves are not best placed to investigate the relationship.

We did not ask our contributors to directly address these issues, and only a few would describe themselves as carrying out analysis either *of* policy or *for* policy (Minogue, 1993). However, each of the six chapters in Part II of this book suggests in different ways some of the connections between research and policy.

The first chapter, by Jo and Peter Mortimore, draws on material from a larger study, evaluating a new educational institution. It focuses on the creation of City Technology Colleges (CTCs) which were designed to provide a scientific and technologically led curriculum. As its subtitle 'Policy into Practice' suggests, it is about the implementation of policy, in particular staffing innovations which sometimes involved the introduction into CTCs of staff recruited from industry with qualifications other than teaching. Here the researchers are cast in the role of evaluator of policies which constitute social experiments. As others have noted, evaluation is not only a mode of research but also a political activity in that, as Minogue (1993) suggests, the failure to

Introduction

evaluate policy can 'contribute further to uncertainties and the unsystematic nature of policy' (p. 23). Evaluation as a research activity has a close relationship to the policy process and may, depending on the results of the evaluation, directly inform the reshaping of policy.

The following chapter by Philip Graham reflects the Mortimores' concern with the effects of policy upon practice, in this case on the clinical work of psychiatrists and clinical psychologists in the field of children's mental health. Surveying this field, as both a clinician and researcher, over the past thirty years, Philip Graham concludes that clinical practice informed by the research evidence is a long way off. Interestingly, one of the reasons Graham gives for this situation is the importance clinicians placed on theory in the period covered by his review which has deflected their attention away from the empirical research results. Other reasons relate to the probabilistic character of many research findings which may prove unhelpful to clinicians in understanding the complexity of particular cases. On the other hand, Graham draws attention to a productive interaction between clinical and research methods, so that researchers are influenced to good effect by clinical approaches, while clinicians benefit from a variety of methods which researchers develop on the basis of in-depth clinical methods. Philip Graham moves on to consider the relationship between research and public policy. Here he is much more optimistic in his assessment and indicates a multiplicity of ways in which research has fed into or served to change public policy.

Martin Richards' chapter again takes the reader a step nearer to public policy in terms of the positioning of the researcher rather than the location of the research itself. Surveying the field of fundamental research on the effects of divorce on children, to which Richards has made a significant contribution, he goes on to analyse a particular piece of legislation which is currently (in early 1996) before Parliament, The Family Law Bill, in the context of recent directions of public policy in relation to family life. His contention is that there has been a shift in family law from public to private ordering which reflects the underlying privatization of domestic relationships. Moreover, he also shows how public policy sets out with one aim, in this case the 'best interests of children', and instead ends up drafting legislation which gives children less protection than before. On the basis of this analysis of the intended and unintended consequences of public policy, Richards, placing himself in an advocate role, makes a number of clear recommendations to policymakers which are informed directly by the research evidence.

The fourth chapter in Part II is closest to an 'insider position' within the policy arena and process. Tessa Blackstone's chapter plots the history of the establishment and operation of an independent 'think tank', the Institute of Public Policy Research (IPPR), which explicitly set out to influence policy, in particular the Labour Party in its role as a future government. The orientation of both IPPR as an institution and its researchers is to the policy arena although, as Tessa Blackstone documents, their actual role changes as the political fortunes of the Labour Party wax and wane. The chapter makes reference to 'the gadfly model' of the relationship between research and policy which, as Thomas (1987) has also suggested, involves the penetration of government and the party political sphere but is independent of these worlds. As Tessa Blackstone demonstrates, in providing an analysis and critique of existing policy and in generating ideas for new policies, the values of the IPPR and its researchers are explicitly partisan though not necessarily directly aligned with those they advise and seek to influence. Indeed, as Weiss has argued, even non-partisan analysis does not mean it does not contain value assumptions (Weiss, 1987, p. 108).

Unlike the other four chapters in Part II, the central concerns of the last two chapters in the book, written by Pat Petrie and Peter Moss, are about the analysis of policy rather than with research. In their role as researchers, these contributors seek to analyse policies across societies and they devote research skills and methods to this end. Both Pat Petrie and Peter Moss examine policy developments across European Union countries; in the former case policies concerning school-age childcare and, in the latter, concerning early childhood services.

Pat Petrie's chapter considers and makes sense of a relatively new and developing policy in the context of another, older, policy area: namely, the education systems in different countries. Petrie's analysis of school-age childcare indicates a multiplicity of policy options across Europe. These include the reinvention of the school to incorporate new curricula and a concern for the whole child. In some cases (France and Sweden) these involve the development of school-age childcare provision and curricula which complement school life, for example concerning expressive activities and interpersonal relationships, and which cover all school children. In other cases, notably Germany, the school curriculum is extended into a separate out-of-school service which is not universal. With the introduction of different forms of school-age childcare across Europe, Petrie's analysis is also suggestive of a changing set of relationships in children's lives with respect to home life and the lives of mothers through their involvement in children's education, that is depending on the complex of specific policies and practices and the way they fit together in each society.

Peter Moss's chapter has a similar orientation both in terms of the type of policy – in his case early childhood services – but also in the orientation of the researchers to European policy, and in the positioning of the researcher. Like Pat Petrie's chapter, Peter Moss's chapter is an analysis of policy provision in a European context. It also involves explicit engagement with the values underpinning policy concerned with services for young children. The particular focus of the chapter is the issue of the quality of services and the way in which a concern with quality raises a consideration of values. Moreover, the chapter goes on to argue that an analysis of values does not simply raise questions about policy, but is also an issue for research. In policy decisions concerning the quality of early childcare services, it is not simply a question of identifying 'desirable developmental universals' as set out in the scientific discourse of child development. The recognition of our own position as stakeholders in services and in relation to research itself means there is a need to focus on the process by which values about quality are constructed. In his role as external researcher, Peter Moss is a player in the policy arena, while as a Coordinator of the EU Childcare Network he also holds an insider status.

Science is not, nor should it be expected to be, value free. Darwin remarked: 'How odd it is that anyone should not see that all observation must be for or against some view if it is to be of any service' (Charles Darwin, quoted in Ralph Ruddock, 1981, *Ideologies*, Manchester Monographs 15, Department of Adult and Higher Education, University of Manchester; also quoted in Minogue, 1993).

Interview with Barbara Tizard

We have in this volume, perhaps indirectly influenced by Barbara Tizard herself, broken with the customary orthodoxy of celebratory volumes. Through a reading of the papers it became clear to us that they were distinguished contributions in their own right, often presenting original data and overviews and assessments of research. What better testimony to Barbara Tizard of the respect held by the authors? It seemed to us that Barbara should not stand outside this gathering of colleagues but be another voice within; to be a subject as well as an object in a book for her. To this end we interviewed Barbara about her research and policy interests. We have reduced the length of the original interview and what we present here is a version edited with Barbara's approval. It was impossible to disguise the fact that the interview was to appear in the book. We discussed the idea of interviewing Barbara with some of the contributors and we were heartened by their enthusiasm. We hope this will be shared by all the authors.

The interview gives some idea of Barbara's determination, energy and commitment in facing and surmounting, often at some cost, the dual responsibility of many women, of family and career. In her own understated way we can glimpse her courage in coming to terms with the tragedy of Jack Tizard's early death and the developing of the Research Unit he founded.

All the contributors we approached to write for this book gladly accepted, despite the diverse calls on their time and energy. And their manuscripts arrived on time. We are most grateful for everything they have done and we are confident that their papers will contribute to our understanding of what has been done and what needs to be done to improve our service to children many of whom are in Britain today in danger of being disadvantaged.

References

MINOGUE, M. (1993) 'Theory and practice in public policy and administration', in HILL, M. (Ed.) *The Policy Process: A reader*, London, Harvester Wheatsheaf.

THOMAS, P. (1987) 'The uses of social research: myths and models', in BULMER, M. (Ed.) *Social Science Research and Government: Comparative Essays on Britain and the United States*, Cambridge, Cambridge University Press.

TIZARD, B., BLATCHFORD, P., BURKE. J., FARQUHAR, C. and PLEWIS, I. (1988) *Young Children at School in the Inner City*, Hove, Erlbaum.

TIZARD, B. (1990) 'Research and policy: is there a link?', *The Psychologist*, **13**, 10, 435–40.

TIZARD, B. and HUGHES, M. (1984) *Young Children Learning: Talking and Thinking at Home and at School*, London, Fontana.

TIZARD, B. and PHOENIX, A. (1993) *Black, White or Mixed Race? Race and racism in the lives of young people*, London, Routledge.

WEISS, C. (1980) 'Knowledge creep and decision accretion', *Knowledge, Diffusion, Utilization*, **1**, 3, pp. 382–404.

WEISS, C. (1987) 'Congressional committee staffs (do, do not) use analysis', in BULMER, M. (Ed.) *Social Science Research and Government: Comparative Essays on Britain and the United States*, Cambridge, Cambridge University Press.

An Interview with Barbara Tizard

Basil Bernstein and Julia Brannen

This interview was conducted with Barbara Tizard during February 1996. The following version, based on a much longer transcript, is the product of the editing of all three of us. Its purpose was to give Barbara a central place in a book which has been written for, and dedicated to, Barbara in recognition of her very considerable contribution to research and in particular her role as Director of Thomas Coram Research Unit (TCRU) from which she retired in 1990. This interview is more than an interchange with a close colleague and friend in the Institute, Basil Bernstein, and with a longtime member of TCRU's research staff, Julia Brannen. It also represents a meeting of disciplines between psychology, Barbara's discipline base, and sociology which is the location of the editors. Set against the background of Barbara's personal and family life (which is only touched on here), the interview covers Barbara's public life, beginning with her entry into higher education, and follows her career in research both before and during her time as a researcher at TCRU, and subsequently as Director of the Unit.

As the interview documents, TCRU was founded by Jack Tizard, Professor of Child Development at the Institute of Education, in 1973, concerned with children and their families. The Unit was set up to pursue policy-relevant research. This aim was fulfilled through the establishment of close links with the Department of Health which, from the Unit's beginning, has provided core funding support as well as grants for specific research projects. However, throughout the life of the Unit, other sources of funding have always supported the research. Indeed in the 1980s, under Barbara Tizard, the Unit became a Designated Research Centre funded by the Economic and Social Research Council (formerly the Social Science Research Council until 1984). From its inception the Unit was designed as a centre for multidisciplinary research. Its charismatic founding Director, Jack Tizard, achieved enormous success in attracting a wide range of disciplines which were harnessed to different types of research endeavour, including intervention and demonstration projects as well as more theoretically based research.

While the themes of TCRU's research programme have varied over the years, its core concerns have been, and continue to be, with children and the variety of settings in which they are cared for, including families, substitute parenting and the organizational and practice contexts of residential care, daycare, health services and schools. TCRU has not only located its research within the policy context: it has been at the forefront in identifying emergent trends and innovative practice, frequently locating its work in relation to research and policy in other countries. Particularly in the field of institutional care and other forms of daycare for young children, its work has sought to advance the UK policy agenda. Under Barbara's direction, the Unit's concern with structural context, with the institutional and family settings which shape children's lives, has ensured that its work has been centrally involved with major issues of our times: with social and economic inequality, with gender and with race and ethnicity.

Early career

Basil   Perhaps we can begin with a little about your family. What did your parents do?
Barbara   My mother was a teacher. She hadn't been to a university, she had been to a teacher training college. My father was a journalist. He had actually been to Cambridge with an ex-servicemen's grant after the First World War. Both of them had working-class parents. My grandfather – my mother's father – was a signalman on the railways and my father's father worked in the mills, I think.
Basil   Would it be true to say that your left-wing formation is very much in terms of grass-roots change rather than intellectual theorizing about change?
Barbara   There were no intellectuals in my family background, except perhaps my father, whom I didn't know. It was very much trade-union socialism. My mother's parents lived in West Ham, which is now Newham. My grandfather was an alderman and active in the NUR as well as the Labour Party. They were all very opposed to the Communist Party, except my grandmother, who started to take the *Daily Worker* in her old age. My mother, who was President of the National Union of Teachers in 1938, was a friend of Aneurin Bevan.
Basil   Was there a history of women working in your family?
Barbara   There were lots of role models of women working. In fact, my grandmother's mother also worked. I think it's wrong to imagine that women only started working quite recently. She was a widow and worked as an unqualified midwife in the village in which she brought up her own family. And my grandmother's sister was also widowed early and supported her family by taking in washing. I think these things must have happened quite a lot. My mother decided we had to go to good schools. So I was put in for all kinds of scholarships. Fortunately I didn't get the one to Roedean! I got a scholarship to St Paul's.

Interview with Barbara Tizard

Basil   Then you went on to Oxford? But you didn't read psychology when you were an undergraduate?

Barbara   No, I didn't. I went up to read medicine and I did a year of medicine and for a whole variety of reasons I decided I would prefer to read PPE. So I changed to PPE – politics, philosophy and economics – and I did my degree in that. Actually, psychology wasn't taught as a degree at that time in Oxford.

Basil   You decided you would switch from medicine. Were there any special circumstances which influenced you to change your subject?

Barbara   I suppose there were, in that my friends were almost entirely not scientists and quite a few of them were doing PPE. Also, of course, I was a very active member of the Oxford Student Communist Party and so, you know, politics, philosophy and economics were exactly what I was interested in.

Basil   How did Jack (Tizard) come into the picture?

Barbara   Oh, well, he came to Oxford on a New Zealand ex-serviceman's grant. He was supposed to be doing a postgraduate degree, but he very much disliked the Oxford atmosphere and he quite soon got a job with Popper at the LSE teaching logic. Popper had been in New Zealand during the war and Jack had been a student of his.

Basil   How was it possible for you to marry Jack (at Oxford) because as I understand it, there was some edict against women marrying when they were undergraduates?

Barbara   There was an edict which was normally enforced. But I think it was perhaps partly because Jack by this time was teaching psychology at St Andrews University – a very long way away – and also the Principal was very kind to me.

Basil   You were at that time a member of the Communist Party?

Barbara   I was, yes. Jack wasn't, in fact.

Basil   I thought from my memory of the CP it was very difficult, so to speak, for members to marry out.

Barbara   Oh, it was. I had long consultations ... about whether I should marry him. I remember going to see a Party member who was married to one of the dons and discussing it with her because she had married out and she thought it was all right. Of course, Jack did subsequently join the Communist Party for a while, but not for very long. It didn't fit in with his kind of Popperian background at all. We both left in the early 1950s.

Basil   We have looked at your academic history so far. In the sixth form you shifted to science. And then we have medicine, then we shift from medicine to PPE and then that arises partly out of boredom with the medical course and partly out of the context of the people that you knew at Oxford and of course driven by your own political orientation at your much earlier formation. Then we get to psychology. But where did you end up reading psychology?

Basil Bernstein and Julia Brannen

Barbara   Well, at that time you were allowed to do a qualifying exam. So I spent the next year after Oxford studying for it at University College. By this time Jack had moved to the Maudsley (Institute of Psychiatry, London) . . . When Bill, my first child, was nine months old, I registered for a part-time PhD at the Maudsley.
Basil   How long did the PhD take you in those days?
Barbara   I think it took me five years because I had two more children.
Julia   What was your PhD on?
Barbara   It was on the psychological effects of brain damage.
Basil   So after you completed your doctorate, we're now into the Maudsley period?
Barbara   No. For three years I worked part-time as a clinical psychologist at the London Hospital. I had no training as a clinical psychologist! . . . But at that time a PhD was an even better qualification. Clinical psychology wasn't properly professionalized at that time.
Basil   So after the London Hospital?
Barbara   Well, then I got bored with it. It was mostly testing, adults and children. . . . And I heard there was a possibility of getting a research grant . . .
Basil   Through Jack?
Barbara   I suppose so – on epilepsy . . . it was in the Children's Department with Desmond Pond, who was a psychiatrist, but his speciality was epilepsy. I can't remember how long that grant lasted, say two or three years. Then I got a lectureship in the Neurophysiology Department as a psychologist. This was an innovation, they had never had a psychologist before. These were all part-time positions. I didn't work full-time until I was fifty . . .
Basil   During your time there you published a number of papers . . .
Barbara   Well, it's partly because you do experimental work quickly and so it's relatively easy to publish papers. And of course there was tremendous pressure to publish anyway – it was a very competitive, high-powered kind of atmosphere at the time. Aubrey Lewis's (Director of the Institute of Psychiatry) influence was all pervasive.
Basil   Did he influence you?
Barbara   Not directly. Perhaps through the very high standards that were expected. I rarely spoke to him. Everybody was terrified of him. Whatever you said he immediately dissected and showed succinctly the falseness of it.
Basil   But that's the kind of practice you often indulge in too!
Barbara   (laughs) It was a very hothouse atmosphere. A very stimulating atmosphere.
Julia   Then we have you now at the Institute of Education. What propelled this move?

Interview with Barbara Tizard

Barbara   A feeling that I wasn't going to get very much further in the field of electrophysiology. But also a feeling that I wanted to get back to something that would have some influence on people's lives.

Research at the Institute of Education and Thomas Coram Research Unit

Basil   Now there is a radical switch in your research focus. What drew you to children – to that focus?

Barbara   Well, it was partly the fact that I had three children and was about to adopt two more. So I felt I knew a bit about them. I think I decided to do research in residential nurseries[1] because about a year earlier we thought about adopting children from care and so we had various experiences of the care of children by public authorities during that time. But also, from a theoretical stance, I wanted to see if Bowlby's views on the dire effects of maternal separation would hold up in modern nurseries which were in many ways of very high quality.

Julia   Did the research have a policy impact?

Barbara   It did *apparently* have an immediate effect on policy. Barnardo's closed all their residential nurseries shortly afterwards. But of course there were other reasons why that happened – the research in their own homes provided them with a justification.

Julia   Residential care was quite a continuous theme of your work from the 1970s to 1994?[5]

Barbara   Well, it was only continuous in the sense that we were following up the children who had been adopted from institutions and were comparing them with those who remained in institutions.

Julia   I have suggested to you (in the past) that you were doing work on children in disadvantaged situations and you said you never thought of it in that kind of way. That really you were a researcher interested in children in different contexts and settings and interactions and you moved from residential care to looking more at children in more 'normal' situations?

Barbara   I think my motives were quite mixed. I *was* concerned that children should have as good a life as possible, I am basically an egalitarian. But also I was interested in the more theoretical issues of the long-term effects of early experience, the influence of the setting on behaviour and so on. My next study[2] was observing children in different forms of day/pre-school centres – playgroups and nurseries – some private and some day nurseries and so on. And that was really to see whether the organizational structure of the nurseries in these settings would also influence the

13

	behaviour of the staff and the children, who were not necessarily disadvantaged.
Julia	And did the . . . policy implications of that emerge from it or was this driven initially by policy concerns?
Barbara	No, I don't think it was. I think it was simply an attempt to shift the earlier theoretical question into a different setting, to see whether you could fit the same kind of model on to it and actually you couldn't (laughs). The only thing of interest to emerge from that study was the evidence on the way in which play reflected gender and social class interactions – the working-class boys stood out as different.
Julia	Did you get involved in any policy issues in this period?
Barbara	No. I think I had a very naïve idea originally. You did some research, wrote it up in psychological journals and everybody would somehow see what its implications were. I only gradually saw that if you wanted to enter the discussion about policy you had to push yourself in there by writing for, and talking to, policy-makers and practitioners.
Julia	So at what point did you become much more conscious of the policy implications of what you were doing?
Barbara	(Pause) Well, the next project I did was very policy-related because it was to do with involving parents in nursery school education.[3] It was a Department of Education grant and it was an action project. It was to see what kinds of parental involvement activities would work, with some attention to outcome in terms of parental attitudes and so on. But the main emphasis was on *how* this kind of work could be done in schools, taking the teachers with you. The project was not of much theoretical interest, although it did highlight the big gap between teachers' and working-class mothers' ideas about child development, play and education. The next project was an observational study of children at home and school,[4] which was funded by the then Social Science Research Council. Which I think had more impact than any other.
Julia	Can you say a bit about that?
Barbara	The study was carried out in the late 1970s, though mostly written up in the early 1980s. It arose from my earlier research in pre-school centres in which I was very struck by the peculiar way in which staff talked to the children, often in a series of 'educational' questions which seemed very artificial and often confused the children. This kind of talk was generated by a belief that working-class children need to be exposed to complex forms of language which they wouldn't be hearing at home. There was a big drive to train pre-school staff to talk like this, and I felt quite sceptical as to whether working-class children were not, in fact, exposed to the forms of language used by the staff, in the currency of everyday life

Interview with Barbara Tizard

at home. Because I couldn't find any studies in which the same children had been observed at home and at school, I decided to do that. And to observe not only the adult language but also the way in which the child was interacting with the adult concerned. So this was a study of differences in setting, with the child as a constant. There were indeed marked differences in the children's language in the two settings, especially the working-class children who tended to be much less forthcoming with the staff than middle-class children. They were clearly less confident in the school setting. And we found that all the mothers, whatever their social class, did indeed use language in the complex ways that were said to be missing from the working-class homes.

Julia   It got taken up by policy, particularly in institutions – schools. Were you happy with the way it was taken up?

Barbara   It did arouse a great deal of hostility from teachers, but I think it must have had a continuing effect on them because I know that in many colleges it's still a set book. The last time I was in Sainsbury's the checkout girl looked at my credit card and said 'Was it you who wrote that book we're doing?' (*Young Children Learning*).

Julia   There seems to have been a sharp difference between your particular research and the general research orientation at TCRU which included an important programme of research on daycare?

Barbara   I suppose it seemed so. But we did not intend to attack daycare or nursery schools as such, we were far from believing that children needed to spend all day with their mothers. Our intention was more to challenge received notions about nursery education, and raise the question of how children's interests and curiosity – what Susan Isaacs called their 'thirst for understanding' – can be fostered, and how the world can be brought into the nursery, which is often set up only for play.

Julia   Did you get caught up in the policy debate about daycare? How did you deal with it? Did you feel it was out of your hands?

Barbara   I think it was absolutely out of our hands. Quite soon after the momentum towards daycare increased, so that all political parties now feel that they have got to pay lip service to pre-school care. They've looked around for research to support that objective. They have all seized on the follow-up study by Lally, Mangione and Honig (1988) of some US pre-school programmes which does appear to show that in the long term pre-school attendance has reduced the rate of delinquency and early pregnancy, the social effects are stronger than educational ones. But British politicians never ever mention that those studies were done on very special populations of deprived children, with very much greater resources than have ever been used in this country: small classes, a structured programme, weekly home visits, etc.

Julia   You then returned to issues of race and identity, which was an earlier concern. What drew you into that in the first place, or was it through Eysenck?

Barbara   Yes, the early 1970s was a period of very fierce debate about racial differences in mean IQ which Jensen and Eysenck argued were genetically determined. On the whole, geneticists didn't accept these arguments and they were politically quite pernicious. It just happened that at that time all the children in the residential nurseries I'd been working in were given IQ tests, I can't remember why. If you looked at the results by race and I suppose because of the general issue of race being highlighted at that time, one did look at them by race, there was no difference in the average. Almost all of the children had been there since birth. I hastily threw that into the debate by writing a letter to *Nature*. It was rather a clever move, because it got international coverage ... Actually I wouldn't have thought of *Nature*, but Mike Rutter suggested it to me. Of course, evidence of that kind is never decisive. Jensen argued that black mothers who put their children in residential nurseries may have higher IQs than white mothers. The racial issue never really left my mind. It never really left the public arena. The Infant School Study[6] was another way of tackling it. Since we know that black children's school achievements at the age of eleven on average are inferior to white children's it is obviously important know at what stage this difference develops. So we assessed children before they entered infant school and we followed them through to the end of infant school by which time racial differences had developed, with the black boys doing the worst and black girls much better. The study was designed to throw light on why that should be. But in fact it didn't.

Julia   Why did you come back to the study of race?

Barbara   Well, as I said, I hadn't ever really stopped being concerned with issues to do with race. The Infant School Study was finishing around the time the study about racial identity[7] was being planned. This arose from a rather different policy issue which was to do with same-race fostering and adoption and we had had a number of discussions about this in the Unit ... I would not have probably taken that project on if Ann Phoenix (a black psychologist) had not wanted to work on it, because there were strong objections from black – and white – social workers to interracial placements and I think if I had had an all-white team they wouldn't have taken any notice of it whatsoever ... But again there was an element of just plain curiosity. The project arose because of its relevance to the policy then prevailing of same-race placement, which was seriously troubling me because it meant that black and, mainly, mixed race children were remaining a long time in residential care. In addition,

Interview with Barbara Tizard

	I had a personal interest, in that I had an adopted mixed race daughter who seemed very comfortable with her colour and her identity despite having white adoptive parents. But there was also the more general issue of how young people not in care cope with a black identity and with a mixed racial identity in a racist society. The general supposition among most psychologists was that they must have a poor self-image and feel stigmatized. And I felt this couldn't be right because the young people I knew who were black or mixed race seemed self-confident and cheerful. So there was a certain element of curiosity to see in what sense race was a stigma for black young people and if it wasn't, how was this possible? The same kind of assumptions are made about elderly people: age is an equally stigmatized condition, in some ways perhaps more so. And I think that there is some evidence that, for the most part, they have quite a positive self-image. I don't believe there is any simple relationship between belonging to a stigmatized group and having a damaged identity. It's much more complex.
Julia	So did the Racial Identity project have much policy impact?
Barbara	Well, again it's hard to tell. I think for a variety of reasons the same-race placement policy was already beginning to be slightly questioned. So I think, as usual, the research just fed into thinking about policy. If research enters in some way into the thinking of policy-makers and practitioners, that's the best you can – and perhaps should – hope for . . . We of course found that the identities children had were very related to their social class and their schooling. And they themselves were aware of this. Some of them say, you know, 'Just because we don't talk black doesn't mean we're not black or because we read The *Guardian* every day or we prefer Beethoven to Blues – people say we're not black.' And many of the mixed-race young people determinedly identified as 'mixed', although aware that they were 'supposed' to regard themselves as black.
Julia	In addition to the projects we have covered, you have also written about issues arising directly from your political involvements: for example, your concern about the consequences of the nuclear threat for children.
Barbara	Yes. Because I was so involved in the anti-nuclear movement I naturally read the material which was coming out about children and nuclear war. There were two kinds of study, apart from clinical studies. There were surveys of the extent of children's anxiety about nuclear war, and whether the nuclear threat was destroying their faith in adults, making them feel helpless, etc. Most of the studies were methodologically poor, but there was clearly evidence that most young people (and adults) worried about the nuclear threat, although most said that they worried more about other

17

issues, problems at school, employment prospects, etc. There really wasn't evidence, other than from case-studies, that this had a very destructive effect on their personalities. So I thought as propaganda this was unobjective and unnecessary: the main issue was the very real threat of the bombs to life. The second kind of study was concerned with how parents and teachers should discuss the nuclear threat with young people. Usually it was argued that we needed to give them more information and generate more concern. But we know from research in health education that these strategies have a limited effect, because stronger influences prevail, for example, peer pressure, a disinclination to believe authority. In the case of the nuclear threat, there was the political issue which the Peace Movement never adequately confronted, the fact that the Soviet Union had nuclear weapons trained on us, as well as the deep 'macho' resistance to giving up weapons. And the moral argument against nuclear weapons, which was very important for somebody like me, always had a minority appeal. So I felt if you were going to try to change young people's attitudes you had to confront these issues. And arousing anxiety is worse than useless beyond a certain point because people become paralysed. That's certainly what happened with the nuclear threat. People felt there was nothing they could do and it was too horrible to think about. So I was really just trying to bring my knowledge as a researcher to bear on these issues. It was a kind of extra-curricular activity.

Julia I think we have covered most of your research, which has always had implicit relevance for policy. Have you ever thought that there should be more of a direct link between research and policy?

Barbara I think I would always have reservations about how direct the link should be between research and policy, because any set of research findings arises out of specific conditions and those limit its generalizability. I think social science research contributes an appeal to rationality, and it may also challenge assumptions and create an 'agenda for concern'. But policy is as much driven by political and moral values, taking into account the resources available.

Julia Would you do your research differently now?

Barbara I would, yes . . . if I was going to do any more research. And one of the things I began to learn from you, Julia, and again I've recently been much more aware of it, is the value of qualitative material and of looking for complexities. Thinking now about the Racial Identity Project, and looking again at some of the transcripts, I feel dissatisfied with the way in which we encouraged people to opt for rather simple identities, rather than expose the contradictions and complexities that there were indications of. We weren't looking for them. And of course the reason you don't look is that they're difficult to quantify and don't lead to a simple answer.

Director of Thomas Coram Research Unit

Julia We're going to move on a bit to your time as Director of Thomas Coram. Was there a point at which you saw yourself on some kind of ladder?

Barbara Yes, I *think* so. After three or four years at the Institute of Education I applied for, and got, a Senior Research Fellowship, although Jack didn't really want me to apply, he thought it would look like nepotism At that time it was quite usual for universities not to allow married couples to work in the same department. And in the year or so before Jack became ill I was looking around for Chairs, though this was a difficult decision, nothing was likely to turn up in London, but how could I leave London with a youngish child, and a husband? In the end, I did apply for a Chair in Sussex, I thought we could live between London and Sussex but about a month after that Jack became ill and I withdrew. So I had been looking for preferment. I thought I had been a backroom researcher too long.

Julia I know that when Jack died (Director of TCRU 1973–79) – it must have been a terrible time – you didn't apply to be Director (of TCRU) in the first round. Why did you eventually decide to go forward?

Barbara Because I thought that nobody else would carry on the Unit in the way that Jack had done. It seemed to me very good in most ways. I had very mixed feelings about applying, though.

Julia What were your concerns about taking it on?

Barbara I'm not sure, looking back. Not measuring up to Jack as a Director and you know perhaps feeling it was a tremendous undertaking. Generally not feeling quite adequate to it, I guess.

Julia Did you feel that, having been very much someone who *did* research, that it hadn't prepared you sufficiently for the role, that you should be prepared in other ways?

Barbara Oh, yes. As I say, I had always been a backroom person, partly because I had worked part-time until recently, and had always taken the main responsibility for the children and the home. I very rarely went to the main Institute building, and I certainly wasn't on any committees – except one set up to help Chilean academics and students, after the coup. Even within the Unit I had kept a very low profile. Jack had held meetings of the project leaders, which I usually didn't attend. I felt, if we didn't agree, this would seem disloyal, and perhaps gossip-worthy. If we did agree, it might seem

19

|||too much like a united front. So apart from my own projects, I had no administrative or management experience at all, and I should certainly have had management training. I think that I couldn't have looked very promising (laughs). I felt my assets were having very high research standards, which I'd partly acquired at the Institute of Psychiatry, and wanting to keep the Unit going on more or less the lines it had before. But it had got a bit ungovernable – it had got very large. There were forty-one academic staff, too many to house on the premises, and a wide range of projects, on mental and physical disability, education, childcare, economics of childcare, paediatrics.

Basil I don't know how accurate this is, but I always had the feeling from the outside that Jack's method of administration – which was essentially decentralized – was to enable him to get on with his own work?

Barbara I don't know what the motivation was. He was a great decentralizer and he was very good at letting people get on with their own thing and not fussing over them. I'm not sure he was very democratic because he more or less devolved power to the senior staff, 'barons'. It wasn't to get on with his research, certainly, because his time was increasingly taken up with administration, international consultancies, government committees, being President of the British Psychological Society, etc. He did get very depressed about this, and said he was nothing but a superior clerk in the Unit, signing papers for others. And as he'd left the Department of Child Development in order to be able to do more research (giving up tenure, incidentally) he felt quite bitter. I think it may have been an inevitable consequence of running such a large and successful Unit, and of seeing it as a duty to take part in public life. But I always remained quite closely involved in research projects, and did much less outside work, although I did do some work for WHO (World Health Organization) and Save the Children.

Julia Did you make a conscious decision to do that?

Barbara I don't know. I wanted to be closely involved in research and that is time consuming, I intensely disliked committees, I don't like being in the public eye, and I had a child to look after. And I thought the Unit could benefit from being rather more tightly held together, and also from pruning. I didn't know enough about paediatrics, or, after Chris Kiernan (Deputy Director of TCRU until 1984) left, disabilities, to effectively supervise those areas. And Jack and I always preferred systems- and context-oriented rather than person-oriented research, so it didn't seem to me appropriate that more or less straightforward clinical research should go on in the Unit. But also our research strategies shifted somewhat. Jack's main research strategies were epidemiology, and demonstration

Interview with Barbara Tizard

projects, which he was tremendously good at. He had the kind of charisma and authority needed to persuade local authorities and charities to put up the large funding required. At that time, in the early and mid-1970s, there was the money, you know. And demonstration projects are tremendously powerful, they show what is *possible*. Jack's ideas were always very bold. For instance, he attempted to set up centres which would provide free education and daycare for all under-fives in an area whose parents wanted to use it, either part- or full-time, as they wished. Unfortunately, no one would fund a demonstration project exactly on those lines. The one project I would dearly have liked to have done would have been a demonstration project in a primary school, in a working-class area, putting considerable resources into trying to raise the children's achievements to middle-class levels: using really small classes, teachers who'd taught, perhaps, in academic private schools and would maintain the same high expectations and choice of books and activities, etc. Then one could have tried to tease out what the problems might be, and got some ideas about how they might be overcome. I think it would have been intellectually exciting, as well as socially important, but I didn't think I had the personality, the enthusiasm and charisma to get it set up, and then deal with the myriad of problems that would follow, especially because at the time primary teachers were generally hostile to a focus on academic achievement.

Basil Jack had created a multidisciplinary empire that was in no sense interdisciplinary. It always struck me that when you came along you saw some of the weaknesses of this structure and you reduced the number of disciplines and tried to set up more interaction.

Barbara Yes, that was certainly one of the changes. A multidisciplinary Unit is always very interesting because you can learn a lot from talking to people in other disciplines. But it's difficult for a Director to supervise work in a discipline about which they're not very knowledgeable. If you have senior staff in other disciplines, the Unit is liable to function in effect as a group of sub-Units, with a life of their own. If you have junior staff only, you may have to call in outsiders to supervise them, or they may in effect not work within their discipline. So a balance has to be struck between having the stimulation of other disciplines, and keeping the Unit manageable. Interdisciplinary research, in which different disciplines jointly formulate a project and decide on its aims and research strategies can be very exciting and creative, and can work if each discipline has a clearly defined responsibility.

Julia Going back to when you took on the Directorship (1980), it was quite rare for a woman to be a Research Director at the time. Was that something you were conscious of, being a woman?

Barbara Well, don't forget it was a very female Unit. Two-thirds of the researchers were women when I took over, and this proportion increased thereafter.

Julia Did it make a difference, being a woman?

Barbara I suspect that as a woman I got paid a lower salary. It's difficult to know, because all professors receive different salaries, which are kept secret.

Julia But you didn't think to do anything at the time?

Barbara Well, I did actually. I could see my salary was much less than Jack had got. I wrote in to this effect and they wrote back offering me an extra £500. I can't say at the time that I thought about it very much, which was foolish, since I knew I'd mostly worked part-time but, like many others, I didn't think ahead to my pension.

Basil When I came to the Institute all the Professors got the same. Elvin (Lionel) (Director, Institute of Education 1954–73) was absolutely adamant on this issue. This is what we were told and had no reason to disbelieve it.

Julia Was it an advantage in some settings to be a woman?

Barbara I think it was, in the sense that I had no hesitation in turning to people for help and advice, which probably most men would have regarded as a sign of weakness. Just as they seem to hate asking passers-by for directions! It was a feminine, rather than a female, way of coping. Lots of woman would have acted differently, but possibly men are readier to help a woman. I also built up a network of fellow academics and people in administration and so on who I felt could be relied on to help the Unit. And as part of this strategy, I set up what Jack had always refused to have, because he thought it would infringe his autonomy – a Unit Advisory Group, which I saw as a source of advice, assistance and protection. It didn't in fact infringe my autonomy, as it took no decisions but gave a lot of support.

Basil That gave you independence from the Institute. Don't you think that was rather important? The actual physical location of Coram (in Coram Fields) gave you a kind of autonomy and there was a very happy relationship between your apparent – you refer often to your lack of social skills in dealing with authority – your very happy relationship in Coram was splendidly removed from the Institute which enabled you to get on with your work without external problems.

Barbara I think another feminine, rather than female, attribute, is that I find it very difficult to cope with people who are hostile to me. Which is partly why I liked to feel there was a network of supportive people I could turn to.

Julia Probably very few people perceived you in that way. They saw you as very independent and resilient and that you didn't actually need

Barbara	people. I always thought of you as a feminist by a kind of natural inclination, but politically are you becoming more of one over time?
Barbara	Well, I don't think I was a feminist in the past. I've become much more sympathetic to feminist thinking since I've retired, and read some feminist writings under the influence of my feminist art history tutor. Of course, I always believed, as my mother and grandmother did, that women get a raw deal in society, that they should have equal opportunities with men, and equal rights to work. Occasionally in the 1970s I went to local feminist groups and found them extremely irritating. To be honest, it seemed to me to be women whingeing about their lot and I thought 'Why don't you do something about it?' I thought that my reasonably successful career showed that I was a liberated woman, which with hindsight I can see was laughably untrue! But spending time at Greenham Common in the 1980s was a feminist experience which, in many ways, was very exhilarating.
Julia	You must have got closer to particular women in that situation than you perhaps had been before.
Barbara	Well, there's nothing like being arrested and shut up in a police cell together for sealing a relationship. Yes, I did, and I was always conscious of the dissonance between my somewhat hierarchical, authoritarian role in the Unit, and the equality, warmth and comradeship of women working together for peace.
Julia	With hindsight, what would you like to have changed, to have been different?
Barbara	I don't know, Julia, I wasn't really comfortable being Director. My problem was that I wanted as far as possible to have a democratic Unit, but there was a limit to what was possible. Also, it was rather an alienating position. You couldn't really have close friendships because you would be seen to have been having favourites and, you know, you didn't really work with anyone as equals. You were alone. I'm sure there are other ways of coping with that. And also because of my domestic responsibilities I had to hurry home, and didn't have that period of relaxed socializing after work. I remember Jack used to go off in the evening with some of the staff to a pub.
Basil	And he socialized in the Institute.
Barbara	Whereas I was always scurrying away home.
Julia	What about in terms of – you had a lot of children – how did you actually manage to combine having five children and all this?
Barbara	Well, by the time I was Director there was only one child left at home, Lucy, who was eleven, and that was difficult enough. You really need a husband, I think. A husband who will share fifty/fifty. And that must be marvellous, or perhaps a mother who's nearby

	who's always willing to help. But when I had all the children, I always worked part-time, and I had (in turn) childminders, daily nannies, au pair girls. I tried everything . . . I usually worked mornings, or two-and-a-half days.
Julia	When you left TCRU, you obviously went on to do a lot of new things. What was it like for you?
Barbara	Well, I suppose it was in many ways a relief because, as I said, I didn't find the position very comfortable although it had its compensations. I was very proud of the Unit, and glad that I'd helped to maintain, perhaps in some ways, improve it. I suppose I continued, as I do now, to feel concern about the Unit, wanting things to turn out right and wanting it really not to be so very different, because it has done such good work. But I perfectly realize that it can't have, and shouldn't have, anything to do with me, so I have tried to distance myself from the Unit's concerns. So I threw myself into other things, and didn't sit around mourning as the analysts would say.
Julia	Did you have a clear vision of what you would do following retirement or did you not pause for breath until it happened?
Barbara	I did have a clear notion because I still had a Department of Health project to finish, and then some work on residential care for children with Ian Sinclair.[8] So I knew that was going to take up about half my time. And I knew I wanted to do a Diploma in the History of Art, part-time, which I am just finishing now. So I did have a reasonably clear idea. I don't think I realized what it was going to mean in terms of daily experiences, especially the lack of social interaction. I think for women who retire – because men are much more likely to have a partner at that age – this is quite a major problem which you can tackle in various ways. I don't think, either, I realized that there would be a problem in organizing intellectual discussion.
Julia	And did the art and the research – have they been two separate bits of yourself or have they had a mutual influence on each other?
Barbara	Yes and no. Hilda Beloff (1994) has written very interestingly about visual images, as a social psychologist. I approached the History of Art as a student, eager to learn. But because I had for several years a tutor who was a strong feminist I found myself reading Lacan, Foucault, semiotics, and thinking about psychological issues in the light of this reading. But I don't think of myself, anyway, as strongly compartmentalized. There's a core part of my identity which is always watching what is going on, and thinking critically about it as a psychologist, as when I worked in a restaurant kitchen for two weeks in the summer.
Basil	You have given an overall picture of how you acted within the arena of research, children and policy. There was your political

	engagement in forms of direct action. Your engagement in the research field against policies which you thought were held too dogmatically on the basis of inadequate evidence. You also took on teachers and social workers whose practice you thought was questionable. So we have a picture of you as a 'grassroots fighter'. Much of your activity in the area of policy is directed towards institutions and practitioners at the level of their practices. You certainly have affected practice by the controversy you produced in challenging various orthodoxies and by providing a much sounder basis for practical decisions.
Julia	But looking back, do you feel pleased with what you've done? Looking at it with your critical eye?
Barbara	I can see weaknesses in everything that I've done . . . I think I have opened up some quite important issues and, yes, drawn attention to them. I wouldn't put it stronger than that, but perhaps that's enough.

References

BELOFF, H. (1994) 'Rending visual rhetoric', *The Psychologist*, **7**, 11, pp. 495–9.

LALLY, J. R., MANGIONE, P. L. and HONIG, A. S. (1988) 'Long-term impact of an early intervention with low income children and their families', in POWELL, D. R. (Ed.) *Parent Education as early Childhood Intervention: Emerging Directions in Theory, Research and Practice*, vol. 4, Norwood, New Jersey, Ablex Publishing Corporation.

Projects directed by Barbara Tizard 1967–94

1 Long-term effects of early institutional care. Funded by Dr Barnado's Society 1967–76. B. Tizard, A. Joseph, J. Rees and J. Hodges.
2 Staff and children in nursery schools and nurseries. Funded by SSRC/DHSS 1971–75. B. Tizard and J. Philips.
3 Parent involvement in nursery education. Funded by DES 1976–79. B. Tizard, B. Burchell and Jo Mortimore.
4 Children's conversations at home and at school. Funded by SSRC 1976–79. B. Tizard, H. Carmichael, G. Pinkerton and M. Hughes.
5 A follow-up study of adolescents whose earliest years were spent in residential care. Funded by Joseph Rowntree Memorial Trust 1982–85. B. Tizard and J. Hodges.
6 Educational achievement in the infant school: The contribution of parents and teachers. Funded by ESRC 1982–88. B. Tizard, P. Blatchford, J. Burke, C. Farquhar and I. Plewis.

7 Social identity in adolescence. Funded by Department of Health 1988–91. B. Tizard, A. Phoenix, A. Brackenbridge, and W. Francis.
8 A review of research on residential care for children. Funded by the Department of Health 1991–94. I. Sinclair and B. Tizard.

Part I

Research

Chapter 1

Specificity of Brain-Behavioural Relationships Revisited: From Epileptic Personality to Behavioural Phenotypes

Michael Rutter and William Yule

An important early phase in Barbara Tizard's career was concerned with research in the field of epilepsy. Her key review of the concept of a characteristic epileptic personality, together with her systematic appraisal of the relevant empirical evidence, did much both to clarify the issues and to cast doubt on the stereotypes that prevailed at the time. Although it is now more than three decades since her review, the paper continues to be cited as marking a significant turning point in the way the topic was thought about (see e.g. Taylor and Eminson, 1994). In her review, Barbara Tizard highlighted five main issues (Tizard, 1962). First, there was the question of whether psychopathological disorders were more frequent among epileptic subjects than in the general population. The evidence at that time was fragmentary and inconclusive but Tizard suggested that there might be a true increase. Second, there was the rather different question of whether such psychological disturbances took a characteristic form in people suffering from epilepsy. Tizard noted the unsatisfactory quality of much of the evidence but concluded that the disturbances were quite varied in type and there was no indication that there was such a thing as a characteristic epileptic personality. Accordingly, there was a need for research to identify the variables – whether they be psychosocial, neurophysiological or structural – that accounted for the heterogeneity. Third, she considered the possibility that there might be either different levels of psychiatric risk, or different forms of psychopathology, associated with the type of epilepsy, the location of an epileptic focus or the presence of organic brain pathology. She concluded that there might well be associations of this kind but the evidence was insufficient to lead to any kind of firm conclusion. Fourth, she drew attention to the inadequacy of the measuring instruments available to assess either levels of psychopathology or (most especially) specific types of psychological dysfunction. Finally, Tizard underlined the problems of inferences based on selected clinic samples. She urged the need for good epidemiological data using discriminating and well-validated measures.

During the thirty-four years that have passed since Barbara Tizard's review of epileptic personality, considerably better evidence has become available. It has broadly confirmed all the main conclusions she drew in 1962, but it has also served to open up new avenues of research and has led to the development of a number of new concepts. In this chapter we briefly review some of these developments, with particular reference to epidemiological data on the psychiatric risks associated with epilepsy and with other forms of neurological dysfunction; the findings on differences in specificity of psychological sequelae according to the age of the individual at the time of brain injury; the evidence on the validity of highly specific behavioural syndromes (with special reference to autism); and the concept of behavioural phenotypes.

Psychiatric risk and neuro-epileptic disorders

Systematic epidemiological data on the psychiatric risks associated with epilepsy and with neurological disorders in childhood were first provided by the Isle of Wight surveys undertaken during the 1960s (Rutter, Graham and Yule, 1970a; Rutter, Tizard and Whitmore, 1970b). A range of multiple screening measures was used to detect all cases of epilepsy or neurological disorder in children aged five to fifteen years who were resident on the Isle of Wight. Children with neuro-epileptic disorders were compared with those who had physical disorders not involving the brain (such as diabetes, heart disease, asthma, or peripheral sensory deficits) and a random sample of the general population. The whole population was assessed using parent and teacher questionnaires of demonstrated reliability and validity (see Elander and Rutter, 1996). Parents and children were also interviewed using investigator-based standardized assessments of psychopathology; individual psychological testing of the children was undertaken and information was sought from teachers. The results showed convincingly for the first time that the rate of psychiatric disorder was substantially higher in children with brain disorders than in children who were free of physical problems or in children whose physical disorders did not involve the brain. Specific reading difficulties were also more frequent in the neuro-epileptic sample. Because the study was based on epidemiological coverage of the total population, rather than a clinic sample, the strong association between brain disorders and psychopathology cannot have been due to a referral bias. The fact that disorders of the brain carried a much higher psychiatric risk than other physical disorders also strongly suggested that the psychiatric risk derived from brain pathology rather than from non-specific effects that might accompany physical handicap or from having a stigmatizing disorder. Part of the risk seemed to derive from the cognitive impairment that was also more common in the brain disorder group but the psychiatric risk was still much increased even after account had been taken of lower IQ. The inference that it was brain pathology *per se* that led to the increased psychopathological risk was confirmed in a further study undertaken in London (Seidel, Chadwick and Rutter, 1975) in which children with cerebral disorders were compared with a matched group of children whose neurological disorders stem from lesions below the brain stem (such as poliomyelitis). The children with brain disorders were twice as likely to have psychiatric problems, despite the fact that the two groups were similar in both social background and visible crippling, and despite the fact that children with an IQ below seventy were excluded.

In both these epidemiological studies, the brain lesions had been present from infancy or early childhood and it was not possible to examine the effects on psychopathology of a newly acquired brain disorder. Accordingly, a further prospective study of a representative sample of children who acquired a severe head injury was undertaken (Rutter, Chadwick and Schaffer, 1983a); the group was compared, during the course of a follow-up lasting over two years, with a similar sample of children with mild head injuries and a group of children with orthopaedic injuries not involving either loss of consciousness or damage to the head. Data on the children's behaviour before injury were obtained very shortly after the accident and before the sequelae could be evident. The results were clear-cut in showing a much increased rate of psychopathology in the case of severe head injuries but not in the case of mild ones. In parallel with the stereotype of the epileptic personality, effectively contradicted by the findings reviewed by Tizard (1962) in the 1960s, there was the notion that there was a distinctive and characteristic behavioural response to brain injury in childhood (Bakwin and Bakwin, 1967). This was usually equated with some variant of the hyperkinetic syndrome and it was broadened and extrapolated so that the presence of hyperactivity, attention deficits and the like was used to infer 'minimal cerebral dysfunction' (MBD) (Kalverboer, van Praag and Mendlewicz, 1978). So called 'soft signs' was also used to infer organic brain pathology (Yule and Taylor, 1987). Empirical findings showed that the concept of MBD was no better validated than that of the epileptic personality. Not only was it found that children with definite organic brain pathology showed a most heterogenous range of psychiatric disorders but also most children with hyperkinetic disorders lacked unequivocal evidence of neurological dysfunction. The stereotype of MBD stood up to empirical testing no better than the epileptic personality (Rutter, 1982a) and it too has come to be abandoned by most researchers and clinicians.

The next question concerns the factors within the group of children with neuro-epileptic disorders that created an increased psychopathological risk. The question is an important one because some two-thirds of the children did *not* show psychiatric disorder and hence the mere fact of brain injury was clearly not sufficient in itself to give rise to a psychiatric condition. The Isle of Wight study findings showed that structural disorders of the brain (such as cerebral palsy) carried a higher psychopathological risk than did uncomplicated epilepsy. On the other hand, psychiatric disorders were more common among children whose structural brain disorders also involved epilepsy than among those where the brain disorder was not associated with epileptic attacks. Among the children with uncomplicated epilepsy, the rate of psychiatric disorder was highest in those with psychomotor attacks but otherwise the type of epilepsy was not a good predictor of psychiatric risk. Several studies have sought to determine whether the localization of epileptic foci is of psychiatric significance but the findings are contradictory and inconclusive. The inconsistency of findings probably partly derives from the fact the EEG findings on epileptic foci tend to vary over time and over repeated testing (Kaufman, Harris and Schaffer, 1980), in part because the EEG data have been of variable quality and usually non-blind and non-standardized, and partly because few of the samples have been epidemiological. Certainly, it cannot be concluded that either the nature of the epilepsy or the localization of the epileptic focus are irrelevant for the development of psychopathology but, equally, there is no good evidence that either are crucial, with the possible exception of a higher psychiatric risk associated with psychomotor attacks or temporal lobe epilepsy (Goodman, 1994a).

The possible importance of the localization of acquired brain lesions was investigated through a systematic study, using standardized methods of assessment of proven reliability and validity, in a group of children with localized brain lesions confirmed through neurosurgery (Shaffer, Chadwick and Rutter, 1975). No substantial associations were found. On the other hand, the investigation was undertaken before the availability of modern methods of brain imaging and, in their absence, it was not possible to be sure that the observed brain lesion was the only one that was present. The matter remains open. What is much needed is an epidemiological study using high quality standardized imaging methods, and good EEG data, as well as standardized assessments of psychopathology.

A further issue of considerable theoretical, as well as practical, importance is the extent to which non-neurological factors affect psychiatric risk. All the evidence indicates that they play a substantial role (Rutter, Graham and Yule, 1970a; Rutter, Chadwick and Schachar, 1983b; Hermann and Seidenberg, 1989). Thus, serious psychosocial adversity much increases the likelihood of significant psychopathology. It might be thought likely that brain abnormalities and psychosocial risk would act synergistically. That is, it might be supposed that the presence of brain dysfunction would act, in part, through increasing the child's susceptibility to the ordinary run of psychosocial stressors and adversity. The evidence to date of any such interaction remains weak and inconclusive and remarkably little is known on the precise mechanisms by which organic brain dysfunction predisposes to psychiatric disorder.

Age effects on the sequelae of brain lesions

In adult life, there is good evidence that the lateralization of brain injuries makes an important difference to the pattern of cognitive sequelae (Newcombe, 1969; McFie, 1975). Thus, lesions of the dominant hemisphere, but not of the non-dominant one, are associated with loss of language and aphasic-type language abnormalities, together with verbal deficits on cognitive tests. By sharp contrast, this has not been found in relation to brain lesions incurred prenatally or in the infancy or early childhood period. Thus, in Chadwick *et al.*'s (1981) study of localized brain lesions, there was no evidence that the pattern of cognitive deficits was affected by which hemisphere was damaged. Similarly, in their study of children with hemiplegic cerebral palsy, Vargha-Khadem *et al.* (1992) found no differences in cognitive pattern according to whether the left or right hemisphere was involved. Cognitive impairment was substantially greater in the case of individuals with epilepsy as well as cerebral palsy, but the side of the hemiplegia appeared irrelevant. Similarly, lesions of the dominant hemisphere in early childhood do not lead to aphasia in the way that comparable lesions in later child or adult life do (Woods and Carey, 1979). Also, hemispherectomy in children with severe unilateral brain lesions does not have the effects that would be expected on the basis of findings in adults (Heywood and Canavan, 1987). It should not be supposed that these findings mean that brain lesions in early life are less functionally damaging. Neuronal regrowth may be more possible but this can lead to harmful *mis*connections as well as restoration of prior functioning (Schneider, 1979; Rutter, 1982b, 1993a; Goodman, 1994b).

The precise mechanisms involved in plasticity remain uncertain. In some way or other, it seems that either transfer of functions from one hemisphere to the other occurs more readily in the immature brain or, alternatively, there is greater plasticity in the take-up of functions. On the face of it, it would seem to follow that specific behavioural sequelae of brain lesions are not likely to be found with brain disorders developing in early childhood. There are, however, two reasons why there should be caution before accepting this negative conclusion. First, the findings on brain plasticity are confined to transfer, or take-up of functions *across* the two hemispheres. It seems much more dubious whether there is similar plasticity with respect to the transfer of functions *within* a single hemisphere or in response to bilateral brain lesions. Second, although there may not be a great deal of behavioural specificity in relation to localized, lateralized brain lesions, it does not necessarily follow that there will not be specificity in relation to the dysfunction of brain systems. Moreover, it manifestly is not the case that children cannot show specific cognitive or behavioural deficits. The former is evident in terms of specific developmental disorders of language (Rutter, Mawhood and Howlin, 1992) and the latter in terms of autism.

Specific 'organic' behavioural syndromes

Autism has come to constitute the best validated of all specific behavioural syndromes for which there is strong evidence of some kind of basis in organic brain dysfunction (Rutter, 1979; Bailey, Phillips and Rutter, 1996). The specificity is evident in several different ways. First, several studies have shown that there is a significant clustering together of the communicative deviance, the social deviance and the stereotyped patterns of repetitive behaviour that constitute the syndrome. Second, twin data indicate the high likelihood that the co-twins of autistic individuals will show a similar pattern of behaviour (Bailey et al., 1995). Third, family studies similarly indicate the extent to which there is a familial loading of the characteristic social and communicative abnormalities (Bolton et al., 1994). The development of epileptic seizures in about one in five of autistic individuals without prior evidence of neurological abnormality constituted the first evidence that it was likely that autism would prove to have an organic basis of some kind (Rutter, 1970). Subsequent research has confirmed this conclusion (Bailey, Phillips and Rutter, 1996). Family and twin data have gone on to show that genetic factors predominate in etiology (Rutter et al., in press a). Moreover, although a diverse range of medical conditions have been associated with occasional cases of autism, there is some limited diagnostic specificity. Thus, for example, autism seems to be particularly associated with tuberous sclerosis and, to a lesser extent, with the fragile X anomaly, whereas it is much less frequent with either Down syndrome or cerebral palsy.

It may be concluded that, as illustrated by autism, children can show highly specific and unusual behavioural syndromes in which the etiology is to be found in some form of organic brain dysfunction. Nevertheless, the same evidence shows that, despite this characteristic specificity, there is substantial variation in both the severity of the handicap and the details of the symptomatology. Thus, in the British general population twin studies, Le Couteur et al. (1996) found that in monozygotic pairs concordant for autism the two twins could differ as much as fifty points in IQ, as well as in the details and severity of symptomatology. It should be added that the same varied manifestations are seen with the neurological features of many single gene Mendelizing disorders. For example, tuberous sclerosis may be manifest only in a few difficult-to-detect hypomelanotic macules or in multiple calcified brain tumours. Equally, the IQ ranges from severely retarded to above normal. The same degree of clinical variability is evident with neurofibromatosis. Even closely circumscribed genetic disorders exhibit a surprising diversity of clinical phenomena. Evidently, both specificity and generality of the sequelae of brain disorders need to be accounted for.

Behavioural phenotypes

The evidence leading to dismissal of the stereotypes of the 'epileptic personality' and 'brain damaged child' led many people to conclude that there were no behavioural specificities associated with brain pathology. Similarly, evidence accumulated that cast doubt on comparable stereotypes associated with, for example, Down syndrome (Rutter, 1971). It was not that there were no differences between the medical conditions in their behavioural correlates but none of the findings seemed sufficiently striking to be useful either in practical management or in the understanding of brain mechanisms. Along with a general distrust of medical approaches to mental retardation, and an antipathy to the use of diagnostic labels, it came to be thought by many that mental retardation was associated with undifferentiated cognitive and behavioural patterns and that subdivisions were not very useful (Ellis, 1969). In recent years, there has been a substantial change in prevailing views and there has been a growing interest in what have come to be termed specific 'behavioural phenotypes' (Broman and Grafman, 1994; Flint and Yule, 1994; Dykens, 1995; O'Brien and Yule, 1995a).

Quite probably the most important stimulus for the concept of behavioural phenotypes arose from Nyhan's (1976) description of the Lesch-Nyhan syndrome. The crucial feature of Nyhan's description was the recognition that specific behavioural features could constitute the pathognomonic defining characteristics of an organic disorder. Almost as soon as children with Lesch-Nyhan syndrome have teeth, they show an unusual form of self-mutilation in which they bite themselves so severely that they frequently lose portions of their lips and tongues and may even sever their fingers. The children also bite other people and show verbal and physical aggression. The self-mutilation is very resistant to environmental interventions and is qualitatively different from the self-injurious behaviour seen in many other mental retardation syndromes (see Oliver, 1995). The syndrome is due to a lack of the enzyme hypoxanthine phosphoribosyltransferase (HPRT). Evidence from a mouse model of HPRT deficiency has shown that this abnormality of purine metabolism leads to self-mutilation. The concept of a behavioural phenotype, then, resides in the notion of qualitatively distinct behaviour that occurs exclusively as a direct consequence of some specific medical condition (Flint, 1995; O'Brien and Yule, 1995b).

The second major stimulus derived from the rapid advances in molecular genetics that has allowed identification of the specific genes responsible for various syndromes of mental retardation, as well as other medical conditions (Flint and Yule, 1994). Thus, it has been shown that the phenotypic manifestations of a fragile X anomaly are due to deletion of the FMR-1 gene deriving from large hypermethylated trinucleotide repeat sequences (see review by Hagerman, 1995; Simonoff, Bolton and Rutter, 1996). As well as mental retardation, individuals with the fragile X anomaly usually show striking behavioural abnormalities. At first, it was thought that these frequently took the form of autism, but it is now clear that, although fragile X individuals can show autism, more frequently they exhibit somewhat different behavioural patterns (Turk, 1992; Hagerman, 1995; Rutter *et al.*, in press a). Gaze avoidance, hand flapping, perseverative and dysfluent speech, social sensitivity and attentional problems seem particularly frequent.

The Prader-Willi syndrome provides a parallel example. This syndrome is characterized by marked foraging for food that begins during the preschool years, persistent overeating and marked obesity. The condition is due to a microdeletion on chromosome 15, the condition being manifest when the chromosome has been transmitted through the father with paternal imprinting (see review by Simonoff, Bolton and Rutter, 1996). The specificity of the gene-phenotypic connections is strikingly illustrated by the finding that when a comparable microdeletion in the same region of chromosome 15 is inherited through the mother, a quite different behavioural syndrome (Angelman syndrome) develops. There is no overeating or obesity in this syndrome but instead there are unusual jerky movements and unprovoked paroxysms of laughter.

The third stimulus for the concept of specific behavioural phenotypes derived from a rather different source: namely, the appreciation that psychiatric disorders defined in purely behavioural terms may have a specific genetic basis (Harris, 1987). Autism constitutes the prototypical example of this kind (Bailey, Phillips and Rutter, in press; Rutter et al., in press a). The syndrome, first described by Kanner (1943), is characterized by qualitatively distinct abnormalities in communication and in social relationships, combined with particular forms of repetitive and stereotyped behaviour. These features are different in kind from the symptomatology shown in other psychiatric disorders, or which accompany mental retardation. As discussed above, twin and family data indicate an extremely strong and highly specific, genetic component. There is every reason to suppose that the clinical features derived fairly directly from the underlying organic abnormality, even though the pathogenic mechanisms are as yet unknown. Rett Syndrome constitutes the other, somewhat different, prototypical example (Rett, 1966; Hagberg et al., 1983; Rett Syndrome Diagnostic Criteria Working Group, 1988). The syndrome differs from autism in that the diagnostic features include neurological abnormalities (deceleration of head circumference, deterioration of motor and cognitive skills and often, but not always, gait apraxia and epilepsy). The earliest manifestations, however, are usually behavioural, with stereotypic mid-line hand-wringing movements beginning in the second year of life the most striking feature. Over the course of the next few years, together with a loss of purposive hand movements, teeth-grinding, breath-holding and hyperventilation are all very common. The condition occurs only in girls. The pathogenesis of the disorder remains unknown but it is thought highly likely that it will prove to be a specific genetic disorder, possibly due to an abnormal gene on the X chromosome, behaving in a dominant fashion.

The fourth stimulus for the concept of behavioural phenotypes was provided by the various parental self-help groups who were concerned that professionals should recognize that some of the behaviours exhibited by children with biologically based mentally handicapping disorders are organically determined (see O'Brien and Yule, 1995a).

As increasing attention has come to be paid to the phenomena of behavioural phenotypes, there has been the development of improved, and much more specific, behavioural measures. It was clear from Tizard's (1962) review that the measures available at that time (mostly questionnaires and projective tests) were seriously inadequate for testing hypotheses about specific behaviours that might be associated with particular medical conditions. The last thirty years has seen a major movement for the development of high quality, discriminating interview and observational measures of behaviour. The Child and Adolescent Psychiatric Assessment (CAPA) provides an example of a standardized investigator-based interview for the measurement of a wide range of child and adolescent psychopathology (Angold and Costello, 1995; Angold *et al.*, 1995) and the Autism Diagnostic Interview (ADI) (Le Couteur *et al.*, 1989; Lord, Rutter and Le Couteur, 1994) and the Autism Diagnostic Observation Schedule (Lord *et al.*, 1989; DiLavore, Lord and Rutter, 1995) provide examples relevant for the behavioural phenotype field of research. It would be a mistake, however, to assume that standardized methods, whatever their quality, provide a general answer. It is likely that careful clinical observations will always provide the first lead on the possible presence of behavioural phenotypes and systematic, specially devised, quantified observations will frequently be necessary to test the hypothesis. Thus, for example, these methods were invaluable in showing that the social and speech abnormalities that were most characteristic of fragile X individuals were rather different from the features usually associated with autism (Cohen *et al.*, 1989; Wolff *et al.*, 1989; Sudhalter *et al.*, 1990). It would also be an error to assume that psychological phenotypes should be confined to behavioural patterns. Distinctive cognitive patterns may be at least as important. Thus, it appears that there may be cognitive features that are relevantly distinctive in fragile X individuals (Mazzocco, Hagerman and Pennington, 1993). Individuals with different sex chromosome anomalies also vary to some extent in the distinctive behavioural and cognitive profiles they exhibit (Ratcliffe, 1994). Similarly, individuals with Williams syndrome appear relatively distinctive in both their behavioural characteristics and their cognitive profile (Udwin and Yule, 1990; Bellugi, Wang and Jernigan, 1994; Karmiloff-Smith *et al.*, 1995) Most have some degree of general cognitive impairment but they are chatty, socially disinhibited, overly affectionate towards adults, and appear to have a good command of language with an extensive vocabulary. They tend to be very proficient at face recognition, theory of mind skills, rote memory and many complex aspects of language forms. By contrast they are markedly impaired on tasks requiring the integration of visual spatial information, on number skills, on problem-solving and on general speed of information-processing.

Where should we go from here?

Empirical research findings over the last decade or so have clearly demonstrated much greater specificity in brain-behaviour relationships than seemed at all likely in the studies available thirty to forty years ago. There are several important practical implications. First, it has become very clear that progress has been inhibited by both a tendency to view mental retardation as an undifferentiated homogeneous grouping and by a relative disregard of the value of medical approaches to mental retardation (Medical Research Council, 1994; Rutter, 1995). This has been the case especially in the field of mild mental retardation in which it is now clear that pathological causes of various kinds account for a substantial proportion (albeit a minority) of cases (Rutter, Simonoff and Plomin, in press b; Simonoff, Bolton and Rutter, 1996). The study of specific behavioural and cognitive phenotypes has well demonstrated both the heterogeneity of mental retardation and also the value of investigating brain-behaviour relationships.

The second important implication is that attention needs to be paid to the likelihood that some of these phenotypic features derive fairly directly from organic brain pathology. That does not mean that they are not open to environmental influences but it certainly does imply that interventions need to be devised with an appreciation of the important role of biological etiological factors.

A third message concerns the potential value of using an unusual behavioural or cognitive phenotype as a starting point. That constitutes a very real change from the situation in the 1950s and 1960s. The relative failure to find specificity in brain-behaviour relationships at that time derived in large part from the fact that the research started with very broadly defined medical groupings (such as epilepsy or cerebral palsy or obstetric complications) which themselves involve major biological heterogeneity. The advances in molecular genetics now mean that it is possible to have much more closely defined, and biologically meaningful, medical starting points. Nevertheless, that does not necessarily imply that the way ahead lies in a search for distinctive behavioural features for each and every genetic condition that comes along. Instead, in many cases, it is likely to be preferable to begin with an unusual and highly distinctive behavioural or cognitive phenotype and to use that as the jumping-off point to examine its possible biological origins.

From an educational and clinical point of view, it will also be important to take into account these important individual differences in behaviour and patterns of cognitive performance in deciding how best to foster the development of the children concerned and how best to plan services that can provide the degree of individual tailoring that will be needed.

It is also necessary to appreciate that very few of the specificities in behaviour and cognitive patterns that have been demonstrated to be connected with specific medical conditions follow the usual psychiatric diagnostic guidelines. It is not, on the whole, that the medical conditions with associated specific behavioural phenotypes have an unusually high rate of, say, anxiety states, or hyperkinetic disorder, or major depression. There are some differences in the frequency of associated psychiatric diagnoses but what is really distinctive concerns the qualitatively unusual behaviours, and not the distribution of traditional psychiatric diagnoses.

The situation with respect to the theoretical value of the demonstrated specific brain-behaviour relationships is substantially more complicated. The promise lies in the potential for identifying the processes involved in the pathways from genotype to phenotype (Flint and Yule, 1994; Flint, 1996). There can be no doubt that that constitutes a most important research objective and the discovery of the mechanisms involved (they are likely to be multiple and chain-like in many instances) would be most important for theory and practice.

The great need for caution derives from several considerations. The first is that there is a considerable danger of overstating the specificity of the behavioural phenotypes. Although it is true that a few (such as the Lesch-Nyhan syndrome) are both highly specific (meaning that the behaviours rarely occur in the absence of the medical condition) and are highly consistent (meaning that the great majority of sufferers from the condition show this behavioural phenotype), that is the exception rather than the rule. Thus, the insatiable overeating and obesity found with the Prader-Willi syndrome undoubtably appears most distinctive but it is, as yet, not clear that it is qualitatively different from the overeating found in other disorders. Also, many of the supposedly characteristic phenotypes are actually surprisingly variable in their manifestations. Thus, although individuals with the fragile X anomaly appear distinctive in their behaviour and cognitive profile as a group, they are immensely variable individually. There is a risk that unwarranted stereotypes will build up. We need to recognize the important specificity but it is equally important that we do not overlook the marked individual variations.

A related point is that the somatic phenotypes associated with single gene disorders are often equally varied and there is no reason to suppose that the situation would be any different with behavioural profiles. For example, as noted above, the somatic manifestations of tuberous sclerosis and of neurofibromatosis extend so widely that some cases require highly skilled observations to detect whereas others are so gross as to be identifiable by the man in the street.

It is also necessary to appreciate that the associations between a genetic condition and a behavioural pattern are open to several rather different explanations. For example, the association between tuberous sclerosis and autism is probably closer than that for any other medical condition (Rutter *et al.*, in press a). That could mean that one or other of the two genes known to be linked with tuberous sclerosis might be directly implicated in the genesis of autism. Alternatively, it could be that those genes are situated very close to susceptibility genes for autism, although quite different genes are involved. But the association might have nothing to do with the genes as such. Thus, the cases of tuberous sclerosis that are associated with autism usually involve both mental retardation and epilepsy. It could be that the association with autism derives from a particular severity or distribution of brain pathology rather than from is genetic origin. Also, some individuals with tuberous sclerosis are not in the least bit autistic-like in their social functioning. What is the explanation for the marked behavioural differences within the group of sufferers from this condition?

The situation is yet more complex in the case of multigene disorders. Thus, one of the hopes for molecular genetic research with multifactorial disorders is that this could lead to the better understanding and identification of the various separate risk mechanisms that may be involved in the etiology of particular medical conditions (Sing and Reilly, 1993). Although indeed it may, so far it has not succeeded in reaching that objective. For example, it seems highly likely that several (but probably not very many) genes are involved in the etiology of autism. It would seem reasonable to suppose that one might find that the condition stems from the combination of, say, a gene concerned particularly with communication, and another with social relationships, and yet another with repetitive stereotyped behaviours but the evidence to date does not seem to support that possibility (Le Couteur *et al.*, 1996). The difficulty is part of a broader problem in the integration of different levels of research inquiry (Bailey, Phillips and Rutter, 1996). There have been many attempts over the years to hypothesize about the specific neural origin of autism on the basis of some aspect of symptomatology. The language abnormalities would seem to suggest a dominant hemisphere disorder but the socioemotional abnormalities are more consistent with a right hemisphere disorder. The executive-planning deficits would seem to point to a frontal lobe disorder whereas other parts of the brain appear to be implicated in other facets of the cognitive problems. It is certainly not the case that an integration is impossible but the difficulties are considerable.

A further hope that derives from the study of behavioural phenotypes concerns the possibility that the study of the abnormal will be helpful in casting light on normal development and functioning because the unusual clinical picture pulls apart variables that ordinarily go together (Rutter, 1993b). The study of cognitive across-domain associations has proved highly worthwhile in the delineation of the different processes involved in memory (see e.g. Tulving, 1983; Baddeley, 1990). Would the comparison of different behavioural phenotypes (e.g. Williams Syndrome and Down Syndrome or tuberous sclerosis and the fragile X anomaly) be equally informative? It is too early to tell but, provided there is proper attention to the numerous conceptual and methodological hazards, this does seem likely to be a productive mode of inquiry (Broman and Grafman, 1994).

If this research approach is to be effective, however, it will be essential that it involves effective integrative collaboration between people representing different areas of expertise (such as molecular genetics, basic neuroscience, cognitive psychology and clinical science). In one sense, the topic of possible specificity in brain-behaviour relationships has moved an exceedingly long way since Barbara Tizard's (1962) thoughtful and critical review of the concepts and findings on a supposed epileptic personality, but it would be equally true to say that the considerations she identified as important over thirty years ago remain as relevant today as they were then. The investigative tools available to us are incomparably better but the need to harness research enthusiasm and research caution remains.

Acknowledgements

We are grateful to Gregory O'Brien for allowing us access to the manuscript of *Behavioural Phenotypes* in advance of publication.

References

ANGOLD, A. and COSTELLO, E. J. (1995) 'A test-retest reliability study of child-reported psychiatric symptoms and diagnoses using the Child and Adolescent Psychiatric Assessment (CAPA-C)', *Psychological Medicine*, **25**, pp. 755–62.

ANGOLD, A., PRENDERGAST, M., COX, A., HARRINGTON, R., SIMONOFF, E. and RUTTER, M. (1995) 'The Child and Adolescent Psychiatric Assessment (CAPA)', *Psychological Medicine*, **25**, pp. 739–53.

BADDELEY, A. D. (1990) *Human Memory: Theory and Practice*, Hove & London, Erlbaum.

BAILEY, A., LE COUTEUR, A., GOTTESMAN, I., BOLTON, P., SIMONOFF, E., YUZDA, E. and RUTTER, M. (1995) 'Autism as a strongly genetic disorder: evidence from a British twin study', *Psychological Medicine*, **25**, pp. 63–77.

BAILEY, A., PHILLIPS, W. and RUTTER, M. (1996) 'Autism: towards an integration of clinical, genetic, neuropsychological, and neurobiological perspectives', *Journal of Child Psychology and Psychiatry, Annual Research Review*, **37**, pp. 89–126.

BAKWIN, H. and BAKWIN, R. M. M. (1967) *Clinical Management of Behavior Disorders in Children*, 3rd Edn, Philadelphia, W. B. Saunders.

BELLUGI, U., WANG, P. P. and JERNIGAN, T. L. (1994) 'Williams Syndrome: an unusual neuropsychological profile', in BROMAN, S. H. and GRAFMAN, J. (Eds) *Atypical Cognitive Deficits in Developmental Disorders: Implications for Brain Function*, pp. 22–83, Hillsdale, NJ, Erlbaum.

BOLTON, P., MACDONALD, H., PICKLES, A., RIOS, P., GOODE, S., CROWSON, M., BAILEY, A. and RUTTER, M. (1994) 'A case-control family history study of autism', *Journal of Child Psychology and Psychiatry*, **35**, pp. 877–900.

BROMAN, S. H. and GRAFMAN, J. (Eds) (1994) *Atypical Cognitive Deficits in Developmental Disorders: Implications for Brain Function*, Hillsdale, NJ, Erlbaum.

CHADWICK, O., RUTTER, M., THOMPSON, J. and SHAFFER, D. (1981) 'Intellectual performance and reading skills after localized head injury in childhood', *Journal of Child Psychology and Psychiatry*, **22**, pp. 117–39.

COHEN, I. L., VIETZE, P. M., SUDHALTER, V., JENKINS, E. C. and BROWN, W. T. (1989) 'Parent-child dyadic gaze patterns in fragile X males and in non-fragile X males with autistic disorder', *Journal of Child Psychology and Psychiatry*, **30**, pp. 845–56.

DiLAVORE, P. C., LORD, C. and RUTTER, M. (1995) 'The Pre-Linguistic Autism Diagnostic Observation Schedule', *Journal of Autism and Developmental Disorders*, **25**, pp. 355–79.

DYKENS, E. M. (1995) 'Measuring behavioral phenotypes: provocations from the "New Genetics"', *American Journal on Mental Retardation*, **99**, pp. 522–32.

ELANDER, J. and RUTTER, M. (1996) 'Use and development of the Rutter Parents' and Teachers' Scales', *International Journal of Methods in Psychiatric Research*, **6**, pp. 63–78.

ELLIS, N. R. (1969) 'A behavioral research strategy in mental retardation: defense and critique', *American Journal of Mental Deficiency*, **73**, pp. 557–66.

FLINT, J. (in press) 'Pathways from genotype to phenotype', in O'BRIEN, G. and YULE, W. (Eds) *Behavioural Phenotypes*, pp. 75–89, London, MacKeith Press.

FLINT, J. and YULE, W. (1994) 'Behavioural phenotypes', in RUTTER, M., TAYLOR, E. and HERSOV, L. (Eds) *Child and Adolescent Psychiatry: Modern Approaches*, 3rd Edn, pp. 666–87, Oxford, Blackwell Scientific Publications.

GOODMAN, R. (1994a) 'Brain disorders', in RUTTER, M., TAYLOR, E. and HERSOV, L. (Eds) *Child and Adolescent Psychiatry: Modern Approaches*, 3rd Edn, pp. 172–90, Oxford, Blackwell Scientific Publications.

GOODMAN, R. (1994b) 'Brain development', in RUTTER, M., and HAY, D. F. (Eds) *Development Through Life: A Handbook for Clinicians*, pp. 49–78, Oxford, Blackwell Scientific Publications.

HAGBERG, G., AICARDI, J., DIAS, K. and RAMOS, O. (1983) 'A progressive syndrome of autism, dementia, ataxia, and loss of purposeful hand use in girls: Rett's syndrome: report of 35 cases', *Annals of Neurology*, **14**, pp. 471–9.

HAGERMAN, R. (1995) 'Lessons from fragile X syndrome', in O'BRIEN, G. and YULE, W. (Eds) *Behavioural Phenotypes*, pp. 59–74, London, MacKeith Press.

HARRIS, J. C. (1987) 'Behavioural phenotypes in mental retardation: unlearned behaviours', *Advances in Developmental Disorders*, **1**, pp. 77–106.

HERMANN, B. P. and SEIDENBERG, M. (Eds) (1989) *Childhood Epilepsies: Neuropsychological, Psychosocial and Intervention Aspects*, Chichester, Wiley.

HEYWOOD, C. A. and CANAVAN, A. G. M. (1987) 'Developmental neuropsychological correlates of language', in YULE, W. and RUTTER, M. (Eds) *Language Development and Disorders*, pp. 146–58, London, MacKeith Press.

KALVERBOER, A. F., van PRAAG, H. M. and MENDLEWICZ, J. (Eds) (1978) *Minimal Brain Dysfunction: Facts and Fiction*, Basel, S. Karger.
KANNER, L. (1943) 'Autistic disturbances of affective contact', *Nervous Child*, **2**, pp. 217–50.
KARMILOFF-SMITH, A., KLIMA, E., BELLUGI, U., GRANT, J. and BARON-COHEN, S. (1995) 'Is there a social module? Language, face processing, and theory of mind in individuals with Williams Syndrome', *Journal of Cognitive Neuroscience*, **7**, pp. 196–208.
KAUFMAN, K. R., HARRIS, R. and SCHAFFER, D. (1980) 'Problems in the categorization of child and adolescent EEGs', *Journal of Child Psychology and Psychiatry*, **21**, pp. 333–42.
LE COUTEUR, A., BAILEY, A., GOODE, S., PICKLES, A., ROBERTSON, S., GOTTESMAN, I. and RUTTER, M. (1996) 'A broader phenotype of autism: the clinical spectrum in twins', *Journal of Child Psychology and Psychiatry*, **37**.
LE COUTEUR, A., RUTTER, M., LORD, C., RIOS, P., ROBERTSON, S., HOLDGRAFEN, M. and MCLENNAN, J. (1989) 'Autism Diagnostic Interview: a standardized investigator–based instrument', *Journal of Autism and Developmental Disorders*, **19**, pp. 363–87.
LORD, C., RUTTER, M., GOODE, S., HEEMSBERGEN, J., JORDAN, H., MAWHOOD, L. and SCHOPLER, E. (1989) 'Autism Diagnostic Observation Schedule: a standardized observation of communicative and social behavior', *Journal of Autism and Developmental Disorders*, **19**, pp. 185–212.
LORD, C., RUTTER, M. and LE COUTEUR, A. (1994) 'Autism Diagnostic Interview-Revised: a revised version of a diagnostic interview for caregivers of individuals with possible Pervasive Developmental Disorders', *Journal of Autism and Developmental Disorders*, **24**, pp. 659–85.
MAZZOCCO, M. M. M., HAGERMAN, R. J. and PENNINGTON, B. F. (1993) 'The neurocognitive phenotype of female carriers of fragile X: additional evidence for specificity', *Journal of Developmental and Behavioral Paediatrics*, **14**, pp. 328–35.
MCFIE, J. (1975) *Assessment of Organic Impairment*, London, Academic Press.
MEDICAL RESEARCH COUNCIL (1994) *Mental Handicap Research: New Technologies and Approaches*, report of the MRC workshop held at the University of Warwick on 29/30 July 1993.
NEWCOMBE, F. (1969) *Missile Wounds of the Brain: A Study of Psychological Deficits*, New York, Oxford University Press.
NYHAN, W. L. (1976) 'Behavior in the Lesch-Nyhan syndrome', *Journal of Autism and Childhood Schizophrenia*, **6**, pp. 235–52.
O'BRIEN, G. and YULE, W. (Eds) (1995a) *Behavioural Phenotypes*, London, MacKeith Press.
O'BRIEN, G. and YULE, W. (1995b) 'Why behavioural phenotypes?', in O'BRIEN, G. and YULE, W. (Eds) *Behavioural Phenotypes*, pp. 1–23, London, MacKeith Press.
OLIVER, C. (1995) 'Annotation: self-injurious behaviour in children with learn-

ing disabilities: recent advances in assessment and intervention', *Journal of Child Psychology and Psychiatry*, **30**, pp. 909–27.

RATCLIFFE, S. G. (1994) 'The psychological and psychiatric consequences of sex chromosome abnormalities in children based on population studies', in POUTSKA, F. (Ed.) *Basic Approaches to Genetic and Molecular Biological Developmental Psychiatry*, pp. 99–122, Berlin, Quintessatz Verlags.

RETT, A. (1966) 'Über ein eigenartiges himatrophisches Syndrom bei Hyperammonämie in Kindesalter', *Weiner Medizinische Wochenschrift*, **116**, pp. 723–6.

RETT SYNDROME DIAGNOSTIC CRITERIA WORKING GROUP (1988) 'Diagnostic criteria for Rett Syndrome', *Annals of Neurology*, **23**, pp. 425–8.

RUTTER, M. (1970) 'Autistic children: infancy to adulthood', *Seminars in Psychiatry*, **2**, pp. 435–50.

RUTTER, M. (1971) 'Psychiatry', in WORTIS, J. (Ed.) *Mental Retardation: An Annual Review III*, pp. 186–221, New York, Grune & Stratton.

RUTTER, M. (1979) 'Language, congnition and autism', in KATZMAN, R. (Ed.) *Congenital and Acquired Cognitive Disorders*, pp. 247–64, New York, Raven Press.

RUTTER, M. (1982a) 'Syndromes attributed to "minimal brain dysfunction" in children', *American Journal of Psychiatry*, **139**, pp. 21–33.

RUTTER, M. (1982b) 'Developmental neuropsychiatry: concepts, issues and problems', *Journal of Clinical Neuropsychology*, **4**, pp. 91–115.

RUTTER, M. (1993a) 'An overview of developmental neuropsychiatry', in BESAG, F. M. C. and WILLIAMS, R. T. (Eds) *The Brain and Behaviour: Organic Influences on the Behaviour of Children*, Special issue *Educational and Child Psychology*, **10**, pp. 4–11.

RUTTER, M. (1993b) 'Developmental psychopathology as a research perspective', in MAGNUSSON, D. and CASAER, P. (Eds) *Longitudinal Research for Individual Development: Present Status and Future Perspectives*, pp. 127–52, Cambridge, Cambridge University Press.

RUTTER, M. (1995) 'Mental handicap: a resurgence of research interest?', *Science and Technology*, Spring, pp. 15–19.

RUTTER, M., BAILEY, A., SIMONOFF, E. and PICKLES, A. (in press a) 'Genetic influences and autism', in VOLKMAR, F. and COHEN, D. (Eds) *Handbook of Autism*, New York Wiley.

RUTTER, M., CHADWICK, O. and SCHACHAR, R. (1983b) 'Hyperactivity and minimal brain dysfunction: epidemiological perspectives on questions of cause and classification', in TARTER, R. E. (Ed.) *The Child at Psychiatric Risk*, pp. 80–107, New York, Oxford University Press.

RUTTER, M., CHADWICK, O. and SHAFFER, D. (1983a) 'Head injury', in RUTTER, M. (Ed.) *Developmental Neuropsychiatry*, pp. 83–111, Edinburgh, Churchill Livingstone.

RUTTER, M., GRAHAM, P. and YULE, W. (1970a) *A Neuropsychiatric Study in*

Childhood, Clinics in Developmental Medicine, **35/36**, London, S. I. M. P./Heinemann.

RUTTER, M., MAWHOOD, L. and HOWLIN, P. (1992) 'Language delay and social development', in FLETCHER, P. and HALL, D. (Eds) *Specific Speech and Language Disorders in Children*, pp. 63–78, London, Whurr Publishers.

RUTTER, M., SIMONOFF, E. and PLOMIN, R. (in press b) 'Genetic influences on mild mental retardation: concepts, findings and research implications'. *Journal of Biosocial Science*.

RUTTER, M., TIZARD, J. and WHITMORE, K. (Eds) (1970b) *Education, Health and Behaviour*, London, Longman.

SCHNEIDER, G. E. (1979) 'Is it really better to have your brain lesion early? A revision of the "Kennard Principle"', *Neuropsychologia*, **17**, 557–83.

SEIDEL, U. P., CHADWICK, O. F. D. and RUTTER, M. (1975) 'Psychological disorders in crippled children. A comparative study of children with and without brain damage', *Developmental Medicine and Child Neurology*, **17**, pp. 563–73.

SHAFFER, D., CHADWICK, O. and RUTTER, M. (1975) 'Psychiatric outcome of localized head injury in children', in PORTER, R. and FITZSIMONS, D. W. (Eds) *Outcome of Severe Damage to the Central Nervous System*, Ciba Foundation Symposium, **34**, pp. 191–213, Amsterdam, Excerpta Medica.

SIMONOFF, E., BOLTON, P. and RUTTER, M. (1996) 'Mental retardation: genetic findings, clinical implications and research agenda', *Journal of Child Psychology and Psychiatry*, **37**, pp. 259–280.

SING, C. F. and REILLY, S. L. (1993) 'Genetics of common diseases that aggregate, but do not segregate in families', in SING, C. F. and HARRIS, C. L. (Eds) *Genetics of Cellular, Individual, Family and Population Variability*, pp. 140–61, New York, Oxford University Press.

SUDHALTER, V., COHEN, I. L., SILVERMAN, W. and WOLF-SCHEIN, E. G. (1990) 'Conversational analyses of males with fragile X syndrome, Down Syndrome and autism: comparison of the emergence of deviant language', *American Journal on Mental Retardation*, **94**, pp. 431–41.

TAYLOR, D. C. and EMINSON, M. (1994) 'Psychological aspects of chronic physical sickness', in RUTTER, M., TAYLOR, E. and HERSOV, L. (Eds) *Child and Adolescent Psychiatry: Modern Approaches*, 3rd Edn, pp. 737–48, Oxford, Blackwell Scientific Publications.

TIZARD, B. (1962) 'The personality of epileptics: a discussion of the evidence', *Psychological Bulletin*, **59**, pp. 196–210.

TULVING, E. (1983) *Elements of Episodic Memory*, London and New York, Oxford University Press.

TURK, J. (1992) 'The fragile X syndrome. On the way to a behavioural phenotype', *British Journal of Psychiatry*, **160**, pp. 24–35.

UDWIN, O. and YULE, W. (1990) 'A cognitive and behavioural phenotype in Williams Syndrome', *Journal of Clinical and Experimental Neuropsychology*, **13**, pp. 232–44.

VARGHA-KHADEM, F., ISAACS, E., VAN DER WERF, S., ROBB, S. and WILSON, J. (1992) 'Development of intelligence and memory in children with hemiplegic cerebral palsy: the deleterious consequences of early seizures', *Brain*, **115**, pp. 315–29.

WOLFF. P. H., GARDNER, J., PACCIA, J. and LAPPEN, J. (1989) 'The greeting behavior of fragile X males', *American Journal of Mental Retardation*, **93**, pp. 406–11.

WOODS, B. T. and CAREY, S. (1979) 'Language deficits after apparent clinical recovery from childhood aphasia', *Annals of Neurology*, **6**, pp. 405–7.

YULE, W. and TAYLOR, E. (1987) 'Classification of soft signs', in TUPPER, D. E. (Ed.) *Soft Neurological Signs: Manifestations, Measurement, Research and Meaning*, pp. 19–43, New York. Grune & Stratton.

Chapter 2

Varied Destinies: A Study of Unfulfilled Predictions

Alan Clarke and Ann Clarke

For well over four decades we have enjoyed Barbara Tizard's friendship and admired her as a scientist. During this period she has exercised her creative, critical and analytic ability in several areas of psychology, has been a devoted wife and mother and latterly, as a widow, took over responsibility for the Thomas Coram Research Unit founded by Jack Tizard. It is a pleasure and privilege to offer a chapter for this book, the contents of which reflect her wide range of interests and important contributions to psychology and social policy.

The establishment of cause-effect relations and their accurate prediction has been the hallmark of the scientific method, nowhere more obvious than in the physical sciences where it originated. Yet Heisenberg in 1927, after making vital contributions to quantum mechanics, stated his Uncertainty Principle which was to have a major effect on scientific thinking. Gleick (1992) summarizes Heisenberg's narrow definition: 'a particle cannot have both a definite place and a definite momentum,' adding that the implications seemed to cover a broader territory than the atom and its interior (p. 429). Thus entered into science an element of unpredictability which challenged earlier views, more recently augmented by chaos theory.

Behavioural science by its very nature has to live with a good deal of uncertainty. Psychologists tend to get excited about correlations as low as 0.50 between childhood and adult characteristics, even though this accounts for only 25 per cent of common variance. Immediate reliability on tests or other assessments of 0.90 or a little above is very acceptable, but test-retest reliability virtually never approximates to 1.00. This failure to maintain precise rank order arises from personal fluctuations which may be important in screening programmes, but are of relatively little significance in developmental predictions. Such fluctuations can be cancelled out by repeated assessment over fairly short periods, yielding greater predictive power than from a single 'snapshot'. But if in a longitudinal study only before and after measures are available, such transitory variations may indicate a trend where none exists, or indeed conceal a 'true' change, depending on the direction of the two 'errors'. These latter are usually thought somehow to reside in the test as opposed to the individual. However, true test error can occur, sometimes dramatically, where, within a test, different standard deviations are found for different ages, or where there are differences between different assessment devices.

In complex systems (and this includes individual development) alteration in one or more variables can affect the whole and thus reflect, or impinge on, the life path. This view becomes obvious when, even from an armchair viewpoint, we consider our description of fundamental parameters of development (Clarke, 1982). First, the biological trajectory may wax or wane at different periods and may differ for different processes. The adolescent growth spurt is one example, and the growing heritability for IQ in adolescence is another (Wilson, 1985). Second, there is a psychosocial trajectory which, too, develops and changes for the individual, whether in the micro-, meso- or macro-environment. Third, there are interactional/transactional processes. To varying extents individuals both affect and reflect environmental influences (Scarr and McCartney, 1983) in feed-forward and feedback processes. In some sense they unwittingly play a causal role in their own development. Finally, chance encounters (Bandura, 1982) or chance events can sometimes alter the direction of the life path. Consideration of these interacting complexities suggests a degree of unpredictability for the individual, a principle of developmental uncertainty.

In determining whether predictions are likely to be strongly or only partially fulfilled, account must be taken of the process involved; thus, much higher correlations have been found for indices of IQ than for any single personality variable. Furthermore, much will depend on the time span over which forecasts are made: the longer the time period, the less accurate in all but the most deviant conditions. Above all, it is important to note whether broad or narrow predictions are required. Dividing a population into top and bottom 50 per cent will lead to fewer changes in category compared with splitting the distribution into ten bands.

Two or three variables taken together (and sometimes suitably weighted) can often yield important long-term predictions of particular characteristics, or life path outcomes. The next step might be to add further measures in the hope of increasing predictive power. In such circumstances a law of diminishing returns operates; multiple correlations are likely to increase but only by small amounts. This reflects the web of related measures, such that the additional variables, correlated with the first two or three, overlap in their predictive power.

Predictions may be based on some sort of a constancy model: that is, with respect to age peers, people change little as they develop. Alternatively, a knowledge of the natural history of a particular condition may suggest an actuarial prediction (e.g. the decline in relative ability of Down's Syndrome children with increasing age). Or again, predictions may rely on knowledge of the common effects of particular events (e.g. divorce), or on the expected outcome of interventions.

We argue that the study of those who defy predictions is of interest in its own right, but may also have a general bearing on our understanding of the dynamics of development. For abnormal conditions, in particular, those who escape their expected destiny may yield evidence on prevention. It is quite

A Study of Unfulfilled Predictions

common to show that some severe adolescent problem yields a very bad adult prognosis, perhaps affecting 80 per cent. The 20 per cent whose adult outcome differed are sometimes brushed aside in discussion, and occasionally circular arguments (e.g. 'the original diagnosis must have been wrong') explain them away. In line with the principle of developmental uncertainty, we indicate that there is nearly always an 'escape' rate from abnormal conditions.

This chapter addresses the question of failures in predicting individual development. Depending both on the particular characteristic, as well as the time span involved, failures of precise prediction may be nearly as common as successes, but owing to the less positive emphasis, are less likely to be discussed directly. Within the constraints of space we outline some recent research findings in just four areas: personality development, early attachment, child sexual abuse and intelligence. Within each, we sample a few of the studies which illuminate the problem of predictive error.

The extent of predictive failures

Personality development

In *Lives Through Time* Block (1971) used a Q-sort method to describe each of 150 subjects in the earlier Oakland and Berkeley Guidance Studies, at the ages of about 15, 18 and 33. Correlating individuals' scores with similar later ones, average correlations of 0.75 (15–18) and 0.55 (18–33) were obtained. Note the lower correlations for the longer period, a customary finding. A wide range of individual correlations was obtained, ranging from considerable constancy at one extreme to complete inconstancy at the other (i.e. no prediction from the early scores). Thus both constancies and changes were exhibited. Before taking these findings at face value, two points need to be made: (1) the original scores, taken years before the analysis, had imperfect reliability; and (2) the later Q-sort would also show imperfect reliability. Taken together, some of the changes would have arisen from these 'errors'. Not surprisingly, these data have been open to different interpretations (Block, 1980; Clarke and Clarke, 1984). While Block argues for continuities, Macfarlane (1964) who had conducted the Berkeley Study, commented with surprise that 'Many of our most mature and competent adults had severely troubled and confusing childhoods and adolescences. Many of our highly successful children and adolescents have failed to achieve their predicted potential... but we were not always wrong! We did have several small groups whose adult status fulfilled theoretical expectations', that is, that personality does not alter and is therefore predictable.

A further *caveat* must be advanced. It may well be that while global personality assesments show both constancies in some, and changes in others, over time, perhaps some dimensions show greater continuities, but are obscured in overall evaluations. This would probably be the view of Kagan who has identified early shyness as showing strong continuities. Nevertheless, Kagan and Snidman (1991) and Kagan (1992) indicate that even with high heritability, a very substantial minority show phenotypic changes over time. Some who were unusually inhibited as infants were no longer so later, while others who had been sociable and fearless had later become shy with adults and children (Kagan, 1992, p. 994). Such changes were presumably the result of intervening experiences. However, the majority of very inhibited children may be at risk of a very introverted adulthood.

A notable addition to the literature on this problem has been provided by Kerr *et al.* (1994) who carried out on a Swedish longitudinal sample a 'conceptual replication' of Kagan's work. Among questions raised were whether extremes of inhibition showed greater stability over time than non-extremes, and whether there are gender differences in stability. We have ourselves (1988) suggested that extremes are likely to have a different developmental history than others.

Data on a large sample consisted of mothers' ratings over a sixteen-year period, and psychologists' ratings over the first six years of life. The former was concerned with perceived shyness towards strangers, and the latter with inhibited behaviour in the testing situation. On the question of temporal stability for the whole group, the findings reflected the two principles to which we have drawn attention over several decades. Correlations increase with increasing age, and the longer the time gap between assessments, the lower the correlation (i.e. the greater the likelihood of change in individual ordinal position). In the context of the present theme, the greatest interest is in whether there are differences in stability between those at the extremes of the distribution versus those in the non-extreme group. For the first six years, stability data supported Kagan's findings. However, 'behaviour did change in the long run ... For most of our subjects the early causes of extremely inhibited or uninhibited behaviour were not long-lasting' (p. 144). Although ratings were more stable for children in the extreme groups, stability into adolescence was only found for inhibited females. Here the authors speculate that culturally shared notions of gender-appropriate behaviour influence the stability of inhibition. This, then, is a study that emphasizes for many of the sample a relative long-term unpredictability of a personality characteristic. We must be aware, however, that overt behaviour may cover up internal inhibitions, and that self-awareness of our own personality may lead to compensatory overt behaviour (Chess and Thomas, 1984). For a useful overview, see Plomin and Dunn (1986).

Using information from the Berkeley Guidance Study, Caspi, Elder and Bem (1988) followed up a group of late childhood shy children at ages thirty and forty. Very significant associations were found, especially for men, with delayed marriage, delayed fatherhood, as well as entry to a stable career. The authors indicate the likelihood that childhood shyness leads to avoidance of novel situations, particularly at life transitions, and point to the reciprocal person/environment dynamics which can maintain behaviour. Although the differences between adult outcomes of shy and non-shy children are often striking, the data make clear that predictions from late childhood are imperfect, with overlaps between these groups. It would be important to know the mechanisms for individual predictive failure. This study is very important in view of the late childhood baseline, a time when in many cases shyness would have become habitual, and also in the very lengthy follow-up to early middle age.

There is a vast literature on prediction from child or adolescent abnormal personality, with some hundreds of longitudinal studies (see, for example, Mednick and Baert, 1981). Here we examine just two. Rodgers (1990) used a thirty-six-year follow-up of a national birth cohort to study the associations between childhood behaviour and personality with affective disorder. The adult criterion was the Present State Examination. The author regards the accuracy of prediction as unimpressive (p. 411), but in a few instances the prognosis was especially poor, notably for bed-wetting frequently at age six, frequent truanting at age fifteen and speech problems at the same age. Even the identification of groups with multiple risk factors failed to yield a high number of cases.

Another study which repays close reading has been reported by Esser, Schmidt and Woerner (1990). In a rather brief longitudinal account of a large cohort of children between the ages of eight and thirteen, around 16 per cent at age eight exhibited moderate or severe psychiatric disorders. The same percentage was found at age thirteen, but the distribution of diagnoses at this later age had changed substantially, with a remarkable increase in conduct disorders, with similar rates for girls as for boys. For us the most interesting finding was the fairly common switch from no disorders at age eight to disorders at age thirteen, and from disorders at age eight to no disorders at age thirteen. Specifically, one half of the disordered eight-year-olds were similarly rated at thirteen, while half were not. Adverse family situations and learning disabilities were associated with new conduct disorders, but more accurate prediction for emotional disorders were the number of life events and adverse family situations. At one extreme, three-quarters of those with conduct disorders at age eight were persistently disordered at age thirteen, but, at the other, early neurotic disorders were likely to remit. Such findings are amply supported by previous work.

Early attachment

This area of research owes its origin to John Bowlby (1951). His views on the importance for mental health of a warm, permanent relationship with the mother were later extended and developed, with strong influences from animal research, especially that of Lorenz. Ainsworth and Witting (1969) extensively elaborated the significance of attachment and created the Strange Situation test. One prediction from these contributions is that children who have not experienced an appropriate early attachment should find difficulty in developing bonds with their own children.

Fonagy, Steele and Steele (1991), Fonagy *et al.* (1994) and Steele, Steele and Fonagy (1995) have reported fascinating material on the intergenerational transmission of attachment behaviour. During first pregnancies mothers and fathers-to-be were asked to describe their own childhood relations with their parents, and were classified as secure/insecure via the Adult Attachment Interview. After the birth of their babies the children were assessed at twelve and eighteen months, enabling them to be classified as secure or insecure in the Strange Situation. Maternal perceptions of their own childhood attachment predicted subsequent infant-mother secure/insecure attachment patterns 75 per cent of the time. Thus a high level of prediction was confirmed. Not only do the authors discuss their successful predictions, but also consider the 25 per cent 'error', examining cases where prenatally reported early attachment security coincided with insecurely attached children, as well as prenatally reported attachment insecurity related to securely attached offspring. Various speculative explanations, including some environmental circumstances, were offered. Such findings illustrate our view that a single criterion (in this case early attachment) is unlikely to provide a wholly satisfactory account of complex behaviour, even when predictively powerful. Although Steele, Steele and Fonagy (1995) discuss temperament briefly, this factor may well be of importance in the Strange Situation, especially at extremes of temperament. This characteristic, with its substantial genetic influence, may well be one of the mediating variables between parents and offspring (see also Goldsmith and Alansky, 1987; Fox, Kimmerly and Schafer, 1991; and Benoit and Parker, 1994).

Fonagy's work is particularly useful in the present context of prediction, suggesting that early attachment may have long-lasting effects. However, it is an open question whether early security/insecurity is a direct causal influence on adult outcome, or whether it is a marker for ongoing influences throughout childhood and adolescence. If temperament is, indeed, one of several mediators, its ongoing continuity in some cases may reflect indirectly from early attachment. In a notable review, Rutter (1995) believes that 'we are very far from having reached an understanding of the development of relation-ships or of the ways in which distortions in relationships play a role in psychopathology... attachment is not the whole of relationships' (p. 566).

Another review concerning insecure attachment has been produced by van IJzendoorn, Juffer and Duyvesteyn (1995). They conducted a meta-analysis of attachment studies on children aged between twelve and twenty-four months. Among other things, they found that interventions are more effective in changing parental insensitivity than in altering children's attachment insecurity. This is reminiscent of the findings of Chess and Thomas (1984) who argued that 'goodness of fit' between parents and young children could be more easily achieved via small change in parents' characteristic behaviour towards them. Van IJzendoorn, Juffer and Duyvesteyn believe that later measures of attachment are more difficult to interpret. Most subjects in attachment studies are very young.

What emerges very strongly from work on late adoption (e.g. Clarke and Clarke, 1976; Tizard, 1977) and from studies of isolated children, discovered late and subsequently habilitated (Skuse, 1984) is that delayed attachments occur and can be maintained. This is just one example of the move away from the notion of critical (rather than sensitive) periods of development.

Childhood sexual abuse

By now there is a vast literature on this problem, and no one can underestimate its seriousness. There is a widespread belief that adverse psychological consequences are inevitable. Such a view is understandable in the light of both the incidents themselves and the probable type of family context in which many of them occur. But since most of the studies have been retrospective on the basis of clinic samples, it is likely that there may have been a reporting bias; those seriously affected may not be wholly representative of all cases of childhood sexual abuse.

Some recent and powerful evidence on this problem has been produced by Mullen *et al.* (1993, 1994). A postal questionnaire was sent to 2250 randomly selected New Zealand women. Information was sought on a range of sociodemographic and family factors, as well as screening for the subjects' experience of sexual and physical abuse during childhood and adulthood. Included was the twenty-eight-item General Health Questionnaire, as well as other measures. Two groups were selected for interview, 298 who reported childhood sexual abuse and an equivalent number who had not so reported. Very detailed information was recorded. As might be expected, a history of child sexual abuse was associated with increased psychiatric problems in later life. While the focus was on mental health difficulties, 'it should not be overlooked that many victims gave no account of significant psychiatric difficulties in adult life' (Mullen *et al.*, 1993, p. 728). In other words, they had escaped the usual prediction. Furthermore, the authors go on to state that 'The overlap between the possible effects of sexual abuse and the effects of the matrix of social disadvantage ... were so considerable as to raise doubts about how often, in practice, it operates as an independent causal element'.

The authors' second contribution amplifies the picture in detailing risk factors for the ill effects of such abuse. It is of interest that only 53.8 per cent of the women attributed long-term effects directly to abuse. Fear of men, lack of trust, damage to self-esteem and self-confidence, as well as sexual problems were among the difficulties they described. Much of the adult *sequelae* may arise from these factors and may be second-order effects (Mullen *et al.*, 1994, p. 45) and therefore potentially preventable.

Turning to the other half of the problem, there is a widespread belief that perpetrators of child sexual abuse have themselves inevitably been abused as children. If this were so, then very precise predictions might be made. Again, there may have been a reporting bias for such beliefs. An important three-year Scottish study by Waterhouse, Dobash and Carnie (1994) indicates, among other things, that the conventional view is simplistic and to an extent incorrect.

The first part of this research involved quantitative analyses of the records of 501 cases of child sexual abuse, drawn from social work, criminal justice and health service files. One of the problems was the uneven amount of information available on the abusers, so that for a particular question there might be either full data recorded (e.g. employment/unemployment) or particular information for some but not for others. Thus, for the central question here, we find that in only 201 out of 501 was there an indication as to whether the abusers had suffered some form of sexual or physical abuse as children. Only 23 per cent were so recorded; this leaves a question mark over the remainder where nothing specifically relevant was noted, perhaps through lack of investigation, or through lack of perceived importance, or because it had not occurred.

The second part of the study is more revealing about our chosen theme. It used one- to two-hour skilled, in-depth interviews with fifty-three abusers, mainly in prison, a reasonably representative sample of this population. Again, a large amount of important information emerged. Here we note only that almost half described their childhoods as 'unhappy'. Offences were either classified as 'familial' (48 per cent) or 'extra-familial' (52 per cent). The childhood backgrounds of the latter were generally quite different from those abusing within the family. They were more likely to have grown up in disrupted families in which significant parental violence towards them was noted, or where a parental mental health problem existed. They were more likely to have experienced prolonged separations or to have grown up in institutions. They were much more likely to have suffered sexually abusive behaviour as children than were the familial offenders. However, of the total sample of abusers interviewed (fifty-three) only twenty-two (41 per cent) reported early sexual abuse, while thirty-one did not. As noted, these former tended to come from more disrupted families than those who had not so suffered.

The findings of this study confirm, yet again, that for complex behaviour, the search for single causes is unlikely to be successful. In this, as in other fields, there exists a web of interrelated factors which indicate probabilities of varying strengths, not certainties.

Intelligence

Much of the classic longitudinal work on IQ has shown that variability in development was as impressive as constancy, and that both were involved in any large sample reared under normal conditions (Clarke and Clarke, 1984).

However, it has never been possible in any of the numerous attempts to show environmental correlates of IQ change in the normal population. Thus, these must have been due to individual fluctuations, or to different tests used at different ages, or in a minority to sequential increments or decrements. More recent research, using the Wechsler Intelligence Scale for Children-Revised (WISC-R), has, unlike the earlier work, tended to emphasize constancy over time. Thus, Yule, Gold and Busch (1982) followed a normal sample of Isle of Wight children, assessed on the Wechsler Pre-school and Primary Scale of Intelligence (WPPSI) at five and a half and retested eleven years later at sixteen and a half on the WISC-R. Results correlated a high 0.86. However, 10 per cent of the children changed by more than 13 points from their original score and our rough calculations suggest that around 30 per cent would have altered by more than half a standard deviation either way, our arbitrary standard of significance. Another example has been provided by Tew and Laurence (1983) reporting a 0.92 correlation between IQs at age five and age sixteen for spina bifida children. Nevertheless, almost 30 per cent varied by more than 10 points and 16 per cent by more than a standard deviation over this eleven-year period.

A further example comes from research reported by Moffitt et al. (1993). Using a New Zealand sample of 794 children, assessed at ages seven, nine, eleven and thirteen on the WISC-R, these authors suggest that overall IQ change is either negligible in amount, unreliably measured or both. However, a good deal of intra-individual variability occurred. Thus 107 children (13.5 per cent of the sample) showed changes which via cluster analysis could be grouped into six reliable patterns. There were no significant correlates of changes. While this variability was marked, the amount of cumulative and sequential change averaged only 5.3 IQ points across the seven years. Only one of the six patterns showed a monotonic trajectory, that of IQ increment, applying to only 3 per cent of the sample. 'In general, then, patterns of IQ change appear to conform to recovery curves and seem to reflect level-maintaining or even level-seeking phenomena ... IQ appears to be elastic rather than plastic' (p. 496). These findings surprised the authors, being for them unfulfilled predictions.

While these three examples tend to emphasize that only in a minority do sustained, sequential changes take place within relatively constant environments, we wish to underline 'relatively'. Quite significant alterations in children's circumstances do not influence IQ, although they may well impinge on other characteristics. However, where children are rescued from dire circumstances, the situation is entirely different, for gross environmental deprivation may have very marked detrimental effects which in certain better circumstances may be reversed (Clarke and Clarke, 1992).

The predictive value of infant tests has until recently been largely written off (including by ourselves) on the grounds of very low correlation with later IQ due, it has been assumed, to the total lack of correspondence between the content of early and later measures. In addition, growth is so fast in the first year of life that fluctuant abilities may predominate. During the last decade, however, there has been increasing interest in the predictive power of infant information-processing, including response to novelty, habituation and other aspects of perception. Correlations as high as 0.61 have been reported (Slater *et al.*, 1989) between length of fixation to a novel stimulus at the age of six months and the WISC at eight years, although the majority of predictive indices fell well short of this value. (See also Slater (1995) for an overview.)

McCall and Carriger (1993), in their meta-analysis, gave a raw median correlation of 0.45 between habituation and recognition memory assessments in the first year of life and IQ measured at between one and eight years of age. It must be remembered that any sizeable correlation is surprising when we consider the low reliabilities reported for the early measures. There is a degree of controversy surrounding these results. A troubling finding is an association between sample size and predictive correlation. These authors report a -0.60 correlation on the basis of a collation of data assembled by Bornstein and Sigman (1986), and in their own meta-analysis -0.56 for all samples, -0.79 for habituation samples and -0.46 for recognition. It has been suggested that extreme scores, particularly for at-risk infants, might account, at least in part, for the results.

Laucht, Esser and Schmidt (1994) studied a sample of 226 three-month old infants recorded as 'at risk', using habituation-dishabituation methods of assessment. Cognitive development was assessed at the age of two and four and a half. There was a significant prediction of outcome, as expected, but correlations from the more conventional infant tests such as the Bayley were higher. Many have claimed the superiority of early information-processing over the latter. The authors also found that early biological and social factors better predicted later IQ. Laucht, Esser and Schmidt attribute the many recently reported higher correlations between the new infant tests and later IQ to small sample sizes, leading to differential publication of high versus low correlations, a suggestion also considered by McCall and Carriger (1993). The debate will continue.

In conclusion, recent work suggests that, under normal circumstances and using individual Wechsler tests, relatively accurate broad prediction of adolescent IQs may be made around age five. Such predictions become more precise with increasing age. It might be added that educational measures are more variable, and we would remind readers that the IQ was originally designed to predict educational ability.

Discussion and conclusions

We have already noted three possible assumptions upon which predictions may be based: (1) a constancy model; (2) a knowledge of the natural history of particular conditions; and (3) an awareness of the common effects of particular events or interventions. In the areas we have sampled, such assumptions are to varying extents imperfect; internal and external influences are at work and changing throughout the life span. In successive reviews over the last four decades we have pointed to growing evidence for this conclusion. Nor are we alone in holding this view. Yet, as Kagan (1992, p. 993) points out:

> the indefinite preservation of a young child's salient qualities, whether intellectual ability or a secure attachment, remains an ascendant assumption in developmental work... There is an inconsistency between the contemporary commitment to the importance of the local context which changes, and a belief in the capacity of early encounters to create immutable structures which will be preserved.

Prediction of individual development will continue to be seen as necessary and useful, but there needs to be a greater awareness of the likelihood of false positives and false negatives. Obviously some abnormal conditions such as severe mental retardation or autism imply accurate and gloomy prognoses for, for example, independent living. Even here, however, we should be aware that for some handicapped persons, a wide range of outcomes is possible. For example, Carr (1994) found a 60-point IQ range in Down's Syndrome adults.

In a wide-ranging yet succinct review of 'Pathways from childhood to adult life', Rutter (1989) drew attention to personal life transitions where psychological changes are likely, and where a reinforced pathway may continue, or a new one may be established. He goes on to write 'Not only will behaviour be shaped by the biological substrate, genetically or non-genetically determined, as well as by psychosocial influences, but equally the past and present are likely to have effects. Most crucially they are not independent of one another' (p. 146). Rutter also refers to the unduly simplified question of whether a person's behaviour is the result of past or present experiences.

It is of interest that in what must have been one of his last contributions, Bowlby (1988) had developed a life-span point of view, rejecting the idea of an early and necessary predetermination of development and emphasizing ongoing interactions throughout life. Such reformulations must have occurred through his awareness of increasing evidence against his earlier views.

It might well be argued that in view of the complexity of human development, the degree of accurate prediction so often achieved for behavioural measures is surprisingly good. Reverting to the simple model proposed at the outset, four parameters were suggested: biological and social trajectories, both of which may be non-linear across time, interactional/transactional processes in which individuals may play some part in influencing their own development and, finally, chance encounters or events which can sometimes divert the predicted life path. While one or two writers have discussed the latter (Bandura, 1982; Lewis, 1990), there appears to be a dearth of empirical studies on the role of chance. However, some researchers have made it clear that chance has played a part in the lives of members of their samples. For example, Rutter, Quinton and Liddle (1983) have indicated that for those seriously at risk for pathology (having been taken into care from disastrous backgrounds and then reared in children's homes), chance events such as a relationship with a stable partner may divert the individual from a predictably undesirable outcome.

We have argued (Clarke and Clarke, 1988) that greater continuities across time are to be expected in seriously deviant conditions compared with less abnormal development, pointing to the sometimes heterogeneous aetiologies for particular syndromes, with multifactorial influences combining in individual cases. The presence of an organic component appears greatly to narrow the range of reaction between constitution and environment, and we warned that increasing social and family disruption may increase the prevalence of conduct disorders, adjustment disorders and school failure.

In all of these, however, there will be a minority who escape the prediction. There is excellent documentation of 'spontaneous' recovery and escape from disadvantage, without any formal interventions (e.g. Kolvin et al., 1990; Pilling, 1990). The factors associated with such unfulfilled predictions include, in broad terms, individual attractiveness, problem-solving ability, an internal locus of control, networks of social support, schools where children are valued and learning is encouraged, a peer group which is prosocial and a capacity for purposeful planning. Conversely, factors likely to militate against escape from disadvantage are individual irritability, low IQ, low emotional security, few emotional ties and chaotic family (Clarke and Clarke, 1992). We should add to these a gender effect in withstanding stress, boys being more vulnerable than girls up to puberty, and vice versa thereafter. In evaluating predictions, we must once again note the relevance of length of follow-up. In a study of the background of a New Zealand sample of multiple-problem adolescents, reared in seriously disadvantaged environments, 87 per cent had by age fifteen developed at least one behavioural or mental health problem (Ferguson, Horwood and Lynskey, 1994). So 13 per cent had not. However, reviewing the literature, the authors go on to indicate that 'with the passage of time young people with serious problem behaviours grow out of these problems, or at least modify the ways in which problem behaviours are expressed'. Having left 'their original family environments they may be exposed to further life and socialization experiences which may overwrite their social learning processes accumulated during childhood' (p. 1137). This is a rather optimistic view.

While we have suggested factors promoting escape from disadvantage, what about the unfulfilled predictions for children reared in ordinary circumstances? Here there are a number of sometimes interacting factors. First, imperfect test reliability which usually represents individual fluctuations or the 'unreliability' of persons. Second, the use of non-comparable assessments at different ages; third, the length of time over which predictions are made.

Fourth, the changing internal or external influences leading in some cases to sequential cumulative alterations, sometimes affecting and sometimes reflecting the life path.

In an earlier publication (1992, p. 154) we summarized our orientation as follows:

> We see development as a series of linkages in which characteristics in each period have a probability of linking with those in another particular period. But such probabilities are not certainties, and deflections for good or ill are possible, but always within limits imposed by genetic, constitutional and social trajectories.

From time to time we have urged that development is *potentially somewhat* open-ended. We have italicized two words, the first to indicate that all too often people can get locked into a life path from which they have neither the need, nor the desire, nor even the ability or temperament, to escape. The second reiterates that there are clear constraints to change, whether from genetic 'ceilings', from aging effects or from social pressures. Radical departures from predicted outcomes are for most people unusual. But the imperfections of precise prediction are increasingly obvious. Perhaps the last word could come from a Russian writer of the 1920s, Zamyatin (quoted by Stone, 1993): 'Man is like a novel: one does not know until the very last page how it will end.'

References

AINSWORTH, M. D. S. and WITTIG, B. (1969) 'Attachment and exploratory behaviour of one-year-olds in a strange situation', in Foss, B. M. (Ed.) *Determinants of Infant Behaviour*, **4**, pp. 113–16.

BANDURA, A. (1982) 'The psychology of chance encounters and life paths', *American Psychologist*, **37**, pp. 747–55.

BENOIT, D. and PARKER, K. C. H. (1994) 'Stability and transmission of attachment across three generations', *Child Development*, **65**, pp. 1444–56.

BLOCK, J. (1971) *Lives Through Time*, Berkeley, CA, Bancroft Books.

BLOCK, J. (1980) 'From infancy to adulthood: a clarification', *Child Development*, **51**, pp. 622–3.

BORNSTEIN, M. H. and SIGMAN, M. D. (1986) 'Continuity in mental development from infancy', *Child Development*, **57**, pp. 251–74.

BOWLBY, J. (1951) *Maternal Care and Mental Health*, Geneva, World Health Organization.

BOWLBY, J. (1988) 'Developmental psychiatry comes of age', *American Journal of Psychiatry*, **145**, pp. 1–10.

CARR, J. (1994) 'Long-term outcome for people with Down's Syndrome', *Journal of Child Psychology and Psychiatry*, **35**, pp. 425–39.

Caspi, A., Elder, G. H. and Bem, D. J. (1988) 'Moving away from the world: life course patterns of shy children', *Developmental Quarterly*, **24**, pp. 824–31.

Chess, S. and Thomas, A. (1984) *Origins and Evolution of Behavior Disorders*, New York, Brunner/Mazel.

Clarke, A. D. B. and Clarke, A. M. (1984) 'Constancy and change in the growth of human characteristics', *Journal of Child Psychology and Psychiatry*, **25**, pp. 191–210.

Clarke, A. M. (1982) 'Developmental discontinuities: an approach to assessing their nature', in Bond, L. A. and Joffee, J. M. (Eds) *Facilitating Infant and Early Childhood Development*, pp. 58–77, Hanover, New England University Press.

Clarke, A. M. and Clarke, A. D. B. (1976) (Eds) *Early Experience: Myth and Evidence*, London, Open Books.

Clarke, A. M. and Clarke, A. D. B. (1988) 'The adult outcome of early behavioural abnormalities', *International Journal of Behavioural Development*, **11**, pp. 3–19.

Clarke, A. M. and Clarke, A. D. B. (1992) 'How modifiable is the human life path?' *International Review of Research in Mental Retardation*, **18**, pp. 137–57.

Esser, G., Schmidt, M. H. and Woerner, W. (1990) 'Epidemiology and course of psychiatric disorder in school age children – results of a longitudinal study', *Journal of Child Psychology and Psychiatry*, **31**, pp. 243–63.

Ferguson, D. M., Horwood, L. J. and Lynskey, M. (1994) 'The childhoods of multiple problem adolescents: a 15-year longitudinal study', *Journal of Child Psychology and Psychiatry*, **35**, pp. 1123–40.

Fonagy, P., Steele, H. and Steele, M. (1991) 'Maternal representations of attachment predict the organization of infant-mother attachment at one year of age', *Child Development*, **62**, pp. 891–905.

Fonagy, P., Steele, M., Steele, H., Higgitt, A. and Target, M. (1994) 'The Emanuel Miller Memorial Lecture, 1992. The theory and practice of resilience', *Journal of Child Psychology and Psychiatry*, **35**, pp. 231–57.

Fox, N. A., Kimmerley, N. L. and Schafer, W. D. (1991) 'Attachment to mother/attachment to father: a meta-analysis', *Child Development*, **62**, pp. 210–25.

Gleick, J. (1992) *Genius: the Life and Science of Richard Feynman*, New York, Pantheon Books.

Goldsmith, H. H. and Alansky, J. A. (1987) 'Maternal and infant temperamental predictors of attachment: a meta-analytic review', *Journal of Consulting and Clinical Psychology*, **55**, pp. 805–16.

Kagan, J. (1992) 'Yesterday's premises, tomorrow's promises', *Developmental Psychology*, **28**, pp. 990–7.

Kagan, J. and Snidman, N. (1991) 'Temperamental factors in human development', *American Psychologist*, **46**, pp. 856–62.

KERR, M., LAMBERT, W. W., STATTIN, H. and KLACKENBERG-LARSSON, I. (1994) 'Stability of inhibition in a Swedish longitudinal sample', *Child Development*, **65**, pp. 138–46.

KOLVIN, I., MILLER, F. J. W., SCOTT, D. McL., GATZANIS, S. R. M. and FLEETING, M. (1990) *Continuities of Deprivation?: the Newcastle Thousand Family Study*, Aldershot, Gower House.

LAUCHT, M., ESSER, G. and SCHMIDT, M. (1994) 'Contrasting infant predictors of later cognitive functioning', *Journal of Child Psychology and Psychiatry*, **35**, pp. 649–62.

LEWIS, M. (1990) 'Development, time and catastrophe: an alternate view of discontinuity', *Life-span Development and Behavior*, **10**, pp. 325–50.

MACFARLANE, J. W. (1964) 'Perspectives on personality consistency and change from the Guidance Study', *Vita Humana*, **7**, pp. 115–26.

McCALL, R. E. and CARRIGER, M. S. (1993) 'A meta-analysis of infant habituation and recognition performance as predictors of later IQ', *Child Development*, **64**, pp. 57–79.

MEDNICK, S. A. and BAERT, A. E. (1981) (Eds) *Prospective Longitudinal Research: an Empirical Basis for the Primary Prevention of Psychosocial Disorders*, Oxford, Oxford University Press on behalf of the WHO Regional Office for Europe.

MOFFITT, T. E., CASPI, A., HARKNESS, H. R. and SILVA, P. A. (1993) 'The natural history of change in intellectual performance: who changes? How much? Is it meaningful?', *Journal of Child Psychology and Psychiatry*, **34**, pp. 455–506.

MULLEN, P. E., MARTIN, J. L., ANDERSEN, J. C., ROMANS, S. E. and HERBISON, G. P. (1993) 'Childhood sexual abuse and mental health in adult life', *British Journal of Psychiatry*, **163**, pp. 271–332.

MULLEN, P. E., MARTIN, J. L., ANDERSEN, J. C., ROMANS, S. E. and HERBISON, G. P. (1994) 'The effect of child sexual abuse on social, interpersonal and sexual function in adult life', *British Journal of Psychiatry*, **165**, pp. 35–47.

PILLING, D. (1990) *Escape from Disadvantage*, London, Falmer Press.

PLOMIN, R. and DUNN, J. (1986) (Eds) *The Study of Temperament: Changes, Continuities and Challenges*, New York, Erlbaum.

RODGERS, B. (1990) 'Behaviour and personality in childhood as predictors of adult psychiatric disorder', *Journal of Child Psychology and Psychiatry*, **31**, pp. 393–414.

RUTTER, M. (1989) 'Pathways from childhood to adult life', *Journal of Child Psychology and Psychiatry*, **30**, pp. 23–51.

RUTTER, M. (1995) 'Clinical implications of attachment concepts', *Journal of Child Psychology and Psychiatry*, **36**, pp. 549–71.

RUTTER, M., QUINTON, D. and LIDDLE, C. (1983) 'Parenting in two generations: looking backwards and looking forwards', in MADGE, N. (Ed.) *Families at Risk*, London, Heinemann Educational.

SCARR, S. and McCARTNEY, K. (1983) 'How people make their own environ-

ments: a theory of genotype-environment effects', *Child Development*, **54**, pp. 424–35.
SKUSE, D. (1984) 'Extreme deprivation in childhood. II. Theoretical issues and a comparative review', *Journal of Child Psychology and Psychiatry*, **25**, pp. 543–72.
SLATER, A. (1995) 'Individual differences in infancy and later IQ', *Journal of Child Psychology and Psychiatry*, **36**, pp. 69–112.
SLATER, A., COOPER, R., ROSE, D. and MORISON, V. (1989) 'Prediction of cognitive performance from infancy to early childhood', *Human Development*, **32**, pp. 158–66.
STEELE, H., STEELE, M. and FONAGY, P. (1995) 'Associations among attachment classifications of mothers, fathers and their infants', *Child Development*, **67**, pp. 541–55.
STONE, M. H. (1993) 'Long-term outcome in personality disorders', *British Journal of Psychiatry*, **162**, pp. 299–313.
TEW, B. J. and LAURENCE, K. M. (1983) 'The relationship between spina bifida children's intelligence test scores on school entry and at school leaving: a preliminary report', *Child Care: Health and Development*, **9**, pp. 13–17.
TIZARD, B. (1977) *Adoption: a Second Chance*, London, Open Books.
VAN IJZENDOORN, M. H., JUFFER, F. and DUYVESTEYN, M. G. (1995) 'Breaking the intergenerational cycle of insecure attachment: a review of the effects of attachment-based interventions on maternal sensitivity and infant security', *Journal of Child Psychology and Psychiatry*, **36**, pp. 225–48.
VIZARD, E., MONK, E. and MISCH, P. (1995) 'Child and adolescent sex abuse perpetrators: a review of the research literature', *Journal of Child Psychology and Psychiatry*, **36**, pp. 731–56.
WATERHOUSE, L., DOBASH, R. P. and CARNIE, J. (1994) *Child Sexual Abuse*, Edinburgh, The Scottish Office Central Research Unit.
WILSON, R. S. (1985) 'The Louisville Twin Study: developmental synchronies in behaviour', *Child Development*, **54**, pp. 298–316.
YULE, W., GOLD, D. R. and BUSCH, C. (1982) 'Long-term predictive validity of the WPPSI: an 11-year follow-up study', *Personality and Individual Differences*, **3**, pp. 65–71.

Chapter 3

The Natural History of Early Non-attachment

Jill Hodges

There exists only a small body of information on the development of children who have had no opportunity to form an attachment relationship in the first few years of life. Such conditions of upbringing are, fortunately, rather uncommon, but they are interesting for the developmentalist in terms of their impact on later functioning. In 1971, Barbara Tizard published a study of the development of young children in residential nurseries (Tizard and Tizard, 1971), the first in what became a longitudinal series of studies of these children's development. More than twenty years later, this series of studies forms a good part of the information which exists on the development of children who have had no opportunity to form first-attachment relationships at the normal time. This paper sets out and discusses some of the main findings of these studies, from the particular viewpoint of the growing research based on attachment theory.

As attachment research has increased, a good deal of knowledge has accumulated on the development and consequences of secure and insecure attachment relationships. But relatively little information exists on the consequences of what Lieberman and Pawl (1988) called 'non-attachment', where the infant has had no opportunity to develop an attachment relationship organized around a particular caregiver.

Currently, four main classifications of attachment relationships are used (Carlson and Sroufe, 1995). These are based initially on infant behaviour in the Strange Situation (Ainsworth *et al.*, 1978), a standardized sequence of brief separations and reunions between mother and infant, involving also an adult 'stranger' unfamiliar to the child. The infant's behaviour in this situation reflects an internalized regulatory pattern based on expectations derived from the history of the parent-infant interaction.

Infants whose attachment relationships are categorized as 'secure' typically show freely exploratory behaviour with the mother present, are happy to see her after a brief separation, and actively seek comfort from her when distressed, showing a clear preference for her over the stranger. The 'insecure-avoidant' category describes children who typically do not show wariness of the stranger, or a preference for the mother, and who do not actively initiate interaction on reunion after a separation, rather appearing to avoid the mother. Children showing the 'insecure-resistant' pattern do not become

63

engaged in exploration, showing wariness of the novel surroundings and the stranger; on reunion with the mother after a separation, they show a mixture of active contact-seeking and angry, unhappy behaviour and remain uncomforted and unsettled. Both 'insecure-avoidant' and 'insecure-resistant' infants are thought to be uncertain about the reliable availability of the mother as a source of comfort and reassurance, although 'insecure-avoidant' children are thought to have adopted the 'avoidant' strategy to prevent further alienation of the parent which might occur if the negative effect were displayed openly as in the 'insecure-resistant' children.

A fourth category, 'disorganized/disoriented' attachment, has been described, in which, unlike the three patterns already outlined, no coherent strategy towards the mother as a source of security is evident, and the child shows disorganized and seemingly undirected behavioural responses in the Strange Situation. It is thought that the experience of these infants has led them to see the mother at times as a source of fear, so that when she is also needed as a source of reassurance, the child is put into an impossible conflict of motivation where no organized response is possible (Main and Hesse, 1990).

In other words, 'insecure-attachment' relationships, just like 'secure' ones, are organized around a key adult caregiver, and expectations of interaction with this caregiver. This is so even if this key caregiver is unresponsive or ill-attuned to infant cues (as tends to be the pattern for 'insecure-avoidant' infants) or inconsistent (as for 'insecure-ambivalent' infants). Even the 'disorganized/disoriented' category, though describing the lack of any organized response, none the less takes the centrality of the attachment figure as a given. It is only in extraordinary circumstances that a child has no such central figure, at the time when attachment relationships would normally develop. These extraordinary circumstances are to be found in certain types of institutional care, which provide natural experiments for research.

Bowlby (1965) characterized maternal deprivation as 'not uncommonly almost complete in institutions ... where the child often has no *one* person who cares for him in a personal way and with whom he may feel secure' (p. 14). This was true of the nursery institutions which Tizard studied. Generally, in the institutions studied earlier (e.g. Spitz, 1945, 1946a, 1946b; Dennis, 1973) and even in some studied more recently (e.g. Hakimi-Minesh, Mohdehi and Tashakkori, 1984; Kaler and Freeman, 1994), 'maternal deprivation' was confounded with gross physical and social deprivation and lack of stimulation. It was therefore impossible to know how far 'maternal deprivation' by itself was responsible for the observed damage to the children's development. In contrast, the nurseries which Tizard studied provided excellent physical care, stimulation and play facilities for the children. However, these young children's caregiving experiences were quite extraordinary in comparison to children reared at home; compared to the earlier studies, this was maternal deprivation in a rather pure form. I should add that this form of care is no longer current – partly as a result of Tizard's work.

The nursery environment

Salient features of the nursery environment are here drawn from the research reported by Tizard and Joseph (1970), Tizard and Tizard (1971) and Tizard (1977).

Children in the nurseries received very little continuity of care, although staffing levels were high. By age two, an average of twenty-four different caregivers had looked after the children for at least a week. Even within the course of a single five-day period, an average of six different caregivers, *excluding* night staff, worked with each 'family group' of six children. The reason for such great discontinuity was because the nurseries functioned as training institutions for Nursery Nurse Examination Board (NNEB) students. As part of their training, staff rotated between 'family groups' of children. They went on and off duty, to college, on holiday, and eventually they left for good. All these moves were unpredictable from the point of view of the children. In this most basic of all parameters for the development of an attachment relationship, the nurseries were utterly unlike an ordinary family.

Besides this fundamental discontinuity, two other features stand out as important. The first is that unlike most children at home, the institutional children had to compete with the other five young children in their group for the attention of the caregivers. Tizard (1977) quotes a nurse who commented 'You see, you can't give the child really individual attention, as you would in a normal family, if you had, say, a toddler and a baby. If one of the group comes over to you, when the others see it they come too. It seems as if they don't like another child to get attention.' Behaviour towards other children was often extremely rivalrous and aggressive.

The other important feature is that caregiving in the nurseries was not only discontinuous and short-term, but also emotionally detached. The contrast between an expectable parent-child relationship, and staff-child relationships in the institutions, is conveyed strikingly by Tizard's observation:

> a child who tried to get affection or special attention from a nurse would generally be distracted . . . Indeed, as an observer one could confidently predict that if a child and an adult in a nursery were paying close and prolonged attention to each other, then either the child or the adult or both were not part of the nursery establishment.
> (Tizard, 1977, p. 33)

Unlike mothers of young children, staff very rarely reported feeling anxious about a child, or angry with them. It was extremely rare for staff to express pleasure or affection, or displeasure or anger, in talking with children; and affectionate physical contact was just as rare. The development of a close attachment between children and the staff who cared for them was explicitly discouraged, since a child who became strongly attached to one adult tended to disrupt the smooth running of the groups. It was also thought unfair both to children and to staff members to allow attachments to develop since they would inevitably be broken when the staff member left.

There is a marked contrast between this detached staff caregiving, and the type of parental behaviour associated with secure attachment. Ainsworth and her colleagues (1978) found various aspects of the mothers' interaction with their infants at the end of the first year of life – subsumed under the construct of maternal sensitivity – to be related to the infants' attachment security. In some respects the interaction of the childcare staff with the children resembles the interactions observed between mothers and infants assessed at one year as showing 'anxious-avoidant' patterns of attachment relationship. Consistently, these mothers were averse to close bodily contact and showed a lack of emotional expression, parallelling the rarity in the nurseries of physical affection and of emotionally expressive talk to the children. They were also 'intrusive', not so much intentionally as because their interaction with the infant tended to cut across the infant's own cues. The nursery care may have produced somewhat the same effect, because of its more rigid routine; because of the need to attend to other infants; and because it is more difficult for a new caregiver to attune to the cues of a particular infant than it is for a caregiver who has had close and continuous contact. Mothers of 'anxious-ambivalent' infants show some of the same features of inaccessibility, unresponsiveness, or inappropriate responsiveness to the infant's cues (Ainsworth *et al.*, 1978; Bretherton, 1987), but behave more inconsistently and less intrusively.

Parallels between maternal behaviour styles and institutional caregiving must be treated cautiously. A mother's style of handling reflects her individual personality and in particular her state of mind with regard to her own experiences of being parented as a child (Main, Kaplan and Cassidy, 1985; Fonagy, Steele and Steele, 1991), while for the nursery staff, the interaction did not necessarily reflect the attitudes and personal characteristics of the staff, but the institutional ethos and climate within which they worked. Thus subtler cues given by mothers might well differ from the cues given by staff; for instance, mothers of 'anxious-avoidant' infants show underlying attitudes of hostility and rejection, overt or covert. None the less, the behaviour itself may well be important regardless of attitude. Grossman *et al.* (1985) in a North German sample found a disproportionately high proportion of 'anxious-avoidant' attachment patterns, though no greater proportion of insecure patterns overall. This finding was attributed to cultural pressure to encourage independence as early as the middle of the first year, suggesting that in infancy it is the withholding of close bodily contact – with or without an underlying attitude of rejection – which leads to the 'anxious-avoidant' pattern (Crittenden and Ainsworth, 1989).

A second reason for caution in comparing styles of maternal interaction with the caregiving style of the nursery staff is that infants with their mothers form an attachment relationship organized around the expected behaviour and responses of a particular individual; the institutional children experienced a large number of different individual caregivers, the behaviour of each conforming more or less to the same pattern. Their attachment behaviour may have becomes organized around a *style of caregiving*, a generalized pattern which represented the common denominator of expectable care, rather than the expectations of a particular caregiver.

It is not surprising that an upbringing so atypical of home-reared infants resulted in a pattern of attachment responses unlike any of the patterns shown by home-reared children. Although the nursery children did not show gross behavioural disturbance, when assessed in the institutions at twenty-four months, and much of their development differed little from children who had been brought up at home, their relationships were most unlike those of a comparison group of a family-reared two-year-olds.

They showed evident 'insecure' patterns in their attachment behaviour. Most would run to be picked up when almost any nurse came into the room, and would cry and try to follow when she left; whereas two-thirds of the family children did not show such behaviour and 'took mother's coming and going from the room as a matter of course' (Bowlby, 1973). As Crittenden and Ainsworth (1989) summarize it, a child who cannot rely on the mother's accessibility, 'is vigilant for any indications of decreased proximity, and displays more distress at little everyday separations or threats thereof'.

Other aspects of behaviour were very unlike even usual 'insecure' attachment patterns. The nursery children were diffusely affectionate towards a large number of people – virtually anyone familiar, although they had a clear hierarchy of preferences. They generally showed a preference either for a particular nurse, or for the mother in those cases where she visited at least weekly. But compared to children in their families, they had extremely little contact with their preferred adults; on most days they would see their preferred nurse for only a few minutes or the mother not at all. At the same time, they were shy and wary of strangers. In contrast the family-reared children showed attachment behaviour to a small number of people – an average of four, the principal attachment figure usually being the mother – and were relatively at ease with strangers, reflecting their experience with a much wider social network.

Subsequently, aged between two and seven approximately, most of the children left the institutions and were placed in families. Most of the children were adopted; some were 'restored' to their biological parent. For most children this was their first opportunity to make close, selective, mutual attachments to a consistently available adult. They were followed up at four years of age (Tizard and Rees, 1974, 1975) and again at eight (Tizard, 1977; Tizard and Hodges, 1978) and at sixteen (Hodges and Tizard, 1989a, 1989b). The study thus took the form of a natural experiment. It is rare for a child to undergo such a profound change in the emotional and caregiving environment, and this allows an examination of whether the period of institutional care did have lasting effects, and whether they were still reversible up to a given age.

Jill Hodges

Family placement and subsequent childhood development; the children at four and a half years old

Tizard and Rees (1974) studied twenty-four four and a half-year-old children who had been adopted, fifteen who had been 'restored' and twenty-six still in institutions. These included children assessed in the previous studies by Tizard and Joseph (1970) and Tizard and Tizard (1971). All the children had been uninterruptedly in institutional care from four months or earlier until at least two years of age, and generally had joined their families soon after three, 'restored' children on average being placed a few months later than adopted children. Children placed with a biological parent were usually not moving to live with a familiar figure; most parents, if they visited at all, had not maintained regular contact.

Adoptive families differed from the families of 'restored' children in several ways: they were two-parent families, usually middle-class, and less likely to have other children. Over half the mothers of 'restored' children were single parents, and they were generally younger and less secure financially than adoptive families. The impact of these family differences on the children's development will be discussed later. The ex-institutional children had all been in their new homes for at least six months when they were assessed. Their development was compared with the group of family-reared London working-class children who had also formed a contrast group in the study of two-year-olds.

As the children joined their new families, what did the development of their attachments look like? At first they tended to be clinging and to follow their new parents around. By four and a half, this was no longer true of most of the adopted children, but the majority of the 'restored' children were still very clinging, and this seemed related to a continuing sense of insecurity; many of their mothers had been ambivalent about reclaiming them, and many threatened the child with being sent back to the nursery. Both adopted and restored children were more demonstratively affectionate and attention-seeking than children who had always lived within their families. Adopted children had the lowest mean number of behaviour problems, and twenty out of the twenty-four adoptive mothers felt their child was deeply attached to them.

Some adopted and 'restored' children were said by their mothers to be over-friendly towards strangers, and would also allow strangers to put them to bed or to comfort them if they were hurt. This was not reported for any of the family-reared children. This indiscriminate friendliness after institutional care has been noted before, up to adolescence (Goldfarb, 1955; Provence and Lipton, 1962). In a group of children adopted from Romanian orphanages and assessed at a median age of thirty months, Chisholm *et al.* (1995) found that this overfriendliness was not related to security of attachment to the adoptive parent, and suggested that 'it may be that just as the indiscriminate friendliness of the normal four-month-old is both endearing and reinforcing to adults, indiscriminate friendliness also serves an adaptive function for children developing an attachment later than usual' (p. 293), though they recognized that its persistence into later childhood might be more problematic.

Of the twenty-six children remaining in institutions at four and a half, 70 per cent were said by the staff 'not to care deeply about anyone', and they tended to be immature and clinging in their attachment behaviour and more attention-seeking than the children who had joined families. For most of these children, the turnover of caregivers had continued; an average of twenty-six (and as many as forty-five) staff had worked with them for at least a week in the last two years.

The children's development at eight years old

When the children were eight years old, they were followed-up again (Tizard, 1977; Tizard and Hodges, 1978). By this time most had been adopted or restored, and only eight children remained in institutions. A total of twenty-five adopted children, plus three children in long-term quasi-adoptive foster placements, was seen, and thirteen 'restored' children.

As was the case at four and a half, the great majority of adoptive mothers, like the mothers of the contrast children who had always lived at home, said they felt their eight-year-old was closely attached to them. Compared to children who had always lived at home, adopted children remained more demonstratively affectionate to their parents. The adoptive parents generally welcomed this 'cuddliness'. They did not feel that it was based on a sense of insecurity and there was little evidence of insecurity or clinging in other respects. The adopted children had grown less indiscriminate in their relationships to adults – for instance, they would no longer accept comfort from a stranger if upset. However, about a third were still said to be over-friendly towards strangers.

The 'restored' children's relationships had developed rather differently by eight. Only half of the mothers of the 'restored' children felt their child was closely attached to them. 'Restored' children were no longer more physically affectionate to their parents than the comparison children; in fact they were *less* cuddly towards their parents than any other group. Parents of 'restored' children also reported much more difficulty than adoptive parents in feeling closely attached, and in showing affection, to their child. The children were still more likely than other groups to accept comforting, as well as affection, from strangers.

There was no evidence that this difference was due to differences in the children prior to placement; rather, it seemed related to the very different family settings offered by the adoptive and the biological parents. Adoptive parents were predominantly middle-class two-parent families, and older than the usually working-class biological parents, who were often single parents with few resources and other children claiming their attention. But the differences extended beyond demographic ones. Adoptive families had very much wanted a child, and put much time and energy into shared activities with their child (more so than other middle-class families) as a way of building up the relationship. Many of the parents of 'restored' children had spent years deciding to reclaim the child from the institution; they felt ambivalent about the child and guilty about the time in care. These parents spent *less* time in shared activities with the child than other working-class parents. Intensity of subsequent stimulation in reversing the effects of early deprivation is important in relation to social development (see MacDonald, 1985, for review), and while the adopted children entered a particularly enriched environment, the 'restored' children entered a rather impoverished one.

The parent's feelings and expectations about the child may also have had other effects. Perhaps because many of the adoptive parents had initially wanted to adopt a baby, they often tolerated and even welcomed dependent behaviour, at least initially – behaviour which normally would have been inappropriate for a child of that age. In contrast, the biological parents expected much greater independence in their young child, once they had left the institution to join the family, than did the working-class parents whose children had always lived at home.

This contrast in parental responsiveness to 'younger' dependent attachment behaviours may well be important for these children, who were developing their first attachments later than normal. It may also explain why at age eight a tendency for later placement to be associated with less attachment to the mother was found in the 'restored' group, but *not* in the adopted one (Tizard and Hodges, 1978). Since much physical care and attention is indispensable for a very young child, it may be that 'restored' children are at particular risk if they return to the family at a slightly older age, when more autonomous functioning can be required of them. In other words, the hypothesis is that adopted children received the responsive attention and care likely to lead to attachment regardless of their age; 'restored' children were likely to receive it if they entered their families still as very young children, but not if they were slightly older and apparently able to manage more independently (Hodges, 1991). Chisholm *et al.* (1995) put forward a similar hypothesis in their study of children adopted from Romania, suggesting that 'there may be an optimal age during which a child's attachment behaviours are considered "normal" by parents, whereas at later ages the same behaviour may be considered overly demanding' (p. 284). The effect may have been enhanced because 'restored' children tended to be the oldest child, with younger step-siblings requiring the parents' care, while adopted children were more likely to be singletons or younger children themselves, without such competition from younger siblings.

In all, there were a number of characteristics of the parenting style of the 'restored' children's parents which somewhat resembled the style of institutional caregiving, though without its discontinuity; while adoptive parents were more responsive, more accepting of dependency and bids for affection and attention, more ready to give physical affection, and spent much more time in one-to-one interactions with the child.

Despite these great differences in family relationships, adopted as well as 'restored' children still showed indiscriminate overfriendliness and attention-seeking behaviour towards adults. Otherwise, their parents reported no more behaviour problems than in family-reared children. However, in school the children's teachers reported considerably more problems, notably attention-seeking behaviour (towards the teacher and other adults), restlessness, disobedience, quarrelsome behaviour and unpopularity with peers. Difficulties were particularly marked in the 'restored' group, but both ex-institutional groups showed more difficulties than classmates or the comparison children. Being one in a class of many other children may for the child have repeated some of the elements of the nursery 'family group', leading to a similar pattern of competitive attempts to gain the attention of the teacher and poor relationships with other children.

Development in mid-adolescence: family relationships

At sixteen, the children were followed-up again (Hodges and Tizard, 1989a, 1989b). The family relationships of most of the adopted sixteen-year olds seemed satisfactory for them and for their parents, and differed little from non-adopted matched comparisons who had never been in care. By sixteen, the adopted children were no longer significantly more 'cuddly' towards their parents than were the non-adopted comparisons; the great majority, as at eight, were seen by parents as closely attached to them. In contrast, the 'restored' group still suffered difficulties and poor family relationships much more frequently than either the adoptees or their own comparison group. They and their parents were less often attached to each other than adoptees or comparisons, and where there were siblings their mothers tended to prefer them to the 'restored' child. 'Restored' sixteen-year-olds still showed less affection to their parents than did any other group, as had been the case when they were eight-year-olds, and their parents, equally, found difficulty in showing affection to them. There were also indications that they wanted less involvement in family discussions than other groups, and identified themselves less with their parents.

Both ex-institutional groups tended to have more difficulty with siblings than their comparisons. The 'restored' group had particularly great difficulty, probably because most of the 'restored' children had entered their families to find younger siblings already there. It would not generally be considered appropriate to place a young child for adoption where there are already younger children in the family, and it seems that placing the 'restored' children with younger half-siblings, previously unknown to them, contributed to sibling relationships which were still difficult years later in mid-adolescence.

Jill Hodges

Development in mid-adolescence: relationships with peers and adults outside the family

The great difference in family relationships between the adopted and the 'restored' children stands in striking contrast to the similarities in their relationships to peers and to adults outside the family. Adopted and 'restored' children were two very distinct groups as regards the development of their family relationships, but in relation to peers and other adults they resembled each other, and contrasted with their matched comparisons who had never been in care. Bowlby's view was that the central ill-effect of 'maternal deprivation', such as was found in an institutional upbringing, was the inability to make deep emotional relationships. While many of these children, especially the adoptees, had developed strong relationships with their parents, in regard to peers and other adults there were indeed indications of some such effect, though this was not inevitable.

At eight, some of the ex-institutional children had shown indiscriminate overfriendliness to adults. This was no longer reported as a problem at sixteen, but the ex-institutional adolescents were still more often oriented towards adult attention than comparison adolescents. Teachers believed adult approval to be particularly important for half the ex-institutional group, but for less than one-fifth of their matched comparisons. It is important to recognize the role of developmental transformations; behaviour is not isomorphic over time (Sroufe and Rutter, 1984). There was no relationship between whether or not the children were indiscriminately overfriendly towards adults at age eight, and how friendly they were towards strangers at sixteen. But in contrast there was a significant association between overfriendliness to *adults* at age eight, and unselective friendliness towards *peers* at sixteen.

This unselective friendliness – being friendly to any peer who was friendly towards the child, as opposed to choosing friends – was not usually seen as a problem by the parents of the adopted and 'restored' adolescents. But parents reported it 'definitely' in one-fifth of the ex-institutional adolescents, and less certainly in another fifth, whereas not one of the parents of comparison adolescents described their sixteen-year-olds thus. Ex-institutional adolescents were also likelier to have difficulties in peer relations than comparison adolescents. The picture was similar to that at eight years, with 'restored' adolescents again tending to show rather greater difficulties than adoptees. Teachers described the ex-institutional group as more quarrelsome, irritable, less liked than other children, and as bullying other children.

In adolescence, the importance of peer relationships increases relative to family relationships, and this shift to the development of close ties with friends appears to play an important part in protecting the individual against the psychological effects of stress (Monck, 1991). Ex-institutional adolescents were less likely than comparisons to have a same-sex special friend. They also tended to see their friendships as 'special' more often than their parents did, in contrast to comparison children. This suggests that the parents of the ex-institutional group may have perceived the friendship as lacking something which the parents regarded as part of the definition of a 'special' friend.

The ex-institutional group were less likely to see peers as a source of emotional support, in that they were only half as likely as comparisons to turn to a peer as a confidant when they were anxious. Even where they did have a special friend, they were less likely to confide in a peer for support. These findings regarding friendships and orientation towards adults recall Yarrow et al.'s (1974) data on ten-year-olds, which suggested that disruption of a caregiving relationship after six months of age had long-term negative effects on the capacity to establish discriminating relationships, i.e. different levels of relationships with people.

If these five characteristics are considered together – orientation towards adult attention, poor peer relationships, less likelihood of a special friend, less turning to peers as confidants, and unselective friendliness towards peers – ex-institutional adolescents are very much more likely to show four or five of them than comparison adolescents. In this sense, we can regard them as an ex-institutional syndrome, which does not appear to be merely a reflection of general behavioural and emotional disturbance. The pattern of these differences very much resembles the picture when the children were eight years old. However, despite being much more common in the ex-institutional group, this syndrome still occurs in only half their number; and it should also be emphasized that in general the behaviour characteristics it represents are *differences* from the comparison group and do not all imply difficulties.

The teachers of the ex-institutional group described them as tending to show quarrelsome, irritable behaviour, to bully others and to be unpopular with peers, and also as often restless, distractable and resentful if corrected by adults. This overall pattern of difficulties, shown by 35–50 per cent of the group, resembles that described by Goldfarb (1943a, 1943b) in ex-institutional six to ten- and ten to fourteen-year-olds, and the aggressive, antisocial and distractable behaviour described by Bowlby in his 1951 report as part of the 'affectionless and psychopathic character'. It seems that although the institutions studied by Tizard were good of their kind, and a world away from the intensely depriving settings studied by earlier researchers, the children's early lack of secure, continuous attachments still had effects by mid-adolescence.

While the adopted adolescents as well as the 'restored' group show significantly more difficulty in school than a matched comparison group, it must also be emphasized that differences between the adopted and the 'restored' groups were consistently in favour of the former. The 'restored' group showed a higher rate of anti-social behaviour and were twice as likely as adoptees to reach the cut-off point for maladjustment on the school behaviour scale. Significantly more had been referred for psychological or psychiatric help. They were more often aggressive towards their teachers than adoptees or comparisons. Further, improvements were shown by most of the adoptees, but none of the 'restored' group, who had shown considerable problems at school when they were eight. All this points to the importance of the later family environment as well as the continuing effects of early institutional care.

It is interesting that the development of attachments within the family appears to have had some modifying effect in the area of peer relationships. If the adequate development of an attachment relationship with the parent is taken as a normal precondition for later peer relationships (Freud, 1966), the ex-institutional children had their first opportunity to develop these close attachments around an age when most children have already done so. They may have continued to lag somewhat behind in the broadening of their social horizons beyond the family. There is some support for this in the findings that better peer relationships, and selectivity in friendships, at sixteen were related to close attachment to the mother at eight; and that it was children who were parent-oriented and not particularly peer-oriented at eight – strongly attached to their parents, but described as preferring to be solitary and uninvolved with other children rather than as having a group of special friends – who apparently had the best peer relationships by sixteen. Although it might be expected that children who were managing peer relationships well by eight would also have the most satisfactory peer relations at sixteen, if only because of peer reinforcement of existing adaptive behaviours, this did not seem to be the case. This is unlike Sroufe, Carlson and Shulman's (1993) finding that good peer functioning in middle childhood predicted peer relationships in adolescence; Sroufe's sample was a high-risk group, but one with neither the early institutional experience, nor the late start to the development of an attachment with a parent.

Work in attachment theory suggests that social relationships with peers are particularly vulnerable to difficulties in early attachment. Sroufe and his co-workers (Waters, Wippman and Sroufe, 1979; LaFreniere and Sroufe, 1985; Sroufe, 1988) found that children who as infants had been assessed as having 'insecure' attachment relationships with their mother, had more difficulties in peer relationships at three and a half and five years old than children with 'secure' attachment histories. They were less popular and more likely to be victimizers or victims than securely attached children, and their relationships with peers were shallower and likely to be tinged with hostility. There are clear parallels between the difficulties shown by these insecurely attached younger children, and the unpopularity and aggressive behaviour found in the ex-institutional group at older ages.

There are also parallels with the greater adult-centredness of the ex-institutional group. Sroufe, Fox and Pancake (1983) found that four- to five-year-old children who had earlier shown insecure patterns of attachment to parents were over-dependent in preschool, in the sense that their need for contact, approval and attention from adults interfered with other developmental tasks, including peer relationships.

As described earlier, the caregiving pattern in the institutions, in so far as it could be characterized in terms of usual, non-institutional mothering, showed parallels with the mothering styles associated with insecure attachments and in particular with 'anxious-avoidant' children. The ex-institutional children's tendency in school to bully others also recalls children with 'insecure-avoidant' histories (LaFreniere and Sroufe, 1985). Sroufe also hypothesized that with time, 'anxious-avoidant' children would cease to reveal their dependency as clearly as at this early age, but that it might 'go underground', showing up later in a fear of interpersonal closeness. This speculation aligns interestingly with the finding that the ex-institutional adolescents were less likely to have a special friend or to confide in peers.

Can the effects of the early institutional experience on school difficulties be differentiated from those of illegitimate or adopted status alone? The National Child Development Study (NCDS) cohort at sixteen (Maughan and Pickles, 1990) included adoptees and also illegitimate children living in their families, paralleling the 'restored' group. In a similar pattern to the ex-institutional children, the NCDS adoptees had rather fewer difficulties than the illegitimate group, but both showed more difficulties than legitimate children living in their families. Comparison with this study suggests that alongside this similar pattern there was a rather higher overall level of school problems in the ex-institutional adoptees, which may be attributable to the institutional experience (Hodges, 1991).

The types of problem shown by the ex-institutional children at school also compare interestingly with the NCDS data. The high problem scores of the NCDS illegitimate group represented a broad spectrum of behaviour difficulties, like those of the 'restored' children; they had worse scores than the legitimate group on restlessness/distractibility, anti-social/conduct disorder and peer relations items but, again like the 'restored' group, did not show higher scores on anxiety. However, NCDS adoptees showed a narrower range of difficulties. They did not differ from the legitimate group either on restlessness and distractibility, or on anti-social/conduct disorder items. But they had the highest scores on items reflecting unhappy, anxious behaviour, and also had significantly greater problems with peers. The ex-institutional adoptees showed these difficulties, but also showed restless and distractible behaviour and aggression to a significant degree. In this respect they resemble the ex-institutional 'restored' group more than they resemble the NCDS adoptees. This behaviour may represent the effect of institutional care rather than of adoptive status.

Comparison with the NCDS and others underlines that the difficulties of the ex-institutional groups cannot be attributed solely to their earlier institutional experience. Other risk factors seem to be involved both in illegitimate status, or initially 'unwanted' status, and in adoption. However, there are indications that early institutional experience may somewhat increase the overall level of disturbance in school, and may also contribute to particular kinds of difficulty, in particular aggressive and antisocial behaviour – recalling the early descriptions by Bowlby (1951) and Goldfarb (1943a, 1943b).

Conclusion

The children's early experiences of institutional care could be expected to result in an internal model of the 'common denominator' of caregivers, somewhat along these lines: 'Caregivers are unreliable, transient, arbitrary figures who are unlikely to provide affection or close attention and whose attention has to be very actively and repeatedly claimed, in competition with other children.' Subsequently, some parents spent much time closely involved with the child, providing responsive attention and affection, and over a long period reliably fostered the child's sense of being securely wanted. This was true of most of the adoptive parents. Given this experience, it seems that most children could develop a specific model of their adoptive parents which was sufficiently uncontaminated by the earlier institution-based model to allow apparently secure attachments. Where the parent was much less involved with the child, and the interaction paralleled some of the characteristics of the institutional style of caregiving, the child was less able to do this, despite now having one or two continuing caregiving figures.

It is almost as if it takes an effort on the part of the environment actively to disconfirm the child's expectations, to counteract this internalized model of the 'common denominator' of caregiver. But despite the development of alternative internalized models of particular attachment figures, such as adoptive parents, this general model may still persist over time, with effects evident in the social relationships and behaviour of the ex-institutional group. These effects are stronger for the 'restored' group, who have lacked the conditions which could strongly disconfirm the original model; in some respects, as described, their family experience may have confirmed some aspects of the internalized model based on the institutions. But effects of this internalized model are also evident in the adoptees, despite their much more favourable family settings.

Sroufe and Rutter (1984) point out that an adaptation which may be serviceable at one point in development may later compromise the child's ability to draw to the full upon the environment in the service of more flexible adaptation. They give an example which is very appropriate to the social relationships of the children in this study:

> Thus, a given pattern of early adaptation could lead a child to isolate himself from peers or to alienate them, to avoid emotionally complex and stimulating social commerce, or to respond to such complexity in an impulsive or inflexible manner. Even such patterns may not be viewed as pathological (in the clinical sense) and certainly may be viewed as 'adapted' in the sense that the child continues to strive toward a 'fit' with the environment. But if the adaptation compromises the normal developmental process whereby children are increasingly able to draw emotional support from age-mates (as well as give it) and to stay engaged in social commerce despite the frequent

emotional challenge of doing so, the individual may be sacrificing an important buffer against stress and, ultimately, psychopathology.

Acknowledgment

I wish to thank Dr Miriam Steele for discussion of an earlier draft of this chapter.

References

AINSWORTH, M. D. S., BLEHAR, M., WATERS, E. and WALL, S. (1978) *Patterns of Attachment*, Hillsdale, New Jersey, Erlbaum.
BOWLBY, J. (1951) *Maternal Care and Mental Health*, Geneva, World Health Organisation.
BOWLBY, J. (1965) *Child Care and the Growth of Love* (2nd Edn) Harmondsworth, Penguin Books.
BOWLBY, J. (1973) *Attachment and Loss, Vol. 2: Separation, Anxiety and Anger*, London, Hogarth Press.
BRETHERTON, I. (1987) 'New perspectives on attachment relations: Security, communication and internal working models', in OSOFSKY, J. (Ed.) *Handbook of Infant Development* (2nd Edn), New York, John Wiley.
CARLSON, E. A. and SROUFE, L. A. (1995) 'Contribution of attachment theory to developmental psychopathology', in CICCHETTI, D. and COHEN, D. (Eds) *Developmental Psychopathology*, New York, John Wiley.
CHISHOLM, K., CARTER, M. C., AMES, E. W. and MORISON, S. J. (1995) 'Attachment security and indiscriminately friendly behaviour in children adopted from Romanian orphanages', *Development and Psychopathology*, **7**, pp. 283–94.
CRITTENDEN, P. M. and AINSWORTH, M. D. S. (1989) 'Child maltreatment and attachment theory', in CICCHETTI, D. and CARLSON, V. (Eds) *Child Maltreatment: Theory and Research on the Causes and Consequences of Child Abuse and Neglect*, New York, Cambridge University Press.
DENNIS, W. (1973) *Children of the Crèche*, New York, Appleton-Century-Crofts.
FONAGY, P., STEELE, H. and STEELE, M. (1991) 'Maternal representations of attachment during pregnancy predict the organisation of infant-mother attachment at one year of age', *Child Development*, **62**, pp. 891–905.
FREUD, A. (1966) *Normality and Pathology in Childhood: Assessments of Development*, London, Hogarth Press.
GOLDFARB, W. (1943a) 'Infant rearing and problem behaviour', *American Journal of Orthopsychiatry*, April, pp. 249–65.
GOLDFARB, W. (1943b) 'The effects of early institutional care on adolescent personality', *Journal of Experimental Education*, **12**, pp. 106–29.

GOLDFARB, W. (1955) 'Emotional and intellectual consequences of psychologic deprivation in infancy: A re-evaluation', in HOCH, P. and ZUBIN, J. (Eds) *Psychopathology in Childhood*, New York, Grune & Stratton.

GROSSMAN, K., GROSSMAN, K. E., SPANGLER, G., SUESS, D. and UNZER, L. (1985) 'Maternal sensitivity and newborn orienting responses as related to quality of attachment in Northern Germany', in BRETHERTON, I. and WATERS, E. (Eds) *Growing Points of Attachment Theory and Research*, Monographs of the Society for Research in Child Development, **50**, 1–2, pp. 233–56.

HAKIMI-MINESH, Y., MOHDEHI, J. and TASHAKKORI, A. (1984) 'Short communication: Effects of environmental enrichment on the mental and psychomotor development of orphanage children', *Journal of Child Psychology and Psychiatry*, **25**, 4, pp. 643–50.

HODGES, J. (1991) *Adolescent Development Following Institutional Care in the Early Years*, unpublished PhD thesis, University of London.

HODGES, J. and TIZARD, B. (1989a) 'IQ and behavioural adjustment of ex-institutional adolescents', *Journal of Child Psychology and Psychiatry*, **30**, 1, pp. 53–76.

HODGES, J. and TIZARD, B. (1989b) 'Social and family relationships of ex-institutional adolescents', *Journal of Child Psychology and Psychiatry*, **30**, 1, pp. 77–98.

KALER, S. R., and FREEMAN, B. J. (1994) 'Analysis of environmental deprivation: cognitive and social development in Romanian orphans', *Journal of Child Psychology and Psychiatry*, **35**, 4, pp. 769–81.

LaFRENIERE, P. J. and SROUFE, L. A. (1985) 'Profiles of peer competence in the preschool: Interrelations between measures, influence of social ecology, and relation to attachment history', *Developmental Psychology*, **21**, 1, pp. 56–69.

LIEBERMAN, A. F. and PAWL, J. H. (1988) 'Clinical applications of attachment theory', in BELSKY, J. and NEZWORSKI, T. (Eds) *Clinical Implications of Attachment*, Hillsdale, New Jersey, Erlbaum.

MACDONALD, K. (1985) 'Early experience, relative plasticity, and social development', *Developmental Review*, **5**, pp. 99–121.

MAIN, M. and HESSE, E. (1990) 'Parents' unresolved traumatic experiences are related to infant disorganised attachment status: Is frightened and/or frightening behaviour the linking mechanism?', in GREENBERG, M. T., CICCHETTI, D. and CUMMINGS, E. M. (Eds) *Attachment in the Preschool Years: Theory, Research and Intervention*, Chicago, University of Chicago Press.

MAIN, M., KAPLAN, N. and CASSIDY, J. (1985) 'Security in infancy, childhood and adulthood: a move to the level of representation', in BRETHERTON, I. and WATERS, E. (Eds) *Growing Points in Attachment Theory and Research*, Monographs of the Society for Research in Child Development, **50**, 1–2, pp. 66–106.

MAUGHAN, B. and PICKLES, A. (1990) 'Adopted and illegitimate children growing up', in ROBINS, L. N. and RUTTER, M. (Eds) *Straight and Devious Pathways from Childhood to Adulthood*, Cambridge, Cambridge University Press.
MONCK, E. (1991) 'Patterns of confiding relationships among adolescent girls', *Journal of Child Psychology and Psychiatry*, **32**, 2, pp. 333–45.
PROVENCE, S. and LIPTON, R. C. (1962) *Infants in Institutions*, New York, International Universities Press.
SPITZ, R. A. (1945) 'Hospitalism: an enquiry into the genesis of psychiatric conditions in early childhood', *The Psychoanalytic Study of the Child*, **1**, pp. 53–74.
SPITZ, R. A. (1946a) 'Hospitalism: a follow-up report', *The Psychoanalytic Study of the Child*, **2**, pp. 113–17.
SPITZ, R. A. (1946b) with K. M. Wolf, 'Anaclitic depression: An enquiry into the genesis of psychiatric conditions in early childhood', *The Psychoanalytic Study of the Child*, **2**, pp. 313–42.
SROUFE, L. A. (1988) 'The role of infant-caregiver attachment in development', in BELSKY, J. and NEZWORSKI, T. (Eds) *Clinical Implications of Attachment*, Hillsdale, New Jersey, Erlbaum.
SROUFE, L. A. and RUTTER, M. (1984) 'The domain of developmental psychopathology', *Child Development*, **55**, pp. 17–29.
SROUFE, L. A., CARLSON, E. and SHULMAN, S. (1993) 'The development of individuals in relationships: from infancy through adolescence', in FUNDER, D. C., PARKE, R., TOMLINSON-KEESY, C. and WIDAMAN, K. (Eds) *Studying Lives through Time: Approaches to Personality and Development*, Washington DC, American Psychological Association.
SROUFE, L. A., FOX, N. E. and PANCAKE, V. R. (1983) 'Attachment and dependency in developmental perspective', *Child Development*, **54**, pp. 1615–17.
TIZARD, B. (1977) *Adoption: A Second Chance*, London, Open Books.
TIZARD, B. and HODGES, J. (1978) 'The effect of early institutional rearing on the development of eight-year-old children', *Journal of Child Psychology and Psychiatry*, **19**, pp. 99–118.
TIZARD, B. and JOSEPH, A. (1970) 'The cognitive development of young children in residential care', *Journal of Child Psychology and Psychiatry*, **11**, pp. 177–86.
TIZARD, B. and REES, J. (1974) 'A comparison of the effects of adoption, restoration to the natural mother, and continued institutionalisation on the cognitive development of four-year-old children', *Child Development*, **45**, pp. 92–9.
TIZARD, B. and REES, J. (1975) 'The effect of early institutional rearing on the behaviour problems and affectional relationships of four-year-old children', *Journal of Child Psychology and Psychiatry*, **16**, pp. 61–73.
TIZARD, J. and Tizard, B. (1971) 'Social development of two-year-old children in residential nurseries', in SCHAFFER, H. R. (Ed.) *The Origins of Human Social Relations*, London, Academic Press.

WATERS, E., WIPPMAN, J. and SROUFE, L. A. (1979) 'Attachment, positive affect, and competence in the peer group: two studies in construct validation', *Child Development*, **50**, pp. 821–9.

YARROW, L. J., GOODWIN, M. S., MANHEIMER, H. and MILOWE, I. D. (1974) 'Infancy experiences and cognitive and personality development at ten years', in STONE, L. J., SMITH, H. T. and MURPHY, L. (Eds.) *The Competent Infant*, London, Tavistock Publications.

Chapter 4

Family Conversations and the Development of Social Understanding

Judy Dunn

Among the many papers and books by Barbara Tizard that have provided seminal ideas and key insights for developmental psychologists, one, in my view, has particular significance for those interested in cognitive development. When *Young Children Learning*, written in collaboration with Martin Hughes, was published in 1984, we were given a strikingly new and important window on the nature of four-year-olds' intellectual curiosity and powers of logical thought. We were also shown the potential significance of family conversations for children's cognitive growth. The four-year-olds whose talk is examined in the book engaged in conversations of richness and depth with their mothers at home; moreover, in these conversations they pursued with energy (and a surprising degree of logic) issues that intrigued or puzzled them. Those issues included work, birth, growing up, death and 'such diverse topics as the shape of roofs and chairs, the nature of Father Christmas, and whether the Queen wears curlers in bed' (p. 8). In a particularly vivid way the book alerted us to children's interest in the social world, and to the importance of conversation between children and other family members as contexts for learning. As Tizard and Hughes commented:

> The children seemed extremely interested in other people's viewpoints, and in the way in which they are similar to, and different from their own. Interest in other people – both children and adults – was a characteristic feature of most children in the study, and manifested itself in many different topics... It is sometimes supposed that children of this age have special, childish interests, mainly to do with mothers, babies, dolls, teddies and animals... The conversations in our study suggest that, on the contrary, all human experience was grist to their intellectual mill. (Tizard and Hughes, 1984, p. 128)

The account of four-year-olds' understanding that the book gives us has proved important and prescient in many ways: for instance, in its emphasis on the children's active role in achieving greater clarity over issues they did not understand, in its demonstration that within the framework of mother-child conversations the children showed considerable powers of logical argument, and in its revelation of the notable differences in their conversations at home and at school.

In this chapter the focus is limited to two key issues among the many raised in the book. The first is the nature of young children's understanding of others; and the second, the importance of conversations between children and other family members as contexts for learning. Both of these issues have proved of major interest to developmental psychologists in the decade since the book was published. The new perspective on children's minds and on the social processes implicated in the development of their understanding that is gained from the study of their conversations at home – so dramatically illustrated in *Young Children Learning* – is here explored further in the context of findings from three longitudinal studies of children in the UK and the US.

Two of these studies focused initially on children in their second year who were growing up in Cambridge and the surrounding villages. The children were followed through the preschool years and beyond (Dunn, 1988; Dunn, Slomkowski and Beardsall, 1994); the third (conducted in Pennsylvania in the US) followed fifty children from thirty-three months until seventy-two months of age (Dunn, 1995). The studies investigated links between children's social understanding and their close relationships, and employed both naturalistic observations, interviews and assessments. Conversational analyses were employed in each study. For details of the samples, the families' socioeconomic and educational background and the procedures and measures, see Dunn (1988, 1995).

Understanding other minds and emotions

The first issue considered is the nature of children's social understanding, and the picture of their capabilities that naturalistic studies of their behaviour and conversations at home give us. By four years old, the children in *Young Children Learning* engaged in vivid discussions of people's feelings, and they pursued the topic of why people behave the way they do with enthusiasm. The children were – in some respects – quite sophisticated in their social understanding, and undoubtedly very interested in people and the social world. What developments in the preschool years led up to this comparative maturity?

In the decade since the book was published there has been a great burst of research into the early stages of the development of children's understanding of emotions and mental states, and especially into their grasp of the connection between what someone thinks or believes and their actions (Wellman, 1990; Perner, 1991; Astington, 1994). This research on children's 'theory of mind' has been chiefly based on studying children in experimental settings; the most widely used approach has been to employ a 'false belief' paradigm, in which the child's understanding of how a protagonist's mistaken belief influences their actions is investigated (e.g. Bartsch and Wellman, 1989). There has been much controversy about the limitations that are typical of young children's understanding of inner states, and about the timing of developments in this understanding, but it is generally agreed that major changes take place as children reach their fifth year.

However, studies of children in naturalistic family settings remind us that the foundations for this understanding are being laid much earlier – in their second and third years. A number of lines of evidence support such a view: studies of children's engagement in sharing a pretend world with another (Youngblade and Dunn, 1995), of their attempts to manipulate others' psychological states by teasing, joking and comforting (Reddy, 1991), of their early attempts at deception (Newton, 1994), and their explicit discussion of feelings and mental states (Bretherton and Beeghly, 1982; Dunn, Bretherton and Munn, 1987; Brown and Dunn, 1992).

The development of children's use of causal language, and their references to mental states, illustrates some of the key developmental changes in their interest in inner states over the early years (Dunn and Brown, 1993; Brown, Donelan-McCall and Dunn, 1996). As part of our longitudinal study of children in Pennsylvania, we examined the changes in children's talk about the causes and consequences of people's behaviour and inner states, and their comments on social practices (for details see Dunn and Brown, 1993). We focused in particular on changes between thirty-three and forty months of age – a very short developmental period but one in which the early stages of 'mindreading' were already apparent (Dunn et al., 1991). The results showed that children's causal talk to both mothers and siblings increased dramatically between thirty-three and forty months, doubling in frequency over the seven-month period. And it was causal references to *internal states* that increased over this period, rather than causal talk about overt behaviour or action. To mothers, for instance, the children's causal talk about inner states increased from an average of .78 speaker turns per hour to an average of 2.27 turns per hour. The children, then, were engaging in causal discourse about inner states well before they were four years old – the age considered to be a 'watershed' developmental stage in studies of mindreading that are based on experimental settings.

There are obvious problems with drawing inferences about children's cognitive capacities from their conversations. As Scholnick and Wing (1992) point out in their lucid analysis of children's logical reasoning in conversations with their parents, the reasoning children show in such settings is the product of two people talking, and it is not clear that the children could make such 'if-then' deductions on their own. This is an issue to which we return below, in the next section. But it is beyond question that the evidence from studies of pretend, deception, argument in disputes, as well as causal talk about inner states confirm the general picture: that *when studied within the familiar and emotional world of the family* the early signs of a developing understanding of inner states and their links to action are evident in the third and fourth year.

Shatz's (1994) detailed study of the developing understanding of an individual child makes this point particularly clearly.

Our research also showed that there were systematic links between the children's social understanding as revealed in their interactions with others, and their later performance on the theory of mind tasks. Thus there were correlations between their success on the sociocognitive tasks, and their earlier spontaneous references to mental states (Brown and Dunn, 1996a), and their earlier engagement in joint pretend (Youngblade and Dunn, 1995). There were also correlations between individual differences in their propensity to take account of their interlocutor's point of view in disputes, and their success on these 'theory of mind' tasks (Slomkowski and Dunn, 1992).

Such evidence is important in showing the connections between children's behaviour and understanding in their real-life interactions and their performance in standardized assessments. But it raises the question of why there should be a discrepancy between the data from naturalistic family observations and children's test performance, in terms of the developmental stage at which their understanding is manifest. Several of the children in Newton's (1994) study of deception within the family, for instance, who engaged in apparent deception of their parents as three-year-olds, failed to succeed in conventional theory-of-mind tasks. We have argued that the interest and emotional salience to the children of the situations at home when they demonstrate early understanding of others, and the familiarity of the people involved may all contribute to the maturity of the understanding the children demonstrate in their everyday interaction within the family.

There is a parallel here with the discussion in *Young Children Learning* about why many of the children in that study should have shown much greater capacity within their conversations at home than they did at school. Tizard and Hughes emphasize a number of features of family conversations that are likely to be relevant. Among these are the shared experiences of mother and child, which enable mothers to understand what their children are attempting to say and to help them make sense of their experiences, and the opportunities for prolonged one-to-one conversations and undivided attention. Perhaps most important of all in relation to our own findings on mindreading are the two final features highlighted by Tizard and Hughes. They point out that the contexts in which mother and child converse are situations of great meaning and interest to the child, and that the relationship between mother and child is one of closeness and emotional intensity. The point that Tizard and Hughes stress here is that mothers usually have a great personal concern that their children should learn and understand. It is the intensity of the *mothers'* concern that they emphasize. In terms of the children's own affective state, they note that many of the 'cognitively rich' conversations took place in relatively unemotional contexts in which mother and child were engaged in daily routine activities – putting away the shopping, sorting the laundry, and so on – and that the children were often not *trying to get something done* in terms of their own needs. Rather, these conversations often took place when the children were in a calm, reflective mood. Our own findings indicate, in contrast, that with children a little younger than those studied by Tizard and Hughes, the children's own emotional state and their instrumental needs may be rather importantly implicated with the quality of discourse, and the 'cognitive richness' of the conversation. This brings us to the issue of the social processes implicated in the development of understanding, our second theme.

Conversations and the development of understanding

First, a background note is in order. The significance of dialogue between more and less experienced members of a culture as contexts for learning has long been widely recognized – for instance, in the writings of Vygotsky (1962) and Bruner (1973). More recently, spontaneous talk in everyday situations has been studied for an increasingly wide range of developmental issues – to investigate children's relationships, their understanding of social rules, their self-development, as well as their changing cognitive capacities (see the contributions to Garvey, 1992). The notion of expert-and-novice in dialogue is being explored in a wide range of different cultures (e.g. Rogoff, 1990), and within intervention studies attempting to foster learning. Appleton and Reddy (1996), for instance, reported that they were able to enhance children's performance on mindreading tasks through conversational interventions, in which the key to success was the provision of conversational opportunities and discussion. The attractive Vygotskyan idea of the developmental potential of collaboration between more and less mature members of a culture, rather abstract in formulation in Vygotsky's own writing, is now being given solid support in a variety of domains. Scholnick and Wing (1992), for instance, in the study mentioned earlier show that children who have not yet reached the stage of making 'if-then' arguments when tested on their own, are able to do so within the frameworks that parents set up for them in conversation. And Scholnick and Wing specify what it is that parents do to support children's early logical thought. They provide the initial premises, the prompts for inferences and feedback to the children's attempts. Scholnick and Wing argue that their results demonstrate that 'the origin of logic is collaborative'. In a different domain – understanding of categories – Callanan (1991) has also demonstrated the key significance of parent-child conversations.

In such studies many of the themes of *Young Children Learning* are being further explored. In our own work three particular issues concerning family conversations as settings for learning have been of special interest, and these are briefly discussed next: first, the evidence for over-time associations between participation in conversations and later sociocognitive sophistication; second, the significance of the emotional and pragmatic context of the conversational exchange, and third, the significance of the social partner with whom the child is interacting.

Patterns over time

Our studies of early psychological understanding have repeatedly highlighted the significance of discourse in these developments. First, they show that children in England and the US grow up in a world in which the actions, feelings, intentions, wants, beliefs and knowledge of people are continually discussed. From surprisingly early in their development children are participants in such discourse, as the studies of talk about inner states have shown. Children not only have access to *perceptual* information about others' intentions and desires (Butterworth, 1991), but are exposed to continuous talk about psychological states and their links to action.

Second, there is evidence now from several different studies that children's participation in discourse about feelings is correlated over time with their later understanding of emotions (Dunn, Brown and Beardsall, 1991; Dunn et al., 1991), and similarly their participation in discourse about mental states relates to their understanding of other minds (Brown and Dunn, 1996a). Perhaps the most remarkable pattern of association came from our examination of the understanding of mixed or ambivalent emotions shown by the children in our Pennsylvanian study in their second year at school. This is held to be a developmental achievement of considerable significance in middle childhood; it is not until the early school years that children begin to recognize that experiences may provoke a mix of emotions, both positive and negative. This knowledge is seen as central to other developments in children's understanding of self and the social world. Our longitudinal study showed that children's early family experiences, particularly their participation in family discussion of the causes of people's behaviours, was related over a four-year period to later differences in how well the children understood the experience of conflicting emotions (Brown and Dunn, 1996).

It should be emphasized that the links between early experiences and later understanding are likely to reflect a number of related processes. Children who are specially interested in why people behave the way they do may, for instance, engage others in more frequent discussions of causality than do their peers, and then continue to be particularly sensitive in middle childhood, and astute at understanding complex social and emotional experiences as they grow up. And family patterns of discussion and conversation may continue through childhood. The associations between early experience and later understanding could reflect continuity in the child, in features of the family environment, or a combination of both. While we have to be careful not to draw causal inferences from such correlational data, it should be noted that the discourse measures contributed substantially and independently to the variance in children's scores on mindreading and emotion-understanding tests. The results of the intervention study by Appleton and Reddy (1996) referred to above are also pertinent here.

The emotional and pragmatic context of conversations

A second issue of much interest to us concerning these early family conversations was the question of how the emotional and pragmatic context of children's interactions related to their social understanding. The relation between affect and cognition is a core issue in psychology, and one on which there is much disagreement. In relation to young children, for instance, it is sometimes argued that children show their most sophisticated behaviour when their own immediate interests are touched most closely (Eisenberg, 1992; Stein and Miller, 1993). In contrast it is also suggested that when children are upset or angry they are less able to cope with cognitive demands; as a result they function in a less mature way in situations of negative emotional arousal (Bloom and Beckwith, 1989; Masters, Felleman and Barden, 1981). As already noted, the four-year-olds in the Tizard and Hughes study frequently engaged in their passages of 'persistent intellectual search' in settings of calm, reflective dicussion. Is this a pattern that only emerges as children's powers of metacognition develop? Or do younger children also show particularly mature understanding in situations where they are not upset or excited?

Two general themes stood out in the findings of our Pennsylvanian study. The first was that there were interesting developmental changes in the links between children's emotional state and the social cognitive sophistication they demonstrated. The second was that these patterns differed for different domains of social understanding. The developmental points can be summarized as follows.

First, when the children studied were very young – for instance, in their second and third years – the settings in which their understanding of others' psychological states began to be evident were rarely emotionally neutral. They were frequently settings in which the child's self-interest was threatened and the child was intensely involved (Dunn, 1988). Thus deception, relatively sophisticated excuses, teasing that reflected some grasp of what would annoy or upset another, attempts to deflect anticipated blame on to a sibling, all occurred in situations in which the child's own interests were touched very directly.

There was also evidence that the kinds of conversation that were associated with the fostering of understanding feelings – discourse focused on emotion and its causes – were in fact frequently precipitated by the children's own distress or upset. At thirty-three months, children were more likely to talk about the causes of feelings with their mothers when they were expressing distress or anger than when they were neutral or happy. Their mothers were more likely to discuss feelings, too, when the children were upset (Dunn and Brown, 1994).

However, there were several lines of evidence indicating that as the children's powers of reflective thought increased, the relation of affective state to these aspects of understanding changed. Thus by forty-seven months, in contrast to the thirty-three-month findings, the children's causal talk about inner states was most likely to take place when they were affectively neutral. Over the fourth year, that is, as their powers of reflective thought increased, they began to engage in causal reflection more frequently when not emotionally aroused; at earlier time points it was when they were aroused that they participated in these relatively sophsiticated talks about inner states.

The third point also concerns developmental change. In our longitudinal study in Pennsylvania, the most striking developments in the children's interactions with their mothers came between forty-seven and sixty-nine months, with a marked increase in the children's engagement in reflective discussion with their mothers (Dunn, Creps and Brown, 1996). By this age, more than 50 per cent of their conversational interactions with their mothers was reflective rather than instrumental or playful in nature, and mothers' reflective talk increased in parallel. As children's powers of reflective thought increase, and as they become less dominated by their immediate, urgent needs, reflective conversation becomes a much more important feature of their close relationships.

There is, however, an important *caveat* to be made about any generalizations concerning the significance of the emotional context of interactions and their potential for cognitive development. The link between children's affective state and the cognitive sophistication revealed in their interactions apparently differed in different domains of understanding. Sharing a pretend world with another – a sophisticated act for a young preschooler, which involves the cognitive demands of sharing an imaginary world – was *unlikely* to happen when children were upset or angry, or even very excited. In contrast, in disputes these young children apparently marshalled their most sophisticated argument and reasoning when they were mildly angry or distressed in disputes, and their explicit discussion of feelings took place most frequently when they were similarly upset.

A final *caveat* concerns the pragmatic context of the conversation being examined. In our study of causal conversations we found that the correlations between causal talk and later mindreading ability were not with a simple measure of frequency of participation in such conversations, but with causal talk *in certain pragmatic settings*. For instance, children whose mothers' causal talk was in the context of shared play or positive interaction did well on the later assessments of social understanding. In contrast, those whose mothers' causal talk was in the context of controlling or disciplining them did poorly on the later sociocognitive tasks. The lesson is that we need to examine not just the content of talk, but what the interlocutors are trying to do, in the conversation. It seems that what may be key for later understanding is not only the exposure of the child to another's point of view, in an affectively neutral 'meeting of minds'; the pragmatics and the emotional quality of the interaction may also be important.

Family Conversations and the Development of Social Understanding

Conversations with whom? The significance of social partner

The issue of how far relationships with particular family members – or indeed close friends – may have special significance in the development of social understanding is one of some developmental importance, on which opinions diverge strongly. The role of mothers has been generally seen as of special significance, either because the relationship between mother and child is seen as a crucial template for later relationships, or because mothers are viewed as having both more interest and more opportunity to engage in 'cognitively rich' conversations with their young children than other family members, and more sensitivity to the child's own interests. It is widely assumed that it is within the mother-child relationship that children develop not only emotional security but expectations concerning others' behaviour, and social understanding more broadly considered, as well as styles of relating to peers in later childhood (Parke and Ladd, 1992). However, it has also been argued that interaction with other children may have special significance for the development of social understanding (Piaget, 1965). As part of our investigation of the links between relationships and developing understanding, we systematically compared what happened in conversations between our target children and their mothers, their older siblings and, after the age of four, their close friends. We also examined the links between these conversational measures and the children's scores on mindreading and emotion-understanding assessments. The comparisons led to some surprising findings.

First, not only our studies, but now a number of other projects have shown links between children's experiences with their siblings and friends, and their sociocognitive development. We found, for instance, in our Pennsylvanian study that a key predictor of children's mindreading and emotion understanding was the children's earlier experience of cooperative play with their older siblings (Dunn *et al.*, 1991). These data complement the findings of Perner and his colleagues that children with siblings do better on mindreading tasks than those without siblings (Perner, Ruffman and Leekham, 1994), and those of Lewis and his colleagues that the number of siblings and kin with whom children interact daily relates to their success on such tasks (Lewis *et al.*, 1995)

Second, we found a dramatic developmental change in the patterns of children's interactions with their mothers and siblings over the third year. Between thirty-three and forty-seven months, the time that children spent with their mothers dropped markedly, as did the amount of their conversation. Children's conversational turns to their mothers dropped from an average of 82 turns per hour to 52 turns per hour over this period, for instance. In contrast their interactions with their siblings increased greatly over this period, from an average of 44 to 70 turns per hour. The prominence of siblings, rather than mothers, as conversational partners for these secondborn children showed up in a variety of domains of discourse. Of special interest were the findings on talk about mental states and feelings. Children referred to mental states strikingly more frequently with their siblings as forty-seven-month-olds than they did with their mothers (Brown, Donelan-McCall and Dunn, 1996). And with close friends, the frequency was even higher. Specific attributes of the discourse differed too. In the child-child conversations, the children were more likely to refer to the interlocutor's thoughts and ideas, or to shared ideas, than they were with their mothers.

And the quality of the child-friend and child-sibling relationships were important here, too. Dyads who were particularly friendly and cooperative were more likely to refer to their own and each other's thoughts and ideas as they played together. Among the child-friend pairs, the length of their friendship and the frequency of their interaction (presumably linked to the closeness of their relationship) were positively related to explicit reference to mental processes. It is tempting, in the light of these findings, to underline the role of social interaction between equals or near equals in the development of children's ability to communicate about mental experience. It is certainly interesting that child-child interaction appears to become particularly prominent just at the stage when children's grasp of the psychological bases of human action is becoming firm.

One final point must be highlighted. Studying each child in three different relationships drew our attention to a striking finding: the same child frequently showed very different powers of social understanding within their different relationships. The child who engaged frequently in sophisticated role enactment with a friend did not necessarily do so with a sibling or mother; there were no significant correlations across the relationships in such pretend play: some children participated in joint pretend with sibling but not with friend, some with mother but not with sibling, and so on. Similarly there were no correlations across relationships in children's discourse about mental states, nor in their propensity to take account of the partner's views in disputes. The findings indicate that children's powers of understanding-in-action differ very much within different relationships, and presumably depend on the emotional context and pragmatics of the interaction. We should be wary of thinking about individual differences in sociocognitive capabilities as characteristics of children that will be evident in all their interactions. Again, we are reminded of the important lessons from *Young Children Learning*, concerning the crucial differences in children's communicative and reflective behaviour at home – in the context of a supportive mother-child relationship, and at school, where all too often the adult-child interaction did not have this quality of supportive interest.

Social class and gender differences?

The social class differences that Tizard and Hughes documented in the girls' conversations at school, and the more minor differences they described in complex language use at home, raise the question of how important early differences in language style in middle- and working-class homes may be. The class differences in the girls' conversational (and therefore presumably cognitive) experiences at school were clear; at home, however, the authors point out, the differences were best characterized as differences in style – that is, as differences in the frequencies of various aspects of usage. They argue that such differences would be greatly misrepresented if described in terms of a 'deficit' for working-class children.

In any case, there was in the Tizard and Hughes study, as in others including our own, a wide range of language use within each social class group. What then can be concluded about the longer term developmental significance of such differences in family conversations? At present the picture is still not clear. Most language studies, like *Young Children Learning*, are based on very small samples. With such samples, we only have power to detect large differences, and as expected on the basis of the Tizard and Hughes study, only small differences have been uncovered to date. We still do not know whether or how such style differences may be implicated in the social class differences evident in children's subsequent achievement at school.

What about gender differences in the nature or frequency of 'cognitively rich' conversations at home? Here again the picture remains unclear. Findings from different studies are inconsistent. Some report mothers talking about emotions and inner states more frequently to girls than they do to boys (e.g. Kuebli and Fivush, 1992); others find no gender differences. Gender differences in children's talk about feelings, and understanding of emotions have also been reported (Strayer, 1986; Fabes *et al.*, 1988; Brown and Dunn, 1996b). However, the average differences found are frequently small and explain little of the overall variance. As regards the understanding of mind, there is no consistent evidence to date for gender differences. In terms of the features of discourse on which Tizard and Hughes focused, the authors pointed out that the larger studies of Wells and Davie which included both boys and girls 'found little evidence of many of the common stereotypes about home life' (p. 259). In the decade since the study was published, the picture has not substantially changed. We are left with some intriguing suggestions – such as the possibility that girls' reasoning about the social world may be more directly derived from experiences within close relationships than that of boys (Blum, 1987) – which deserve further study with larger samples of children.

A final comment: to single out one study from Barbara Tizard's research does not do justice to a body of work that has had impact on educational policy, on the care of children in institutions, on the training of nursery staff and of teachers, on thinking about adoption, on the long-term sequelae of early adversity and the resilience or vulnerability of children. Other chapters in this volume reflect the scale and importance of her research in these areas. *Young Children Learning*, too, raised important issues for policy-makers and educationalists, as well as for those concerned with children's cognitive development from an academic standpoint. Perhaps most of all, it deserves our attention for the message it carries about valuing what parents do, and about what we can learn from listening to children.

Acknowledgments

The research described here was supported by the Medical Research Council, and by grants from NIMH (MH 46535), and NICHD (HD 23158).

References

APPLETON, M. and REDDY, V. (1996) 'Teaching three-year-olds to pass false-belief tests: A conversational approach', *Social Development* (in press).
ASTINGTON, J. W. (1994) *The Child's Discovery of the Mind*, Cambridge, MA, Harvard University Press.
BARTSCH, K. and WELLMAN, H. M. (1989) 'Young children's attribution of action to beliefs and desires', *Child Development*, **60**, pp. 946–64.
BLOOM, L. and BECKWITH, R. (1989) 'Talking with feeling: Integrating affective and linguistic expression in early language development', *Cognition and Emotion*, **3**, pp. 313–42.
BLUM, L. (1987) 'Particularity and responsiveness', in KAGAN, J. and LAMB, S. (Eds) *The Emergence of Morality in Young Children*, Chicago, University of Chicago Press.
BRETHERTON, I. and BEEGHLY, M. (1982) 'Talking about internal states: The acquisition of an explicit theory of mind', *Developmental Psychology*, **18**, pp. 906–11.
BROWN, J. and DUNN, J. (1992) 'Talk with your mother or your sibling? Developmental changes in early family conversations about feelings', *Child Development*, **63**, pp. 336–49.
BROWN, J. R., DONELAN-MCCALL, N. and DUNN, J. (1996) 'Why talk about mental states? The significance of children's conversations with friends, siblings and mothers', *Child Development* (in press).
BROWN, J. R. and DUNN, J. (1996) 'Continuities in emotion understanding from 3 to 6 years', *Child Development* (in press).
BRUNER, J. S. (1973) *The Relevance of Education*, New York, Norton.
BUTTERWORTH, G. (1991) 'The ontogeny and phylogeny of joint visual attention', in WHITEN, A. (Ed.) *Natural Theories of Mind*, pp. 223–32, Oxford, Blackwell.
CALLANAN, M. A. (1991) 'Parent-child collaboration in young children's understanding of category hierarchies', in GELMAN, S. and BYRNES, J. (Eds)

(1991) *Perspectives on Language and Cognition: Interrelations in Development*, pp. 440–84, Cambridge, Cambridge University Press.
DUNN, J. (1988) *The Beginnings of Social Understanding*, Cambridge, MA, Harvard University Press.
DUNN, J. (1995) 'Children as psychologists: The later correlates of individual differences in understanding of emotions and other minds', *Cognition and Emotion*, **9**, pp. 187–201.
DUNN, J., BRETHERTON, I. and MUNN, P. (1987) 'Conversations about feelings states between mothers and their young children', *Developmental Psychology*, **23**, pp. 132–9.
DUNN, J. and BROWN, J. R. (1993) 'Early conversations about causality: Content, pragmatics, and developmental change', *British Journal of Developmental Psychology*, **11**, pp. 107–23.
DUNN, J. and BROWN, J. R. (1994) 'Affect expression in the family, children's understanding of emotions, and their interactions with others', *Merrill-Palmer Quarterly*, **40**, pp. 120–37.
DUNN, J., BROWN, J. and BEARDSALL, L. (1991) 'Family talk about feeling states and children's later understanding of others' emotions', *Developmental Psychology*, **27**, pp. 448–55.
DUNN, J., BROWN, J., SLOMKOWSKI, C., TESLA, C. and YOUNGBLADE, L. (1991) 'Young children's understanding of other people's feelings and beliefs: Individual differences and their antecedents', *Child Development*, **62**, pp. 1352–66.
DUNN, J., CREPS, C. and BROWN, J. R. (1996) 'Children's family relationships between two and five: Developmental changes and individual differences', *Social Development* (in press).
DUNN, J., SLOMKOWSKI, C. and BEARDSALL, L. (1994) 'Sibling relationships from the preschool period through middle childhood and early adolescence', *Developmental Psychology*, **30**, pp. 315–24.
EISENBERG, A. R. (1992) 'Conflicts between mothers and their young children', *Merrill-Palmer Quarterly*, **38**, pp. 21–43.
FABES, R. A., EISENBERG, N., MCCORMICK, S. E. and WILSON, M. S. (1988) 'Preschoolers attributions of the situational determinants of others' naturally occuring emotions', *Developmental Psychology*, **24**, pp. 376–85.
GARVEY, C. (1992) 'Talk in the study of socialization and development', *Merrill-Palmer Quarterly*, **38**, pp. 1–149.
KUEBLI, J. and FIVUSH, R. (1992) 'Gender differences in parent-child conversations about past emotions', *Sex Roles*, **27**, pp. 683–98.
LEWIS, C., FREEMAN, N. H., KYRIAKDOU, C. and MARIDAKI-KOSSOTAKI, K. (1995) *Social influences on false belief access: Specific contagion or general apprenticeship?* Presentation at the Biennial Meetings of the Society for Research in Child Development, Indianapolis, March.
MASTERS, J. C., FELLEMAN, E. S. and BARDEN, R. C. (1981) 'Experimental studies of affective states in children', in LAHEY, B. and KAZDIN, A. E.

(Eds) *Advances in Clinical Child Psychology*, Vol. 4, pp. 91–114, New York, Plenum.
NEWTON, P. E. (1994) 'Preschool prevarication: An investigation of the cognitive prerequisites for deception', unpublished PhD dissertation, University of Portsmouth.
PARKE, R. D. and LADD, G. W. (1992) *Family-peer Relationships: Modes of Linkage*, Hillsdale, NJ, Erlbaum.
PERNER, J. (1991) *Understanding the Representational Mind*, Cambridge, MA, MIT Press.
PERNER, J., RUFFMAN, T. and LEEKHAM, S. R. (1994) 'Theory of mind is contagious: You catch it from your sibs', *Child Development*, **65**, pp. 1228–38.
PIAGET, J. (1965) *The Moral Judgement of the Child*, New York, Academic Press.
REDDY, V. (1991) 'Playing with others' expectations: Teasing and mucking about in the first year', in WHITEN, A. (Ed.) *Natural Theories of Mind*, pp. 143–58, Oxford, Basil Blackwell.
ROGOFF, B. (1990) *Apprenticeship in Thinking: Cognitive Development in Social Context*, Oxford, Oxford University Press.
SCHOLNICK, E. K. and WING, C. S. (1992) 'Speaking deductively: Using conversation to trace the origins of conditional thought in children', *Merrill-Palmer Quarterly*, **38**, pp. 1–20.
SHATZ, M. (1994) 'Theory of mind and the development of sociolinguistic intelligence in early childhood', in LEWIS, C. and MITCHELL, P. (Eds) *Children's Early Understanding of Mind*, pp. 311–29, Hillsdale, NJ, Erlbaum.
SLOMKOWSKI, C. M. and DUNN, J. (1992) 'Arguments and relationships within the family: Differences in children's disputes with mother and sibling', *Developmental Psychology*, **28**, pp. 919–24.
STRAYER, J. (1986) 'Children's attributions regarding the situational determinants of emotion in self and others', *Developmental Psychology*, **22**, pp. 649–54.
STEIN, N. and MILLER, C. (1993) 'The development of memory and reasoning skill in argumentative contexts: Evaluating, explaining, and generating evidence', in GLASER, R. (Ed.) *Advances in Instructional Psychology*, pp. 284–334, Hillsdale, NJ, Erlbaum.
TIZARD, B. and HUGHES, M. (1984) *Young Children Learning: Talking and Thinking at Home and at School*, London, Fontana.
VYGOTSKY, L. S. (1962) *Thought and Language*, Cambridge, MA, MIT Press.
VYGOTSKY, L. S. (1978) *Mind in Society*, Cambridge, MA, Harvard University Press.
WELLMAN, H. M. (1990) *The Child's Theory of Mind*, Cambridge, MA, MIT Press.
WOLF, D. (1982) 'Agency and experience: A longitudinal case study of the concept of independent agency', in FORMAN, G. E. (Ed.) *Action and Thought*, New York, Academic Press.

YOUNGBLADE, L. M. and DUNN, J. (1995) 'Individual differences in young children's pretend play with mother and sibling: Links to relationships and understanding of other people's feelings and beliefs', *Child Development*, **66**, pp. 1472–1492.

Chapter 5

Parents, Teachers and Schools

Martin Hughes

Introduction

This chapter is about the relationship between parents and their children's schools. In particular, it is about the different types of role which parents can play in their children's education, and about the ways in which this role is perceived by teachers and other professional educators. It is also about the extent to which professionals are prepared to change their practices in order to involve parents more closely in the educational process.

From a policy point of view, these issues are not new. For the last hundred years at least, there has been considerable interest among British educators in the appropriate role which parents should play in their children's education (see for example Docking, 1990, and David, 1993, for more extensive accounts). One recurring theme during this period has been that parents – or at least, particular groups of parents – should be viewed by professional educators as essentially 'problematic' (Hughes, Wikeley and Nash, 1994). From this point of view, parents are considered to possess certain attitudes, or to bring up their children in certain ways, which make it difficult for professionals to do their job properly. As a result, professionals have frequently been encouraged to change parents' attitudes or behaviour in directions which are considered to be educationally desirable. A more recent – and more positive – approach to parents is to regard them as 'partners' with professionals in the educational process. The notion of partnership assumes some kind of equality: parents and professionals are seen as having different types of expertise, of equal value, which can be brought together to serve the same educational ends. The notion of 'partnership' became particularly prominent in the 1980s, when it was applied both to the increasing presence of parents on school-governing bodies, and to the growing movement to involve parents in the primary curriculum through schemes such as Parents and Children and Teachers (PACT) (e.g. Griffiths and Hamilton, 1984) and Inventing Maths for Parents and Children and Teachers (IMPACT) (e.g. Merttens and Vass, 1990). The 1990s have seen the growing prominence of a third way of seeing parents – that of 'consumers' in the educational market. As we shall see later, the main role for parents as 'consumers' is to make informed choices between schools on the basis of the schools' academic performance.

While the role of parents has received considerable attention from a policy perspective, it has received much less attention from research. A notable exception to this lies in the work of Barbara Tizard. During the 1970s and 1980s, Tizard directed three major studies which made a fundamental contribution to our understanding of the different roles of parents and teachers: these studies will be reviewed in the next section of the chapter. Tizard's seminal work, however, was carried out before the Education Reform Act 1988 and its associated attempt to make a radical change to the relationship between parents and schools. In the second half of this chapter, we look at some recent research on parents and ask whether the conclusions drawn from Tizard's earlier work are still valid today.

Involving parents in nursery education

In 1981 Barbara Tizard published *Involving Parents in Nursery and Infant Schools*, written with Jo Mortimore and Bebb Burchell. The book was based on an action-research project which took place between 1976 and 1979. At that time, there was considerable enthusiasm for the idea of 'parental involvement', an enthusiasm which owed much to the recommendations of the Plowden Report ten years earlier. At the same time, this enthusiasm for parental involvement was accompanied by a lack of clarity over the meaning of the term, by a wide range of practices which might be described as 'involving parents', and by the paucity of systematic attempts to evaluate parental involvement in practice.

The study described by Tizard and her colleagues set out to address these issues. The research took place in seven nursery units (nursery schools or nursery classes in infant schools) which served contrasting catchment areas in and around London. The research team worked closely with the staff of these units over a period of two years, encouraging them to develop activities involving parents, and providing additional resources and support. The researchers also carried out an evaluation of the programme using observations, interviews and questionnaires. In addition, the research team returned one year after the end of the project to see how far the programme had been continued once the additional support had been withdrawn.

In their account of the project, Tizard, Mortimore and Burchell suggested that the intervention programme was only partially successful. It was clear that the schools had developed a range of activities for parents, and that these activities had been generally appreciated by the parents. However, the underlying purposes of the activities were not always realized. Thus several schools intended that the programme would increase parents' understanding of the aims and methods of nursery education: this was only partially achieved. Moreover, at the end of the project nearly half the parents felt that not enough had been done to involve them in their children's education. In particular, parents felt they had not been told enough about how their children were getting on, about the teaching methods used in the schools, or about the ways in which they as parents could help their children at home.

Tizard and her colleagues suggested that one of the main obstacles to successful parental involvement lay in the teachers' sense of their own 'professionalism'. Teachers, they argued, believe that they possess skills and expertise which parents do not and as a result they are reluctant to engage in genuine two-way dialogue with parents. Teachers' professionalism also means that they are likely to restrict parental involvement to routine classroom activities, and fail to draw on the skills and expertise which parents themselves possess. As Tizard, Mortimore and Burchell (p. 114) point out:

> Professionalism is likely to be a serious obstacle to establishing innovations of this kind. At present teachers are often unwilling to listen to the opinions of parents on educational aims and practices, or to accept that parents can make an important contribution to their child's education, on the grounds that the parents lack the requisite knowledge.

The issue is complex, as Tizard, Mortimore and Burchell admit. Professionals do indeed possess skills and knowledge which parents do not. Moreover, there are few parents who would want to challenge this expertise: most parents in their study were happy to leave educational decisions to the teacher. What concerned Tizard and her colleagues was that teachers' professionalism may often prevent them from recognizing that parents too have skills and knowledge, and from finding ways of using these skills and knowledge for the benefit of the children.

The home as a learning environment

The different contributions which parents and professionals can make to children's education was explored further in Barbara Tizard's next book, *Young Children Learning* (Tizard and Hughes, 1984). Although published in the mid-1980s, this book described a study which took place in the late 1970s, and which looked critically at some of the assumptions about parents which were current at that time. In particular, the book examined the widely held assumption that the kind of learning environment provided in the home by parents – and particularly by working-class parents – was impoverished compared to that provided by professional educators in a nursery school or class.

The study described in *Young Children Learning* involved thirty girls a few months either side of their fourth birthdays. Fifteen came from middle-class homes and fifteen from working-class homes. All the children attended a morning nursery school or class, and all spent the afternoons with their mothers at home. Tape-recordings were made over several days of the conversations which took place between the girls and their teachers at school, and between the girls and their mothers at home.

The study revealed that the children were experiencing a rich learning environment at home. For both the working-class and middle-class children, the home conversations were longer, more frequent and more complex than the school conversations. The conversations between the children and their mothers ranged over a wide range of topics – including the shape of roofs, the nature of Father Christmas and whether the Queen wears curlers in bed – and allowed frequent opportunities for the children to explore such topics at length. In contrast, the conversations between the children and the nursery staff had a narrower focus, and often consisted of the children providing brief answers to the teachers' questions.

Tizard and Hughes concluded that assumptions about the value of the home as a learning environment needed to be reconsidered. In particular, they were critical of parent-education programmes in which professionals attempted to change how parents interacted with their children. The book ended (p. 267) with the following comment:

> Indeed, in our opinion, it is time to shift the emphasis away from what parents should learn from professionals, and towards what professionals can learn from studying parents and children at home.

The effect of parents on children's achievements at school

The third major study which Barbara Tizard published in the 1980s was *Young Children at School in the Inner City* (with Peter Blatchford, Jessica Burke, Clare Farquhar and Ian Plewis, 1988). The overall aim of this study was to identify factors – both at home and at school – which might contribute to children's progress and attainment in the infant school. In order to achieve this, the research team followed a cohort of around 300 young children through three years at infant school. The children came from thirty-three schools in Inner London, most of which were in materially disadvantaged areas. A particular focus of the study was on comparing the attainment and progress of black and white children. A range of different types of data was collected using different methods, including standard tests, classroom observations and annual interviews with the parents.

The study revealed that the parents were providing a large amount of help to their children at home, both before and after they started school. Virtually all the parents gave their children help with reading at home, and many parents had started teaching them to read before they started school. The great majority of parents were also helping their children with maths, in areas such as counting, money, addition and subtraction. Most parents were also helping their children with writing, and most children engaged in spontaneous writing activities at home, such as writing stories or letters. Across all these activities, the black parents were giving their children significantly more help with school work than the white parents were.

The study found that much of this parental help was taking place without either the knowledge or the encouragement of the children's teachers. None of the teachers encouraged parents to help their children with maths, either before or after they started school, and only a few teachers encouraged parents to help with writing. Most of the teachers disapproved of parents teaching their children to read before school, although they actively encouraged parental help in reading once the children had started school.

Tizard and her colleagues also found that there was little effective communication taking place between parents and teachers, even though there was a good deal of informal contact between the two groups. Parents were poorly informed about what was happening to their children at school, and few could explain in much detail how their children were being taught to read or do maths. The majority of parents had received no information about their children's progress or behaviour, and black parents in particular had rarely been told how their children were getting on.

What effect did the parents' help have on the children's attainments and progress at school? The research team found that a number of home factors were directly related to the children's basic skills at school entry. For example, children's preschool reading and writing skills were significantly (and independently) related to their mother's educational level, to the amount of parental teaching they had received at home, and to the experiences they had received with books. However, once the children started school, there was no direct relationship between the amount of parental help they received with reading and their progress in reading during the infant years. In other words, children whose parents helped substantially with reading at home made no faster progress with reading at school than children whose parents provided little or no help.

This particular finding appeared to conflict with earlier research which showed that parental help was directly associated with greater progress in reading (e.g. Hewison and Tizard (J.) 1980; Tizard (J.), Schofield and Hewison, 1982). The finding also flew in the face of widely held beliefs about the importance of parental involvement in reading. In trying to explain this discrepancy, Tizard and her colleagues pointed out that the parents in their study had received little or no advice from schools as to how they should help children at home, and suggested that this might be a crucial factor:

> While it would be wrong to conclude from our study that parents cannot help to improve reading, our findings do suggest a need to look more closely at what is going on in both successful and less successful parent involvement schemes. This may help to identify the essential features required for parental help with reading to be effective. (p. 120)

Home and school – two separate worlds?

Taken together, these three studies which Barbara Tizard published in the 1980s have made a major contribution to our understanding of the role which parents can and do play in their children's education. The picture that emerges, however, is one of home and school as two separate worlds. In their different ways, parents and teachers are trying hard to do their best for the children; yet it would seem there is little effective communication between them and little knowledge of what the other is doing.

Tizard's research, for example, suggests that most parents of preschool children provide a rich informal learning environment in the home. Many parents also teach their children the beginnings of reading, writing and maths well before they start school. Once children have started school, most parents continue to help them with their school work; they listen to their children read, they talk about counting and money, and they encourage them with writing. And yet much of this activity is going on in relative isolation from the formal education system. Parents appear to know very little about what their children are doing at school, and receive little information from teachers about their children's progress and behaviour in school. They also receive little guidance from teachers about how they can help most effectively at home. Teachers, for their part, seem to have only a limited awareness of what parents are doing at home. They provide little encouragement for parents' attempts to support children's school learning, and they appear to place little value on parents' skills and expertise. And yet, as Tizard and her colleagues point out in *Young Children at School in the Inner City* (p. 180):

> parents are potentially the teachers' best allies; as we discovered, most parents, especially black parents, value schools and teachers highly, are anxious to help their children, and welcome opportunities to co-operate with teachers to this end.

Clearly, the schools and teachers studied by Tizard and her colleagues were not providing the kind of opportunities for cooperation which their parents were evidently seeking. However, it should be noted that all three studies were carried out in the late 1970s and early 1980s, and so inevitably reflect the policy context in which they took place. In particular, these studies were carried out before the major shift in educational policy which accompanied the Education Reform Act 1988, and which was specifically aimed at changing the relationship between parents and schools. The next section briefly sketches out some of the main features of this changing policy context; this is followed by a look at more recent research on the relationship between parents and schools.

Martin Hughes

The changing policy context

One of the main features of the reforms introduced by the Education Reform Act 1988 has been the explicit encouragement of market forces in education. From this point of view, education is seen as a commodity and schools as rival outlets which compete against each other for parents' custom. The main role for parents, as consumers of education, is to make choices between schools on the basis of publicly available information, such as a school's performance on standardized assessment tests (SATs). The assumption is that schools will have to raise their standards and make public the fact that they have done so, or parents will take their custom elsewhere. And as the funding of schools is now directly related to the number of pupils attending, a school which starts to lose parents' custom is in danger of becoming extinct.

In addition to this general promotion of an educational market, two further (and closely related) developments have taken place. First, there has been the elevation in policy statements of parents' knowledge above that of the professional. This was spelled out most clearly in the 1992 Education White Paper, *Choice and Diversity*. In a key paragraph, it was claimed that:

> Parents know best the needs of their children – certainly better than educational theorists or administrators, better even than our mostly excellent teachers.

The rationale for this kind of statement presumably lies in the need to support the policy of enhanced parental choice. For if choice of school is to be left primarily to parents, it might be objected that many parents would make choices that were not in the best educational interests of their children. Statements like the one quoted above make clear that this cannot happen: if parents 'know best the needs of their children', then whatever choice a parent makes must be the best for their child.

The second related development has been a major drive to provide parents with more information about their children's schools. A key document here has been *The Parent's Charter*, first published in 1991. A central plank of the Charter is the parents' 'right to know', enshrined in five main elements. These consist of an annual written report about each child, regular reports on schools from independent inspectors, publicly available 'league tables' comparing the performance of local schools, a prospectus or brochure about each school and an annual report from the school's governors. Interestingly, while *The Parent's Charter* went to some length to spell out parents' rights and what schools need to do to meet these rights, it contained relatively few mentions of the term 'partnership'.

Taken together, these various policy developments indicate a clear intention to bring about a major shift in the relationship between parents and schools. On the basis of this intention, then, we might expect that schools would be taking more steps to become aware of their parents' views on educational matters, and that they would be more prepared to change their practices to accommodate parents' wishes. We might also expect a greater recognition among professionals of parents' knowledge (particularly in regard to their own children) and a greater desire to find ways of making productive use of this knowledge. In addition, we might expect that parents themselves would now be more knowledgeable about their children's education, and that schools would be actively seeking ways of ensuring that parents were better informed.

Research on parents after the Education Reform Act

During the last few years, my colleagues and I have carried out three studies on the relationship between parents and schools in the context of the current educational reforms. These studies have focused on the early years of school, on the grounds that these are the years when the relationship between parents and schools is likely to be most critical. It is also the period of schooling where many of the recent reforms (such as the National Curriculum and standardized assessment) were first introduced.

One study, carried out with Felicity Wikeley and Tricia Nash, followed a cohort of around 150 children through the first few years of the National Curriculum. The children entered Year 1 in 1989, and in 1991 took part in the first standardized assessment of seven-year-olds in England and Wales. The children came from a wide range of social backgrounds, and their parents were interviewed each year on a number of topics concerned with their children's education. A full account of the methods and findings is provided in Hughes, Wikeley and Nash (1994).

In general, the study found little evidence that the relationship between parents and schools was changing in the immediate aftermath of the Education Reform Act. For example, there was a widespread reluctance among the parents to see themselves as 'consumers' of education. Only a small minority of parents saw themselves unequivocally in this way, and many parents found the idea puzzling or difficult to apply to their particular experiences. There was a general feeling among the parents that they wanted a closer and more interactive relationship with schools than that implied by being a passive consumer. As one parent graphically put it: 'It's not entirely like buying a packet of biscuits – you're putting in as much as you're taking out.'

The study also cast doubt on the assumption that 'parental choice' could be a major vehicle for raising educational standards. For some parents in the study, the amount of choice was virtually non-existent, either because they could not travel to schools other than their nearest school, or because these alternative schools were full. Other parents had the possibility of choice but did not appear to use it, because they were quite happy to send their child to the local school. Even when parents explicitly exercised some degree of choice, they did not necessarily choose on the basis of a school's academic performance. Other factors, such as the school's location, size or friendliness were of equal if not greater importance.

There was also little evidence in the study that the educational reforms had made parents better informed about what was going on in schools. Most parents in the study felt they knew very little about what their children were learning in school, and their knowledge about the National Curriculum and assessment procedures was also extremely limited. This did not seem to be due to a lack of interest, as the parents repeatedly said they wanted to know more about such matters. Most of the parents had hoped that the SATs would provide them with useful knowledge about their children, but in the event, many were disappointed; over two-thirds of the parents felt they had not learned anything new from the SATs.

Teachers' responsiveness to parents' views

The second study was concerned with the extent to which schools were responding to parents' views in the context of the new educational market. This study, which was carried out with Cathie Holden and Charles Desforges, looked at the extent to which teachers were aware of parents' views, and at the extent to which they amended their practice in the light of their knowledge of parents (or assumptions about them). The study examined these issues in the context of the assessment procedures introduced for seven-year-olds at the end of Key Stage One.

The project followed two cohorts of children through the assessment procedures of 1991 and 1992. Each cohort consisted of around 120 children, drawn from a wide range of schools in London, Bristol and the South West. The children's parents and teachers were interviewed both before and after they had taken part in the SATs, and the children were also observed in the classroom. Some findings from the 1992 cohort will be presented here: further details about the project can be found in Holden, Hughes and Desforges (1993), and Desforges, Hughes and Holden (1994, 1996).

The study found that teachers had only a partial awareness of parents' views. On some issues, the teachers were reasonably accurate in their assumptions about parents. For example, most parents in the study said they were generally satisfied with their children's schools. Over two-thirds of the parents (70 per cent) were 'happy' with the school, and only 6 per cent were 'not happy'. This level of parental satisfaction was correctly identified by the teachers in the study, who judged that their parents were generally 'happy with the school'. The teachers' judgments, however, were not based on any systematic attempts to measure parental satisfaction; rather, happiness was usually inferred from a lack of parental complaints. As one teacher put it: 'They're invited to come in any time if they' re not happy, but they don't – so we assume they are happy.'

While they were correct in their assumptions about parental satisfaction, the teachers were less aware of parents' views on other issues. For example, around two-thirds of the parents in the study felt they did not know enough about what was happening to their child at school. As in previous research (e.g. Tizard, Mortimore and Burchell, 1981; Tizard *et al.*, 1988; Hughes, Wikeley and Nash, 1994), parents said they wanted to know more about the curriculum, more about teaching methods and more about their child's progress. Almost all the parents also wanted to know more about the assessment procedures. The teachers, however, were mostly unaware of parents' desire for more knowledge. The predominant perception among the teachers was that parents had little interest in educational matters, and that any additional knowledge would be of little use to them anyway. As with parental satisfaction, teachers' judgments of parents' interest was not based on any systematic survey of parents' views. Instead it was inferred from, for example, low attendance at parents' meetings.

The teachers were also unaware of the extent to which parents wanted to be more involved in their children's education. In particular, they seriously underestimated parents' desire to play an active role in the assessment process itself. Nearly half the parents wanted to be involved in some way in assessing their children – for example, by preparing their children at home before the SATs, or by providing the school with additional information about their children's interests and achievements at home. The teachers, however, were mostly unaware of parents' desire for this kind of involvement. Moreover, most of the teachers felt that it was inappropriate for parents to be involved in this way. Some teachers, for example, were actively opposed to what they saw as parents 'coaching up their children for the tests', while other teachers clearly felt that parents had little of value to offer.

The project also looked at the extent to which teachers said they had amended their practice to take account of parents' views. For example, the teachers were asked whether their perceptions of particular parents had influenced the way they had approached the task of assessing children or preparing reports for parents. For the most part, the teachers claimed that they had not been influenced in any way by their perceptions of parents: indeed, many of them considered it would have been 'unprofessional' to do so. There were, however, some exceptions to this. In almost all these cases, the teacher suggested that the information they had provided for parents was influenced by their perceptions of those parents. However, in each case it was clear that the teachers were acting in what they considered to be the best interests of the child, rather than that of the parents.

In one example, the teacher explained at some length that the parent had low expectations about a child whom she (the teacher) considered to be quite able. She therefore wanted to show the mother that this child was capable of more than the mother expected. As the teacher admitted: 'I'm doing that more for G than for G's mum. I'm desperately trying to build up this child's self-esteem.'

In another example, the teacher explained that she had written the report in a particular way because she was worried the child's father might react violently to a negative report. As in the previous case, the teacher made it clear that she was acting in what she considered to be the best interests of the child: 'I needed to be very positive because I am aware that Dad might be a little physically violent if he wasn't happy with the report. If you think a child might really suffer, you tend to be very careful what you write.'

In general, then, the teachers considered it would be 'unprofessional' to amend their practice in accordance with what they knew (or assumed) about particular parents. Where they made exceptions to this, it was because they saw themselves acting in the best interests of the child, and not primarily in the interests of the parents.

Changing practice in schools

The third project was essentially an extension of the previous one. We wanted to find out how schools might develop their relationship with parents if they were given extra resources and support to do this. We therefore set up an action-research project involving three contrasting schools which had a good reputation for their work with parents. The project team did not prescribe specific ways of working with parents: instead, the schools were asked to address the following questions:

1 What methods can schools use to develop a closer understanding of their parents' views, particularly in regard to the productive use of assessment?

2 How can this information about parents' views be used to develop partnerships aimed at promoting pupils' learning?

Each school was encouraged to develop its own programme of activities, appropriate for the school, which would address these questions. The main phase of the project took place during the school year 1993–4. During this phase the research team provided supply cover, organized termly meetings of all the teachers in the project, and made regular visits to each school. An evaluation was made of the work in each school by means of interviewing teachers and parents, attending meetings and collecting relevant documentary evidence. One member of the research team also returned to each school a year after the project had ended to see which innovations had been sustained despite the removal of external support. A full account of the project is given by Holden, Hughes and Desforges (1996).

All three schools organized meetings with their parents to generate ideas for the programme. Some of the parents' suggestions were rejected because they did not fit with current school policy. For example, the parents in School A asked for more guidance on helping with homework, but this was not taken up as it did not fit with the school's policy of encouraging independent learning. Other suggestions, however, were adopted. School A, for example, introduced regular home visits and set up a 'shadowing' scheme whereby parents could observe their children in the classroom. School B introduced special folders for conveying work and information between home and school, while the teachers also wrote a simplified guide (in 'Childspeak') to the National Curriculum attainment targets in English. School C extended the time available for parent/teacher interviews to allow fuller discussion of children's progress, and instigated regular coffee mornings for improving communication with parents.

The project evaluation suggested that these activities had had a mixed reception. In School A, the shadowing innovation was greatly appreciated by those parents who made use of it; however, the school staff did not think that the parents had gained much from it. Conversely, the home visits were valued much more by the teachers than by the parents. In School B, the simplified guide to the attainment targets was considered to be very useful by the parents, but the home-school folders fell quickly into disuse. In School C, the parents valued the extended parent-teacher interviews, but there was a mixed response to the coffee mornings.

The follow-up interviews conducted a year after the project had ended revealed that only a minority of the innovations had been maintained. In general, activities which provided information for parents had continued longer than those which sought parents' views. The main reason given for this was lack of time and resources. However, one particularly ironic explanation was provided by School A. This school had been inspected by OFSTED during the year and had been highly praised for its work with parents. At the same time, other areas of the school's work had been criticized. The school had reacted to the inspectors' report by switching time and resources to these other areas and away from its work with parents. No adverse reaction had been received from parents as a result of this decision.

In many ways, the findings from this action-research project mirrored those of the action-research carried out by Barbara Tizard and her colleagues some fifteen years earlier. In both projects, the schools developed new ways of increasing the amount of information being provided for parents. However, this communication was essentially one-way. In neither project did the schools show any signs of substantially modifying their practice to take account of parents' views. Nor did the teachers find ways of significantly increasing parents' involvement in their children's school learning.

Plus ça change?

The main conclusion to be drawn from our research is that, despite the intentions of policy-makers, there has been little change over the last ten to fifteen years in the relationship between parents and schools. As in Tizard's earlier studies, we found that the great majority of parents were actively helping with their children's education at home, and many wanted to be more closely involved with their education at school. Like Tizard, we found that most parents had only limited knowledge about what was happening at school, and that many parents wanted to know more. Teachers, for their part, were doing little to meet parents' desire for more involvement and information. Indeed, the teachers in our studies seemed mostly unaware of what their parents wanted and were making few systematic attempts to find out. As Tizard and her colleagues noted some fifteen years earlier, teachers' sense of their own professionalism often prevented them from acknowledging what parents had to offer. Even with the provision of extra resources and support, the schools in our action-research study made no fundamental changes in their relationship with parents.

Why has there been so little change in this relationship, despite the efforts of policy-makers? One of the most obvious reasons is that, since the Education Reform Act 1988, schools in England and Wales have been experiencing an unprecedented number of externally imposed demands for change. These demands have been particularly acute in the early years of school (Key Stage One), where many of the innovations were first introduced. While it is not clear how far these demands have actually led to change in the classroom (see Pollard *et al.*, 1994; Plewis and Veltman, 1996), there is no doubt that they have significantly increased teachers' workloads and lead to high levels of stress (e.g. Campbell *et al.*, 1991). At such a time, it is hardly surprising if teachers concentrate on what they see as their priority – working with the children – and give little attention to developing their relationships with parents.

Such an explanation, however, is only partial. It suggests that schools in other parts of the world, in other policy contexts, might operate differently. Yet there is little evidence that this is the case. For example, a recent summary by Levin and Riffel (1995) of research in the USA and Canada concludes that schools generally do little to seek the views of their 'stakeholders' – such as parents, pupils or the local community. Even when they do, few schools have effective procedures for making use of the information so obtained. As Levin and Riffel point out:

> School systems do not have good processes for learning about and responding to changes in their environments except in a very narrow sense. These limitations are not the result of ill-will or incompetence, but of long-ingrained patterns of thought and behaviour which will not be easy to change, no matter what policy-makers may promulgate. (p. 1)

It is not only on the schools' side of the relationship that there appears to have been little change over the years. When carrying out our research with parents, we were frequently struck by how much the educational reforms appeared to be passing them by. Despite the rhetoric of parental empowerment, the parents in our studies often seemed cut off from their children's schools, to lack understanding about what was happening, and to be uncertain how to express their concerns. Many parents felt that there was no effective organization working on their behalf, either locally or nationally, and that even when they were given a voice, they were not always listened to. Indeed, we must conclude from our research that if the notion of 'parental empowerment' is to become more than just rhetoric, then it must be accompanied by sustained political will at both local and national level. Without this, it seems highly likely that parents and schools will remain two separate and unrelated worlds.

Acknowledgments

The research described in this chapter was supported by the Leverhulme Trust and the Economic and Social Research Council (ESRC).

References

CAMPBELL, R., EVANS, L., NEILL, S. and PACKWOOD, A. (1991) *Worloads, Achievement and Stress*, University of Warwick.
CENTRAL ADVISORY COMMITTEE FOR EDUCATION (1967) *Children and their Primary Schools* (Plowden Report), London, HMSO.
DAVID, M. E. (1993) *Parents, Gender and Education Reform*, Cambridge, Polity Press.
DEPARTMENT FOR EDUCATION (1992) *Choice and Diversity: A New Framework for Schools*, London, HMSO.
DEPARTMENT OF EDUCATION AND SCIENCE (1991) *The Parent's Charter*, London, DES.
DESFORGES, C., HUGHES, M. and HOLDEN, C. (1994) 'Assessment at Key Stage One: its effects on parents, teachers and classroom practice', *Research Papers in Education*, **9**, pp. 133–58.
DESFORGES, C., HUGHES, M. and HOLDEN, C. (1996) 'Parents, teachers and assessment at Key Stage One', in HUGHES, M. (Ed.) *Teaching and Learning in Changing Times*, Oxford, Blackwell.
DOCKING, J. W. (1990) *Primary Schools and Parents*, London, Hodder & Stoughton.
GRIFFITHS, A. and HAMILTON, D. (1984) *Parent, Teacher, Child*, London, Methuen.
HEWISON, J. and TIZARD, J. (1980) 'Parental involvement and reading attainment', *British Journal of Educational Psychology*, **50**, pp. 209–15.
HOLDEN, C., HUGHES, M. and DESFORGES, C. (1993) 'What do parents want from assessment?' *Education 3–13*, **21**, pp. 3–7.
HOLDEN, C., HUGHES, M. and DESFORGES, C. (1996) '"I just want to know what he does all day" Action research with parents and schools', *Education 3–13*, **24**, pp. 42–50.

HUGHES, M., WIKELEY, F. and NASH, P. (1994) *Parents and their Children's Schools*, Oxford, Blackwell.
LEVIN, B. and RIFFEL, A. (1995) 'School system responses to external change: Implications for school choice', paper presented to ESRC/CEPAM Seminar: Research on Parental Choice and School Responses, The Open University.
MERTTENS, R. and VASS, J. (1990) *Sharing Maths Cultures*, Basingstoke, Falmer Press.
PLEWIS, I. and VELTMAN, M. (1996) 'Changes in the classroom experiences of Inner London infant pupils, 1984–1993', in HUGHES, M. (Ed.) *Teaching and Learning in Changing Times*, Oxford, Blackwell.
POLLARD, A., BROADFOOT, P., CROLL, P., OSBORN, M. and ABBOT, D. (1994) *Changing English Primary Schools? The Impact of the Education Reform Act at Key Stage One*, London, Cassell.
TIZARD, B., BLATCHFORD, P., BURKE, J., FARQUHAR, C. and PLEWIS, I. (1988) *Young Children at School in the Inner City*, Hove, Erlbaum.
TIZARD, B. and HUGHES, M. (1984) *Young Children Learning*, London, Fontana.
TIZARD, B., MORTIMORE, J. and BURCHELL, B. (1981) *Involving Parents in Nursery and Infant Schools*, London, Grant McIntyre.
TIZARD, J., SCHOFIELD, W. N. and HEWISON, J. (1982) 'Collaboration between teachers and parents in assisting children's reading', *British Journal of Educational Psychology*, **52**, pp. 1–15.

Chapter 6

From Miscegenation to Hybridity: Mixed Relationships and Mixed-parentage in Profile

Ann Phoenix and Charlie Owen

Racially mixed unions and mixed-parentage are at the intersection of a number of theoretical and social policy debates because they highlight a range of racialized social relations and divisions. 'Mixed-parentage' challenges binary, black-white thinking and demonstrates some of the contestations that are constantly being waged around the terminology of 'race'. Since children of mixed-parentage are more likely than white or black children to spend long periods in local authority care (Bebbington and Miles, 1989), they illustrate most starkly the difficulties caused by the polarization of debates on transracial adoption (Tizard and Phoenix, 1993). There is increasing recogniton that people with one black parent and one white parent do not necessarily suffer from identity confusion because they are neither black nor white. Instead, new, 'mixed' identities have emerged. Barbara Tizard's recent research has played an important part in documenting and analysing the emergence of 'mixed-race' identities among young Londoners (Tizard and Phoenix, 1993).

This chapter first discusses the social construction of black-white unions and mixed-parentage as problematic. It then examines the demographic background which has, at least partly, provided the conditions of possibility for the emergence of 'mixed' identities. Finally, it uses some data from the study of the Social Identities of Young Londoners, conducted with Barbara Tizard, to demonstrate the complex ways in which young people of mixed-parentage think about their racialized identities and how this contrasts with the simplistic ways in which they are often positioned by other people.

The construction of mixed-parentage as problematic

The terms of colour

The construction of 'mixed-parentage' as necessarily problematic can only occur when there is acceptance that there are clearly differentiated 'races' who are, in essence, necessarily polarized. The treatment of people in 'essentialist' ways has been much critiqued in feminist and cultural studies work as well as in social science literature for its obscuring of intragroup differences and commonalities between groups as well as its valorizing of intergroup differences (Hall, 1989; Brah, 1992, 1996). Bipolar constructions of black and white have been responsible for notions that people can be 'between two cultures' or 'neither one colour nor the other' and denials that it is possible to have identities which are 'both/and', rather than 'either/or' (Collins, 1990).

In Britain and the USA, the conceptual polarization of black people and white people has, historically, generally led to those of mixed-parentage being included in the category now commonly called 'black'. It is indicative of the political nature of this categorization that having one white parent has never been sufficient to permit inclusion as 'white', but having one black parent necessarily entailed classification as 'black'. Most states (at one time forty of fifty) in the USA enacted laws against racially mixed unions and marriages. Such laws were not declared unconstitutional until 1967 (Young, 1995). Although the categories forbidden to marry in the various states were not consistent, all forbade marriage between black and white (Reuter, 1931). Definitions of what constituted being black also varied, but, 'in practice – both legal and customary – anyone with *any* known African ancestry was deemed an African American, while only those without any trace of known African ancestry were called Whites' (Spickard, 1992, p. 16). This is what became known as the 'one drop rule' or 'hypodescent'. Common sense would suggest that skin colour was the basis of the black-white differentiation, but some of those of mixed-parentage could be lighter than some whites, but would still be classified as black (Spickard, 1992). One edition of the 'Oprah Winfrey' show (BBC2, Saturday 28 October 1995) vividly demonstrated this essentialist thinking: the featured guests were people living in the USA who had thought that they were white and who had been treated as white. Each had discovered that, in fact, they had black ancestry. They were then called 'black' and treated as black rather than as white. In some cases this included having to change schools – very much in line with the 'one drop' rule.

The binarism that underpinned the 'one drop rule' has 'sedimented into common sense'. Thus, it is not surprising that discussion on the 'Oprah Winfrey' show reflected this old, but still pervasive, construction. Even some of the opposition to transracial adoption from black social workers and other black groups is based on the same principle as the 'one drop rule'. Arguments that people of mixed-parentage have to recognize that, regardless of how they feel, they are black are based on a recognition that racism will differentiate them from white people. Yet such arguments construct black people and white people as cultural and visual opposites rather than either as part of a continuum or as united and/or differentiated by features other than 'race'. Instead of posing a challenge to racism or racialized discourses they (re)produce them, as in the following quote from the black US magazine, *Ebony*:

> Some biracial brothers and sisters might do well to heed advice from Lenny Kravitz [American rock star]. 'You don't have to deny the White side of you if you're mixed,' he says. 'Accept the blessing of

having the advantage of two cultures, but understand that you are Black. In this world, if you have one spot of Black blood, you are *Black*. So get over it.' (Norment, 1995, p. 112)

Although people with one black and one white parent have historically been categorized as black, they have, simultaneously (and contradictorily), been identified as separate from both black and white people. The specific terms commonly used to describe people of mixed-parentage and sexual unions between black and white people tend to pathologize those who cannot easily be fitted into the taken-for-granted racialized binary opposition. Thus, 'half-caste', 'mixed race'; 'biracial'; 'maroon', 'mulatto' (from mule) and 'métis' (French for mongrel dog) all demonstrate essentialism and bipolar thinking. Many are also riven with pathologizing tones of impurity. In the same way, the terms mixed-marriage, intermarriage and 'miscegenation' (meaning 'interbreeding between races, especially sexual union of whites with Negroes', *Oxford Illustrated Dictionary*, 1980; *The Shorter Oxford English Dictionary*, 1983) accept binary notions of 'race' and have negative overtones. The ubiquitous nature of such terms is illustrated in the work of the sociologist Fernando Henriques (1974). Henriques challenged negative views of mixed marriages. Yet he called his book *Children of Caliban: Miscegenation* and wrote about himself as a 'part of the process of miscegenation that I have tried to describe' (p. 6).

Given the increasing numbers of people who are of mixed-parentage and in mixed relationships, it is not surprising that this is an area where terminology has been contested. Although this contestation is perhaps less well known than was the contestation over changing the term 'coloured' to 'black' in the 1960s and 1970s, many people now reject usage of terms such as 'mulatto', 'half-caste' and 'miscegenation'. In the USA, where 'Afro–American' has largely given way to African–American, there is now widespread usage of the term 'biracial' to make general reference to 'mixed-parentage'. In Britain, Small (1986) has argued for dropping the term 'mixed race' because it both accepts that there are 'races' and denies blackness. He advocated use of the term 'mixed-parentage' if 'black' would not suffice. Yet, as with much of the terminology of 'race', terms to describe 'mixed-parentage' are not satisfactory and, for that reason, are likely to continue to change:

> What term adequately describes the relationship between a Black and a White parent? The term 'mixed race' is inappropriate because 'race' carries undertones of biological inferiority and superiority. An alternative term needs to be found but we do not have one to offer. We use 'mixed parentage' but it too has racist undertones. (Early Years Trainers Anti-Racist Network, 1995, p. 11)

One reason for dissatisfaction with the term 'mixed-parentage' to describe those who have one black and one white parent is that it constructs an arbitrary division between those of mixed-parentage and others. Because the populations of the world are almost all intermixed, most people have some mixed-parentage (Small, 1986). Indeed, because of slavery and colonial relationships, many more people are of mixed black-white ancestry than is generally accepted. May Opitz *et al.* (1992) point out that while 'Afro–German' is a new term and people of mixed black-white parentage in Germany are generally viewed as hated war babies, there has been a long history of mixed-parentage as a result of Germany's colonial relationship with Cameroon, Tanzania and Namibia. Augustin Barbara (1989) makes similar points for France, while Peter Fryer (1984), Henriques (1974) and Visram (1986) document the long history of mixed relationships in Britain.

It is difficult to estimate the percentage of white British and US populations which have black ancestry, but it has been estimated that 70–80 per cent of all US black people have some white ancestry (Zack, 1993). Some recent popular interest in the impact of mixed ancestry is demonstrated by the fact that the highly popular US 'Oprah Winfrey' show has dedicated two programmes to white people who have black relatives and vice versa. One of these was also shown on British television (BBC 2, Saturday 28 October 1995).

In recent years, academics in cultural studies have produced terms which attempt to take on board the processual nature of ethnicity. Thus the terms 'hybridity' and 'hybridization' are often used to denote the syncretism and plurality of racialized identities. Hall (1989) refers to 'the process of cultural *diaspora-ization*'. Such terms are not designed to refer particularly to people of mixed-parentage, but they offer ways of thinking about ethnicity which include those of mixed-parentage without pathologizing them. It may seem paradoxical that the term 'hybridity' should be invested with positive connotations when 'miscegenation' is not. The dictionary definition of the term 'hybridity' is the condition of 'being produced by the interbreeding of two different species or varieties; mongrel; cross-bred; half-bred' (*Shorter Oxford English Dictionary*, 1983) as well as 'person of mixed nationality' (*Oxford Illustrated Dictionary*, 1980). Parker (1995) argues that the concept of hybridity 'is an uneasy biologistic metaphor for combination which can connote a state rather than a process . . . The focus should be on specific processes of identity formation rather than subsuming them all into one state of hybridity' (Parker, 1995, p. 26). Similarly, Young (1995, p. 27) argues that:

> There is an historical stemma between the cultural concepts of our own day and those of the past from which we tend to assume that we have distanced ourselves. We restate and rehearse them in the language and concepts that we use: every time a commentator uses the epithet 'full-blooded', for example, he or she repeats the distinction between those of pure and mixed race. Hybridity in particular shows the connections between the racial categories of the past and contemporary cultural discourse.

Nonetheless, given that 'hybridity' is theorized as processes resulting from the combination of peoples and cultures, its use can be seen as part, however unsatisfactory, of the process of reclamation of terms and contestation over meanings which was signalled by the change from 'coloured' to 'black'. The accounts of young people of mixed-parentage interviewed in Barbara Tizard's study of the social identities of young Londoners and of people involved in racially mixed relationships can be said to demonstrate such a shift. Most of their discourses were not pathological constructions of 'miscegenation' and binary oppositions of 'neither one colour nor the other', but instead showed the beginnings of constructions of 'hybridity'.

In keeping with all racialized terms, the terminology of mixed relationships and mixed-parentage thus demonstrates dynamism, contestation of power to define, and historical and geographical specificity:

> There are no terms that are 'right' forever more. Groups define and redefine themselves, their sense of who they are culturally and politically as preferred terms change. Also within a group one person may like a term which another may not. We have to constantly pay attention to changing definitions and to the reasons why they are changed. People need to discover for themselves who they are and not have terms imposed on them. (Early Years Trainers Anti-Racist Network 1995, p. 11)

Opposition to 'racial mixing'

In countries with a colonial history, there have been (and continue to be) contradictory responses to racially mixed unions and children of mixed-parentage. On the one hand, such unions have always existed where people of different colours and ethnicities have coexisted. On the other hand, there has long been a mainly negative orientation to unions between black and white people in countries such as Britain and the USA. In slavery and colonialism, mixed unions were often forced by white colonizers on colonized women (Spickard, 1989). However, there always were some consensual unions. Yet, nineteenth-century white writers frequently denounced 'racial mixing' as indecent or unnatural. Such denouncements were obviously designed to dissuade readers from contemplating mixed unions:

> Who that has any sense or decency, can help being shocked at the familiar intercourse, which has gradually been gaining ground, and which has, at last, got a complete footing between the Negroes and the women of England? ... but to accompany him *to the altar*, to become his wife, to breed English mulattoes, to stamp the mark of Cain upon her family and her country! Amongst white women, this disregard of decency, this defiance of the dictates of nature, this foul,

> this beastly propensity, is, I say it with sorrow and with shame, *peculiar to the English*. (Cobbett, 1804, *Cobbett's Weekly Political Register*, 16 June 1804. Quoted by Fryer, 1984, pp. 234–5)

There is some evidence on the extent of opposition to mixed marriages in modern Britain. For example, on a number of occasions between 1983 and 1991 the British Social Attitudes Survey has asked respondents if they would mind if a close relative married someone of *Asian* origin or of *West Indian* origin. About half of respondents said they would mind, either a lot or a little, although there has been a fall in the number who mind, from 54 per cent in 1983 to 43 per cent in 1991. (For more detail see Owen (in prep).) In a poll conducted for *The Independent on Sunday* (7 July 1991), respondents were asked the extent to which they agreed or disagreed with the following statement: 'People should only marry people of their own ethnic group.' Among *White* respondents, 31 per cent said they agreed; 17 per cent of *Black* respondents and 39 per cent of *Asian* respondents also agreed[1]. More recently, the fact that there is still opposition to black-white relationships was brought home to a British public by media accounts of attacks on black men with white girlfriends (see, for example, *Daily Mail*, 19 October 1993; *The Guardian*, 10 June 1994; *The Sun*, 21 June 1994; *The Sun*, 23 September 1994).

While there has been a long-standing negative orientation to relationships between black and white people and the children from such unions, the nature of that negative orientation has shifted. There has been a shift from eugenic concerns with 'miscegenation' to liberal concerns with the welfare of the children born from such unions, i.e. to expressions of benevolent concerns about the children:

> Many people who are in almost all other respects very tolerant of coloured people defend their objection to mixed marriages on the grounds that the children of such marriages are bound to suffer. (Richmond, 1961, p. 284)

> The prevailing view of mixed race children is that they have identity problems because of their ambiguous social position... the stereotype of the 'tortured misfit'. (Wilson, 1987, pp. 1–2)

Although this appears, at first sight, to be a benign shift, from concerns with miscegenation to liberal concerns, it is, in effect, also negative. This is because it still construes mixed relationships as problematic. However, this apparently benevolent concern masks its deleterious effects in three related ways. First, it prevents charges of racism by deflecting attention from racist discourses on to children of mixed-parentage as misfits. Second, it individualizes the issue by shifting focus on to the problems of identity for the children produced from mixed unions. Finally, it constructs 'regimes of truth' (Foucault, 1980) which are designed to lead to internal, individual regulation of mixed relationships since external controls are neither legal nor currently socially acceptable. Thus, since most parents do not have children with the intention of damaging them, the implication is that concerned, responsible parents should not produce children of mixed-parentage. It thus warrants attempted deterrence of mixed relationships and intrusive comments to those who become parents of mixed-parentage children:

> In a society where our reluctance to become 'involved' leaves tortured children at risk in their own homes and raped women lying in gutters, perfect strangers think they have the right to abuse you, or your partner or your child, because you have different skin colours. (Alibhai-Brown and Montague, 1992, p. 4)

Foreboding about the impact on children of being of mixed-parentage arises from divergent political interests, since such fears are expressed by people who are positioned differently in relation to power and social control. Thus, some white people are concerned that mixed-parentage involves a dilution of their 'race', while some black people are more concerned that it involves consorting with 'the enemy'. Yet these positions coincide in discourses of concern for the welfare of children of mixed-parentage in the same way that black people and white people sometimes apply the 'one drop rule' for different reasons. The construction of mixed-parentage as a social problem represents a conflation of issues constructed as social problems. It is easier to impute causation of problems associated with minority status, discrimination and uncertainty about how to deal with those who do not fit into the artificially created binary division between black and white, to being of mixed-parentage, than to deal with these issues themselves.

While there has been strident opposition to 'racial mixing', it is possible to discern positive as well as negative themes in writing over the last sixty years. In 1937, for example, Stonequist argued in *The Marginal Man*, that people of mixed-parentage would almost inevitably experience a painful lack of belonging to either black or white groups. Mixed-parentage was thus, according to Stonequist, inherently likely to cause negative experiences. By way of contrast, Park (1931), working in the same period, argued that there could be positive benefits of the marginality resulting from mixed-parentage, in that the possessing of two cultures could make the marginal person a 'citizen of the world'. This conceptualization of 'marginality' is, arguably, a forerunner of notions of 'hybridity', although current usage of the latter is intended to connote the forging of new cultures from syncretic blending and does not imply marginal existence.

Demographic trends: an example of contestation in practice

There are few demographic data available on people of mixed-parentage. However, those data available indicate there are a growing number of people in 'racially' mixed relationships and big increases in the number of people of mixed-parentage. Thus, despite negative constructions of mixed-parentage, many people are contesting the social proscription on crossing racialized boundaries. This section considers the demographic data on mixed-parentage available in Britain. The demographic data provide the context within which it is possible to understand ideological and discursive shifts in regard to mixed-parentage.

Prior to the 1991 Census, the main source of data on Britain's ethnic minority populations had been the Labour Force Survey (Owen, 1993). The Census is now the main source, but it is very limited in the information it provides on mixed ethnic backgrounds. In fact, there is only one published table which includes any data on mixed-parentage.

Census

The first British Census to include a question on ethnic group was 1991. The question went through extensive field trials, to get a wording that was both acceptable to those completing the Census form and usable by those who wanted the data:

> To be effective an ethnic classification has to be expressed both intelligibly and acceptably to all sections of the population: it has also to furnish information in the form in which it is needed . . . the various aims are not always compatible and . . . the final design has had to be a compromise between conflicting objectives. (Sillitoe and White, 1992, p. 141)

11	Ethnic group	
		White ☐ 0
		Black-Caribbean ☐ 1
		Black-African ☐ 2
		Black-Other ☐
		please describe
	If the person is descended from more than one ethnic or racial group, please tick the group to which the person considers he/she belongs, or tick the 'Any other ethnic group' box and describe the person's ancestry in the space provided.	Indian ☐ 3
		Pakistani ☐ 4
		Bangladeshi ☐ 5
		Chinese ☐ 6
		Any other ethnic group ☐
		please describe

Figure 6.1 *Question on ethnic group in the 1991 Census*

From Miscegenation to Hybridity

Table 6.1 Numbers identified as of mixed-parentage in the Census and LFS

	Census		LFS	
	N	%	N	%
Black-White	54,569	0.099	570	0.126
Asian-White	61,874	0.113	591	0.131
Other Mixed	112,061	0.204	1,192	0.264
Total	54,888,844	100	451,648	100

Sources: Census 1991, Great Britain; Labour Force Survey, 1989–1991.

The question that was finally used is shown in Figure 6.1.[2] The question is a mix of colour categories (*White* and *Black*) and geographical origins (e.g. *Indian*, *Chinese*, etc.), sometimes used in combination (e.g. *Black-Caribbean*). No simple classification could be entirely satisfactory, but this one does try to enumerate categories which reflect the important dimensions of discrimination in British society. The possibility of ticking more than one box, or of having an explicit category of *Mixed* were both rejected. In the USA a race or ethnic question has been included on the census for many years. That question does not include a mixed category, but there is currently debate about whether to include such an option in the next census (Root, 1996).

In the British Census people who ticked either of the *Black-Other* or *Any other ethnic group* boxes were asked to '*please describe*'. The answers given by those ticking *Black-Other* were assigned to eleven categories; those from the *Any other ethnic group* were assigned to a further seventeen categories. For all (but one) of the published Census tables, these categories were reassigned to larger groups. Of the people who ticked one of these *other* boxes, some described themselves as of mixed or multiple ethnic origins. Table 6.1 shows the numbers involved: those who ticked the *Black-Other* or the *Any other ethnic group* boxes, but who otherwise gave similar answers, have been combined. It can be seen that altogether 228,504 people – out of a total enumerated of almost 55 million – identified themselves (or were identified by others in their household – e.g. by their parents) as being of mixed origin. Before going on to look at these mixed-parentage groups in more detail, we look first at what data the Census has on mixed couples.

Mixed couples

There are no published tables on the ethnic groups of couples, but the Census Sample of Anonymized Records[3] does allow within-household analyses – including by ethnic group. For this chapter we have looked at the percentages with a *White* partner for each ethnic group. The results are shown in Table 6.2.

Table 6.2 Percentages of people in couples with a white partner

Ethnic Group	Male		Female	
	N	%	N	%
White	125,128	99.5	125,128	99.3
Black-Caribbean	222	26.3	102	14.3
Black-African	48	17.5	41	15.8
Black-Other	74	51.0	63	43.8
Indian	133	7.7	70	4.3
Pakistani	41	5.6	9	1.3
Bangladeshi	7	3.2	0	0.0
Chinese	34	13.2	77	24.9
Other Groups-Asian	54	15.1	143	32.2
Other Groups-Other	215	51.2	138	39.2
Total	125,956	96.3	125,771	96.2

Source: Census 1991, Sample of Anonymized Records.

(There were also 100 mixed couples where neither partner was *White*, but too few in any group for statistical analysis.) Over 99 per cent of *White* men and women living with a partner had a *White* partner. For the three *Black* groups, men were somewhat more likely to have a *White* partner than were women. More than a quarter of *Black-Caribbean* men living with a partner were living with a *White* partner; for *Black-Caribbean* women it was 14 per cent. For the *Black-Other* group, more than half the men and almost half the women – who were living with a partner – had a *White* partner. Clearly these mixed relationships are very common.

The percentages of relationships with *White* partners for the three South Asian groups were much lower. Of *Indian* men in couples, about 8 per cent had a *White* partner, 6 per cent of *Pakistani* men and 3 per cent of *Bangladeshi* men. The order was the same for women but the percentages were all lower. For the *Chinese* and *Other Groups-Asian* the percentages were higher, and higher for women than for men: a quarter of *Chinese* women in couples were with a *White* partner. The final category, *Other Groups-Other*,[4] had a large percentage with *White* partners: over half the men and nearly 40 per cent of the women who were in couples had a *White* partner.

Mixed parentage in the census

We have used data from the one published table that includes the full ethnic classification (OPCS/GRO(S) 1993: Table A) to look at those who were classified as mixed. There were 54,569 people identified as *Black-White*: this

From Miscegenation to Hybridity

amounted to less than one tenth of 1 per cent of the population, or 994 persons per million. There were three *Black* groups distinguished by the Census question: these are *Black-Caribbean, Black-African* and *Black-Other*. However, this mixed category of *Black-White* combines all forms of black parentage.

There were 61,874 people identified as *Asian-White*: this is just over one tenth of 1 per cent, or, more precisely, 1,127 persons per million. The main Census classification includes five *Asian* categories: *Indian, Pakistani, Bangladeshi, Chinese* and *Other Groups-Asian*. The mixed group, *Asian-White*, includes all of these in their parentage. Given the relatively low number of relationships with *White* partners among the three South Asian groups it is likely that the children in this group had parents who were either *Chinese* or from the so-called *Other Groups-Asian* group. There was also a group of 3,776 people identified as *Mixed White*, but for all tables these were reassigned to *White* and are ignored here. Finally there is a group of 112,061 labelled as *Other Mixed*, approximately 0.2 per cent of the population or 2,042 persons per million.

Out of a total population for Great Britain of nearly 55 million, these three mixed groups – *Black-White, Asian-White* and *Other Mixed* – combined amount to less than half of 1 per cent. This may seem very small, but it does amount to 8 per cent of the minority ethnic population – i.e. of all those not classified as *White* in the Census. These three groups are the people who ticked one of the *Black-Other* or *Any other ethnic group* boxes (or had it ticked for them) and who wrote in something that could be constructed as mixed-parentage. It cannot be known if the numbers would have been different if explicit *mixed* categories had been offered on the Census form, or if people had been allowed to tick more than one box. The wording of the question actually seems to encourage people of mixed-parentage to identify with one of the main categories: *If the person is descended from more than one ethnic or racial group, please tick the group to which the person considers he/she belongs, or tick the 'Any other ethnic group' box and describe the person's ancestry in the space provided.*

It may seem surprising that *Black-White* is the smallest of the three mixed groups, as this is the group that draws most attention. However, some of the other sub-categories of the *Black-Other* group may include people of mixed ethnic origin, in particular the *Black Other: British* (58,106) and the *Black Other: Other Mixed* (50,668) sub-categories might include people who would have described themselves as mixed *Black-White* had that been offered as a choice. Nevertheless, it is interesting that the comparatively large *Asian-White* group receive much less attention – as does the even larger *Other Mixed* group.

The single Census table that shows the full classification, including the *mixed* categories, gives a population count – down to district level – but no other information, e.g. age, gender, class, household type, etc. However, the Labour Force Survey, which has included a question on ethnic group since 1979, does give more detail on mixed-parentage.

Ann Phoenix and Charlie Owen

The Labour Force Survey

The Labour Force Survey (LFS) is a national sample survey of private households. It collects interviews from around 60,000 households in Great Britain, annually prior to 1992 and quarterly since. Since 1979 the survey has included a question on ethnic origin. Respondents are shown a card and asked to say to which ethnic group they consider they belong. Prior to 1992 the ethnic groups distinguished in the list were: *White, West Indian* or *Guyanese, Indian, Pakistani, Bangladeshi, Chinese, Arab, Mixed Origin* and *Other*. If the respondents replied they were of *Mixed* or *Other* ethnic orgin, the interviewer asked them to describe their ethnic origin in greater detail (Haskey, 1990). From 1992 onwards the LFS has used the same question as the 1991 Census. For this paper data for the three years 1989–1991 will be considered.[5] This gives data from the same period as the Census, but is prior to the change of question, and so includes the explicit choice of *mixed* in the question.

Prior to 1992 the responses to the ethnic question for the LFS had been assigned by OPCS to thirty-six codes: twelve of these include *mixed* in their descriptions (plus *White Mixed*). This classification has more detail than the Census but, even with a sample size of almost half a million (obtained by combining three years), numbers in some categories are very small, and too small to give reliable data. For now, these groups have been combined to give three mixed categories, very similar to those in the Census. The numbers in the three categories are also shown in Table 6.1. In each case the proportion was higher for the LFS than for the Census. This suggests that people are more likely to describe themselves as mixed if that is one of the categories offered. In the USA, where there are numerous occasions on which people have to record racial and ethnic information, the fastest growing category has beome 'other' and, according to the US Bureau of the Census, 'nearly a quarter million people "wrote in" a multiracial designator to the race question' (Root, 1996, p. xvii).

As with the Censuts results, the *Black-White* mixed group is the smallest of the three, slightly smaller than the *Asian-White* group and considerably smaller than the *Other Mixed* group. The *Asian-White* group was made up of four LFS categories: *Indian-White* (252), *Pakistani-White* (79), *Bangladeshi-White* (15) and *Other Asian-White* (245), so that those of mixed South Asian and White origins comprise just over half the *Asian-White* group.

Age structure

Figure 6.2 shows the age structure of the three mixed ethnic groups. Each line shows the percentage of the groups within each five-year age band. For the total population there are approximately equal numbers of people in each age band, but these mixed ethnic groups clearly have a very young age structure:

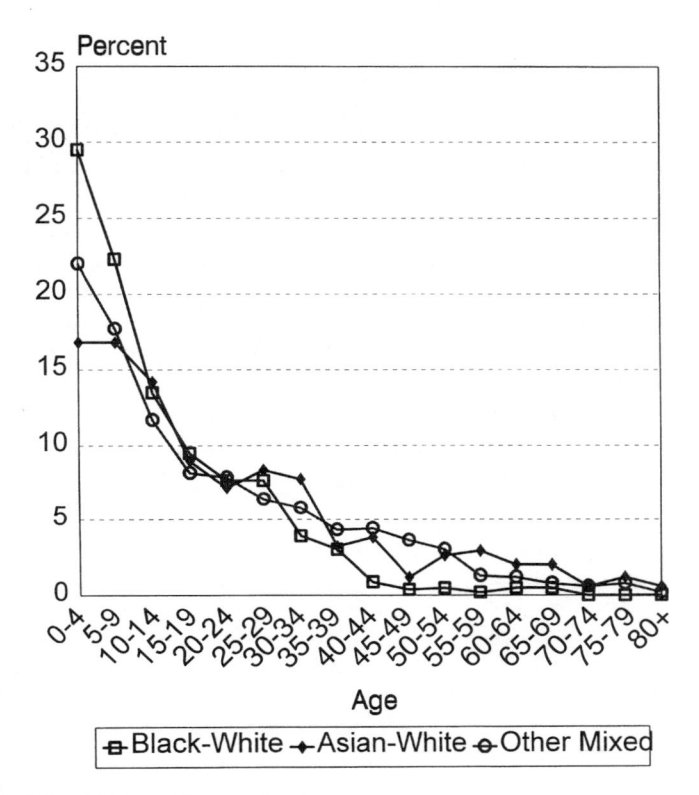

Figure 6.2 *Mixed Ethnic Groups By Age*
Source: Labour Force Survey, 1989–1991.

children younger than sixteen form 70 per cent of the *Black-White* group, 52 per cent of the *Asian-White* group and 56 per cent of the *Other Mixed* group, compared with 23 per cent in the total population. This indicates that the populations of mixed ethnicity are, on average, quite young, so that people of mixed-parentage will form an increasing percentage of the population as they grow older. For example, while these three groups together account for 0.5 per cent of the population overall, they amount to 1.4 per cent of the population of children under the age of sixteen, and 1.8 per cent of under fives.[6]

People of mixed ethnic background are much more likely to have been born in the UK than any other ethnic group except *White*. This partly reflects the young age structure, since only a minority of people who move to a different country are children. However, even among children the mixed-parentage groups are more likely to have been born in the UK than any of the other ethnic groups, except *White*.

Family structure

The rest of this discussion of demographic structure will deal just with the children, aged under sixteen. For all three groups the majority of children are living with two parents, although not necessarily the biological parents. The percentages are shown in Table 6.3, which also includes data on other ethnic groups for comparative purposes. For the *Black-White* group 53 per cent live with two adults acting as parents: this is a lot less than the percentage for *White* children (85 per cent) but a little higher than that for *Black* children (47 per cent). For the *Asian-White* group the percentage of children living with two parents is 82 per cent: this is slightly lower than the percentage for *White* children and 10 per cent below the percentage for *South Asian* children (93 per cent). For the *Other Mixed* group the percentage is 76 per cent: this is below the percentage for all groups except the *Black* group and the *Black-White* mixed group.

Table 6.3 Type of family unit for children aged under sixteen, by ethnic group

| | Couple | | Lone Parent | | | | |
| | | | Mother | | Father | | |
Ethnic Group	N	%	N	%	N	%	Total
White	73,369	84.5	12,305	14.2	1,152	1.3	86,826
Black	578	47.3	624	51.0	21	1.7	1,223
South Asian	4,014	92.7	293	6.8	24	0.6	4,331
Other	637	84.3	173	45.5	5	1.3	756
Black-White	202	53.2	173	45.5	5	1.3	380
Asian-White	250	83.1	51	16.9	0	0	301
Other Mixed	426	62.3	244	35.7	14	2.0	684
Not Stated	1,153	76.1	312	20.6	50	3.3	1,515
Total	80,629	84.0	14,118	14.7	1,269	1.3	96,016

Source: Labour Force Survey, 1989–1991.

For all three groups of mixed-parentage children, more were living with a white mother than with a white father (see Table 6.4). The most common family arrangement was to be living with a white mother in a couple. For the *Black-White* group, though, almost as many children lived with a lone white mother. This family type was uncommon for *Asian-White* children, more of whom lived with a white father than for the *Black-White* group. The *Other Mixed* group was least likely to be living with a white mother in a couple; they were between the *Black-White* and *Asian-White* groups in the percentages living with a lone white mother or with a white father.

Table 6.4 Percentage living with white parents

	White Father		White Mother				
			In Couple		Lone		
	N	%	N	%	N	%	Total
Black-White	62	16.3	133	35.0	110	28.9	380
Asian-White	100	33.2	112	37.2	33	11.0	301
Other Mixed	167	24.4	200	29.2	161	23.5	684

Source: Labour Force Survey, 1989–1991.

Not all the children were living with a white parent. Overall 25 per cent of the *Black-White* group were not living with a white parent, 20 per cent of the *Asian-White* group and 26 per cent of the *Other Mixed* group. Of those not living with a white parent, many were living with at least one parent (or parent figure) who described themselves as *Mixed*: this was true for 14 per cent of the *Black-White* group, 13 per cent of the *Asian-White* and 17 per cent of the *Other Mixed*.

Insider accounts from young people of mixed-parentage

The demographic data demonstrate that people of mixed-parentage constitute a small, but increasing, percentage of the British population. They are, however, a larger percentage of the minority ethnic population. This fact, together with the greater numbers of younger than older people of mixed-parentage, is important to the understanding of the context within which the identities of young people of mixed-parentage are forged and expressed. The more people who are seen to fit into a particular group (ethnic, racialized or otherwise), the more likely it is that at least some will identify as part of that group and resist outsider classification of themselves (Root, 1996).

The demographic data available make clear that there are fewer people of *Black-White* parentage than of *Asian-White* parentage. This is not surprising since there are twice as many people of Asian descent than of African (including African–Caribbean) descent in Britain (3.4 per cent and 1.6 per cent respectively). Historically, *Asian-White* and *Black-White* mixed relationships were both frowned on:

> It would surprise many people to see how extensively these dark classes are tincturing the colour of the rising race of children in the lowest haunts of this locality: and many of the fallen females have a visible infusion of Asiatic and African blood in their veins. They form

a peculiar class, but mingle freely with the others. It is an instance of depraved taste, that many of our fallen ones prefer devoting themselves entirely to the dark races of men, and some who are to them have infants by them. (*London City Mission Magazine*, August 1857, p. 217, quoted in Visram, 1986, p. 62)

In the US, there has been some interest in mixed-parentage arising from relationships between people from a range of ethnic groups. However, in both the USA and in Britain more attention has been given to those born of black-white relationships (with black referring to people of African origin). In Britain, this is the 'racial/ethnic' group most likely to enter, and to stay for longer periods in, local authority care. Children of mixed-parentage have also been central to considerations about 'transracial adoption'.

Transracial adoption: rehearsing the arguments

Over the last decade, there has been heated debate about the adoption and fostering of black children into white families. On the one hand, those in favour of transracial adoption argue that if there is an insufficient supply of black (and, more recently, mixed) adoptive couples, black and mixed-parentage children should be placed with white parents rather than being left for long periods in institutions or foster care. Loving care in a family is argued to be children's primary psychological need while racial identity is less important in developmental terms.

It is often suggested that, for healthy psychological functioning, children and young people from minority ethnic groups need to have secure ethnic identities in order to develop 'positive identities', characterized by high levels of self-esteem (Phinney and Rosenthal, 1992). This notion has been taken up by proponents of what has come to be known as 'same-race' adoption placements. Advocates of 'same race' placements argue that black children brought up in white households may develop well in many ways, but will suffer from 'identity confusion'; they will fail to develop a 'positive black identity' and be uncomfortable with black people. Furthermore, it is argued that white parents will be unable to pass on to black children the strategies they need in order to come to terms with and survive in a society where racism is common and where rejection by white people is likely. According to this argument, transracial adoption is damaging to black children's identity development (Tizard and Phoenix, 1994). Children of mixed-parentage are not differentiated from those who are black by most proponents of this argument.

Both sides of the debate on transracial adoption thus draw on arguments about children's psychosocial development and, to some extent, both find support for their polarized views from the handful of studies that have been done on transracial adoption (see Bagley *et al.*, 1993; McRoy and Hall, 1996). There is, however, little research evidence with which to resolve this controversy (Kirton, 1995) although, taken to the extreme, both sides of the debate have serious shortcomings. On the one hand, it is clear from the study of majority and minority ethnic children that 'race' and racism impinge on the lives of children who have not been adopted (Troyna and Hatcher, 1992; Holmes, 1995). There is, as yet, insufficient research evidence to indicate how continuous care from a loving white family affects, and is affected by, black and mixed-parentage children's experiences and racialized understandings. On the other hand, arguments that the adoption of black and mixed-parentage children by white parents will necessarily have a damaging effect on young people's 'positive black identity' rely on largely outdated theories of identity. There is no evidence, for example, that 'race' is privileged over gender or social class as social identities and it is now common for psychological approaches to view identities as plural rather than unitary and as dynamic rather than determined by particular characteristics. The challenge posed by new theories of identities is to explain how different identities intersect with each other.

The Social Identities Study

This section uses data from a study of the racialized identities of mixed (black-white)-parentage (58), black (101) and white (89) fourteen to eighteen-year-old young Londoners conducted by Barbara Tizard and Ann Phoenix. There were 152 young women and 96 young men in the sample. The sample was more middle class than would have been expected by chance. If social class is assessed using fathers' occupational groupings, 50 per cent of the whole sample and 63 per cent of the mixed-parentage sample came from the middle classes. Using mothers' occupational groupings, the percentage rises to 66 per cent for the whole sample and 70 per cent for those of mixed-parentage. Half the interviews lasted between an hour, and an hour and a half. A quarter were longer and a quarter slightly shorter. See Tizard and Phoenix (1993) for fuller details of the sample and the study and Phoenix and Tizard (1996) for specific discussion of social class.

This study (referred to here as the 'Social Identities' study) aimed to get a good understanding of the identities of non-adopted, non-clinical samples of young people in order to contribute to debates about transracial adoption and racialized identities. In order to avoid prejudging the issue of whether racial identities are necessarily different from other social identities or from more personal identities, the study also focused on gender, social class and personal identities in addition to 'race'. However, given that transracial adoption was the starting point of the study, more attention was paid to issues of 'race'.

In attempting to understand the racialized identities of young people of mixed-parentage, it is important to document the range of ways in which young people of mixed-parentage think about themselves. This section of the chapter uses data from the study to demonstrate that many of the young people had the contradictory experiences of being treated on the one hand as if they are necessarily 'black' and, on the other, as if they are 'neither black nor white'. It argues that many of the young people had complex understandings of their racialized identities in which they used the terms of colour flexibly and shifted identifications over time and from context to context. This could mean that young people resisted using those terms the adults around them told them they should use in describing themselves. As with all other identities, the diversity of mixed-parentage identities makes it untenable always to subsume those with one black and one white parent into the category 'black' (as would be suggested by the 'one drop principle', described above) or to assume that they constitute a unitary group.

Experiencing the legacy of 'one-drop' thinking

In childhood, some of the sample of young people of mixed-parentage reported that they came to recognize that other people found it difficult to accept that they had a white parent. 'People used to say I was adopted because my mother was white, and stuff... It was really horrible.' This reluctance to accept that they could have been born to their mothers is not because young children know or subscribe to the 'one-drop' thesis. In her study of how young children perceive race, Holmes (1995) found that USA kindergarten children consider that children have to be the same colour as their parents unless children are adopted. Since, in Britain, children of mixed-parentage are more likely to have white mothers than black mothers, this may explain why some children of mixed-parentage were subjected to claims that they were adopted. Whatever the reason, however, it is one way in which young children of mixed-parentage learn that they are more likely to be thought of as black than as white.

Young people of mixed-parentage were sometimes surprised to find themselves subject to constructions of them as necessarily and only black. The following account, from a girl of mixed-parentage, who goes to an almost exclusively white private school, makes painfully clear that 'one-drop' thinking has left an identifiable legacy. In her case, a close friend demonstrated an inability to conceive of people with one black and one white parent as having anything in common with white people of the same sex:

Q. Have you ever discussed racism with your friends?
A. Um, I must admit actually it's not a subject that I often talk about with my friends. It doesn't really concern them. Or it does. I mean they're all sort of – you know, you know debate. You know they'll be sort of all for you know – racism is the most disgusting thing in their eyes, but – I remember arguing about, um, I was absolutely furious with my best friend who isn't any more really my best friend. But she said, um, I said 'Who in school do you think I most look like? Which teacher would you say?' And she said, um

'Mr–.' He's the only black teacher in the school. And I said 'Mr–?' And she said 'Well, yeah, because you're black.' And . . . I said, 'I know, but I – that doesn't necessarily mean I look like him.' And we had this really quite nasty argument about it. Well, not really actually. It wasn't very long. It lasted about twenty or thirty seconds. She obviously thought I was grossly over-reacting, but I was extremely hurt because it just shows, it just shows underlying values that people have really about that and I . . . thought about it. It really hurt me, and I thought about it for a long time and I thought – well, I mean I'm half white, you know, so it means that I should look just as much like someone white in the school than black, but no one else would see that. And maybe that's what people do think, you know.

The above example illustrates the intersection of 'race' with social class and school. The young woman's attendance at an expensive public school meant that she hardly saw anybody not from the white majority. Hence, her friend rarely had to think about issues of 'race' and ethnicity. At the same time, the respondent had nobody with whom she could feel that such issues could be discussed from an 'insider' perspective.

It is important to recognize that there are different reasons for the persistence of the 'one-drop' notion. Those black people and social workers who produce arguments such as that described above are unlikely to consider that recognition of mixed-parentage will dilute the purity of whiteness. Instead they are likely to be taking a pragmatic view based on recognition that people of mixed-parentage are highly likely to be on the receiving end of racialized discrimination. Most of the young people of mixed-parentage in the Social Identities study reported that they had experienced racialized discrimination. However, the argument that mixed-parentage people have to accept themselves as black and will, necessarily, be treated as black, ignores the fact that many children and young people of mixed-parentage experience discrimination specific to their mixed-parentage. Thus, many of the mixed-parentage young people in the Social Identities study were called names like 'peanut', 'yellow-belly,' 'half-breed' and 'redskin' that were not used for black children (as well as racialized names to which black children reported that they were subjected). In addition, 20 per cent of them said they were called racist names by black as well as white people. This made a tiny minority of the mixed-parentage young people conscious of themselves, whether they were with white or black people.

Both/and or either/or? Plural identities in practice

It is increasingly common for literature on mixed-parentage to argue that people of mixed-parentage must be allowed to assert their racialized identities in whichever ways they feel are most appropriate. In the USA, there is increasingly an assertion of mixed-parentage identities in the academic work of those who are themselves of mixed-parentage (see, for example, the collection edited by Root, 1996). Root (1996) describes four of the ways in which it is possible to experience, negotiate and reconstruct the 'borders' between 'races': having *both* feet in *both* camps (as opposed to being 'between cultures'); practising 'situational ethnicity and situational race', i.e. changing identifications as the context shifts; 'border identity' and locating in one 'camp' for an extended period of time. Collins (1990) argues for conceptualizing identities as 'both/and'. Similarly, Parker (1995) styles this 'partial identification' and 'subjectivity of conditional belonging'. The emphasis in postmodern approaches on fluid, shifting and multiple identities is also potentially helpful in the conceptualization of mixed-parentage identities.

How, then, did the young people interviewed in the Social Identities study think of their identities as young people of mixed-parentage? Three related points are worth noting in relation to answering the question of whether or not they engaged in notions of 'one-drop' thinking or thought of their racialized identities in more flexible, postmodern ways in which they were able to draw on a variety of constructions of identities:

1 'If you've got one black parent, you must be black'

Many of the young people recognized that they were expected by many to think of themselves as black. For a variety of specific reasons, some responded to this by identifying themselves as black while others rejected it.

2 (Non-)dualist pluralism

It was not uncommon for the young people to explain how they described themselves in different ways at different times and in different contexts. In this they appeared to have a range of ways in which they could individually express their racialized identities that could be said to be congruent with notions of postmodern plurality and flexibility. In expressing these identities, some seemed to accept, and others to reject, the dualism inherent in the treatment of 'black' and 'white' as oppositional categories. Gender and social class both differentiated the discourses of racialized identities used by the young people and the strategies available to them for dealing with 'race' and racism in different contexts (see Tizard and Phoenix, 1993; Phoenix and Tizard, 1996).

Those young people who rejected black-white dualism tended to do so by asserting that they were mixed-parentage and did not think of themselves in any other way. However, the experience of being 'different' whether with white or black people made some of the young people feel that they would like to be visibly either black or white. Since much literature on racial identity suggests that some young black children wish to be white, we asked the young people if they had ever wished to be another colour. Twenty eight per cent of black young people, 14 per cent of white young people and 51 per cent of mixed-parentage young people said that they had, at some time, wished to be a different colour. The high percentage of young people of mixed-parentage saying this generally said that they would have preferred to be either 'black' or 'white' rather than 'mixed' or 'half and half'. Mixed-parentage and black young people who had wanted to change their colour had generally wanted to do so earlier in life in order to avoid racial discrimination or name-calling; in order not to 'be different' or to have the same hair as their white peers. Those young white people who wanted to do so, tended to want to change colour later in life for reasons of style, youth culture or to look as if they were of mixed-parentage (a look many found particularly attractive).

3 Resisting outsider definitions and advice

The young people found numerous ways in which to resist naming or identifying themselves in the ways suggested to them by parents or other people. The issue of whether black parents make their children (black or mixed-parentage) proud to be black is one that is often assumed in debates on transracial adoption. In this study, black young people were much more likely than the other groups to report that they had been told by their parents to be proud to be black (66 per cent black; 40 per cent mixed-parentage and 6 per cent white young people). In interpreting this, however, it is important to recognize that the young people's identities and ways of describing themselves were not simply the result of being told how to define themselves by their parents and others. It was quite clear that young people resisted advice they did not want, either by simply not listening or by continuing to use the terms they chose. Such resistances indicated that 'professional', liberal discourses (from social workers, teachers, etc.) were part of the context in which young people asserted their own racialized discourses, sometimes in opposition.

Conclusions

Black-white unions and mixed-parentage have both been socially constructed as problematic. The historical shift from concern with 'miscegenation' to concern about children of mixed-parentage has not been unambiguously progressive. However, contestation about the terms in which to describe mixed relationships and mixed-parentage helps to illuminate the different ways in which these categories have been constructed and resistance to dominant constructions from 'insiders'. The area of mixed relationships and mixed-parentage is one where demography and social definitions can clearly be seen to intersect. The increasing number of mixed, black-white unions and people of mixed-parentage, particularly young people, has been partly responsible for the emergence of insider-defined 'mixed' categories. These challenge the treatment of black and white racialized categories as binary opposites and the 'one-drop' thesis that anybody with black ancestry is necessarily black.

Most of the young people interviewed in the Social Identities study identified as 'mixed' rather than 'black' or 'white'. Their accounts indicated that they had a range of ways in which they negotiated their racialized identities in different contexts and at different times. They indicated that the ways in which they constructed their identities had changed over time. It is likely, therefore, that the accounts they negotiated in their interviews will change over time. However, most of the young people were clear that they made their own decisions about whether to accept or reject the constructions their parents, teachers and friends attempted to persuade them to use.

Notes

1 Data kindly made available by National Opinion Polls.
2 The question was not included in the Census form for Northern Ireland, so all figures in this section refer to Great Britain.
3 There are two Census SARs: a 2 per cent household sample and a 1 per cent individual sample, each chosen at random from the total population. The samples contain data on individuals in the population, but without identifying those individuals. They were introduced in the UK for the first time in 1991. The SARs make it possible to relate data on different people in the same household, such as couples or parents and children. In this chapter the 2 per cent household SAR has been used. For more detail see Marsh, 1993. The data are Crown Copyright and have been made available through the Census Microdata Unit of the University of Manchester with the support of the ESRC/JISC/DENI.
4 This category includes all those who could not be assigned to one of the other nine Census ethnic group categories, including people who described themselves as North African or Arab. Most people of mixed-parentage are included in this group. See OPCS/GRO(S), 1993.
5 Data for the LFS have been deposited at the ESRC Data Archive of the University of Essex by the Department of Employment, and are used here with permission. The data are Crown Copyright.
6 It might be that children are more likely to be described as of mixed ethnic origin by their parents than they are to so describe themselves when they are adult. This would account for the higher percentages for children. However, this possibility is contradicted by the steady decline in the percentage with age, suggesting a real change rather than a change in reporting. It is possible that people become increasingly less likely to describe themselves as of mixed ethnic origin as they get older, but this seems less likely.

Acknowledgements

We should like to acknowledge the support of the Department of Health, who funded the *Social Identities in Adolescence* project described in this chapter; and of the ESRC, who funded the project *The Changing Social and Economic Circumstances of Families with Children* under their 'Understanding Social and Political Change' Initiative (Award L-303-35-3003), which included the demographic analyses in this chapter. We should also like to thank the schools and the young people themselves who took part in the research. Most of all, we should like to thank Barbara Tizard, who not only inspired the work reported in this chapter, but has provided intellectual leadership and support to both of us over many years.

References

ALIBHAI-BROWN, Y. and MONTAGUE, A. (1992) *The Colour of Love: Mixed Race Relationships*, London, Virago.
BAGLEY, C., YOUNG, L. with SCULLY, A. (1993) *International and Transracial Adoptions*, Aldershot, Avebury.
BARBARA, A. (1989) *Marriage Across Frontiers*, Clevedon, Multilingual Matters.
BEBBINGTON, A. and MILES, J. (1989) 'The background of children who enter local authority care', *British Journal of Social Work*, **19**, pp. 349–68.
BRAH, A. (1992) 'Difference, diversity and differentiation', in DONALD, J. and RATTANSI, A. (Eds) *'Race', Culture and Difference*, London, Sage, pp. 126–45.
BRAH, A. (1996) *Cartographies of Diaspora*, London, Routledge.
COLLINS, P. H. (1990) *Black Feminist Thought*, Cambridge, MA, Unwin Hyman.
EARLY YEARS TRAINERS ANTI-RACIST NETWORK (1995) *The Best of Both Worlds . . . Celebrating Mixed Parentage*, London, EYTARN.
FOUCAULT, M. (1980) *Power/Knowledge*, Brighton, Harvester Press.
FRYER, P. (1984) *Staying Power: The History of Black People in Britain*, London, Pluto Press.
HALL, S. (1989) 'New ethnicities', in MORLEY, D. and CHEN, K.-H. (Eds), 1996, *Stuart Hall: Critical Dialogues in Cultural Studies*, London, Routledge, pp. 441–9.
HASKEY, J. (1990) 'The ethnic minority populations of Great Britain: estimates by ethnic group and country of birth', *Population Trends*, **60**, pp. 35–8.
HENRIQUES, F. (1974) *Children of Caliban: Miscegenation*, London, Secker & Warburg.
HOLMES, R. (1995) *How Young Children Perceive Race*, London, Sage.
KIRTON, D. (1995) *'Race', Identity and the Politics of Adoption*, London, University of East London.

MARSH, C. (1993) 'The Sample of Anonymised Records', in DALE, A. and MARSH, C. (Eds) *The 1991 Census User's Guide*, London, HMSO, pp. 295–311.

MCROY, R. and HALL, C. I. (1996) 'Transracial adoptions: in whose best interest?', in ROOT, M. (Ed.) *The Multiracial Experience: Racial Borders as the New Frontier*, Thousand Oaks, CA, Sage, pp. 63–78.

NORMENT, L. (1995) 'Am I black, white or in between? Is there a plot to create a "colored" buffer race in America?' *Ebony*, August, pp. 108–12.

OPCS/GRO(S) (1993) *1991 Census: Ethnic Group and Country of Birth, Great Britain*, London, HMSO.

OPITZ, M., OGUNTOYE, K. and SCHULTZ, D. (Eds) (1992) *Showing our Colours: Afro-German Women Speak Out*, London, Open Letters.

OWEN, C. (1993) 'Using the Labour Force Survey to estimate Britain's ethnic minority populations', *Population Trends*, **72**, pp. 18–23.

OWEN, C. (in prep.) 'British attitudes to mixed marriages'.

PARK, R. E. (1931) 'Mentality of racial hybrids', *American Journal of Sociology*, **36**, pp. 534–51.

PARKER, D. (1995) *Through Different Eyes*, Aldershot, Avebury.

PHINNEY, J. and ROSENTHAL, D. (1992) 'Ethnic identity in adolescence: process, context and outcome', in ADAMS, G., GULLOTTA, T. and MONTEMAYOR, R. (Eds) *Adolescent Identity Formation*, London, Sage.

PHOENIX, A. and TIZARD, B. (1996) 'Thinking through class: the place of social class in the lives of young Londoners', *Feminism and Psychology*, **6**.

REUTER, E. B. (1931) *Race Mixture: Studies in Intermarriage and Miscegenation*, New York, Whittlesey House.

RICHMOND, A. H. (1961) *The Colour Problem*, Harmondsworth, Penguin Books.

ROOT, M. P. P. (1996) 'A Bill of Rights for racially mixed people', in ROOT, M. P. P. (Ed.) *The Multiracial Experience: Racial Borders as the New Frontier*, Thousand Oaks, CA, Sage, pp. 3–14.

SILLITOE, K. and WHITE, P. H. (1992) 'Ethnic Group and the British Census', *Journal of the Royal Statistical Society A*, **155**, 1, pp. 141–63.

SMALL, J. (1986) 'Transracial placements: conflicts and contradictions', in AHMED, S., CHEETHAM, J. and SMALL, J. (Eds) *Social Work with Black Children and their Families*, London, Batsford, pp. 81–99.

SPICKARD, P. R. (1989) *Mixed Blood: Intermarriage and Ethnic Identity in Twentieth-century America*, Madison, University of Wisconsin Press.

SPICKARD, P. R. (1992) 'The illogic of American racial categories', in ROOT, M. P. P. (Ed.) *Racially Mixed People in America*, Newbury Park, CA, Sage, pp. 12–23.

STONEQUIST, E. V. (1937) *The Marginal Man: A study in Personality and Culture Conflict*, New York, Russell & Russell.

TIZARD, B. and PHOENIX, A. (1993) *Black, White or Mixed Race?* London, Routledge.

TIZARD, B. and PHOENIX, A. (1994) 'Black identity and transracial adoption', in GABER, I. and ALDRIDGE, J. (Eds) *In the Best Interests of the Child*, London, Free Association Books.

TROYNA, B. and HATCHER, R. (1992) *Racism in Children's Lives: A Study of Mainly-white Primary Schools*, London, Routledge.

VISRAM, R. (1986) *Ayahs, Lascars and Princes: Indians in Britain 1700–1947*, London, Pluto Press.

WILSON, A. (1987) *Mixed Race Children: A Study of Identity*, London, Allen & Unwin.

YOUNG, R. J. C. (1995) *Colonial Desire: Hybridity in Theory, Culture and Race*, London, Routledge.

ZACK, N. (1993) *Race and Mixed Race*, Philadelphia, Temple University Press.

Chapter 7

Young Children at School: Inequalities and the National Curriculum

Ian Plewis

Introduction

In this chapter I present some findings on educational inequality, an issue which has been rather neglected in the widespread debate about educational questions during the last decade. I do so from the perspective of a recently completed research project, the main aim of which was to examine changes between the mid-1980s and the mid-1990s in young children's experiences at school. I focus on the relative attainments of African–Caribbean boys and girls in maths, but the methods I use can be generalized to a variety of educational inequalities. The evidence I present suggests that there is cause for concern about, and certainly the need for further investigation into, the impact on inequality of the major changes introduced by the Education Reform Act 1988.

Previous research

Of the many projects Barbara Tizard directed during her career at the Thomas Coram Research Unit (TCRU), the Infant School Project was the largest. It was funded by the Economic and Social Research Council at a time when TCRU was a Designated Research Centre. A cohort of pupils was followed from the time they entered thirty-three multi-ethnic inner London infant schools in 1982 until the end of their three years of infant schooling. The research was written up in *Young Children at School in the Inner City* (Tizard *et al.*, 1988). The project was multifaceted in that it collected data from teachers and parents as well from the pupils themselves, and a variety of methods was used, including interviews, standardized tests and systematic observation. In many ways, the project represented much of what was typical in Barbara Tizard's work; it was located within a tradition of quantitative non-experimental research, the sample was not especially large but it was studied rather intensively, and the study was informed by psychology but not dominated by it. The genesis of the research lay in Barbara Tizard's theoretical interest in the relation between what goes on at home and how well young children get on academically at school, and in her social concern at the apparent gap in the attainment of African–Caribbean (defined later) and white pupils. From the outset, the research team was aware that the ethnic gap might in fact be different for boys and girls and so it turned out. African–Caribbean pupils as a group did *not* have lower attainments than their white peers in these inner London schools, but, at that time, African–Caribbean boys were doing much less well than African–Caribbean girls and also less well than the two white groups. Disappointingly, the research was able to provide only some clues, and not a definitive view, as to why a gender gap of this kind should develop.

The bulk of the research focused on the pupils' experiences and progress during their infant years. However, the cohort was followed up again at the end of their primary schooling (year six) and these results were reported in Plewis (1991). The gender gap in the attainment of African–Caribbean pupils found by the end of infant school (year two) neither widened nor narrowed during junior school for this cohort. However, for the comparable but larger cohort studied in the Inner London Education Authority (ILEA) Junior School Project (Mortimore *et al.*, 1988), there was evidence of a widening gap between African–Caribbean boys and the other three groups. At the end of year six in 1988, the maths attainment of African–Caribbean boys in the TCRU Infant School Project cohort was about one-quarter of a standard deviation unit behind African–Caribbean girls, with essentially no difference between white boys and girls. The relative gender gap was larger for the ILEA Junior School Project cohort at the end of year five in 1983: about half a standard deviation unit. What happens to the attainment gap during secondary school is less clear. The Junior School Project cohort has been followed up, and an analysis of exam results at the end of year eleven suggests that the overall gap between African–Caribbean and white pupils narrowed during secondary school (Sammons, 1995). Unfortunately, in common with a number of studies in this field, there was no published analysis of the effect of the *interaction* between ethnic group and gender on attainment at sixteen years.

The Education Reform Act 1988

The research just described was, however, geographically and temporally restricted: it related to young children being brought up, and going to school, in inner London in the 1980s. By the 1990s, there had been many changes in the way primary education was organized in England and Wales. The Education Reform Act was passed in 1988 and, in 1990, the Inner London Education Authority (ILEA) was abolished. A new education vocabulary was launched; phrases such as National Curriculum, Standard Assessment Tasks (universally referred to as the SATS) and Key Stage, which were non-existent at the time of the Infant School Project, could be heard at the school gates as well in the staff common room. But these changes in vocabulary reflected a more profound change in the way in which the Thatcher government of the time regarded state education. No longer would teachers have the same freedom to determine what they taught, how they assessed their pupils' achievements, and how much they told parents about these achievements. Instead, the state was to have a much greater say in what was to be taught in each subject at particular ages, and how pupils' attainments were to be assessed. Allied to prescribed arrangements for reporting, both to parents in the form of school reports and to the world at large in the form of so-called league tables of schools' results, it was hoped that these major upheavals would lead to an improvement in standards, and would thus enhance the country's economic competitiveness in the world.

All the rhetoric surrounding the Education Reform Act (and a good deal of educational debate before then) was about raising educational standards, and not about reducing educational inequalities. The architects of the reforms expected the introduction of a National Curriculum, regular assessment of pupils, and ranking schools by results, to produce higher standards across the board, and to bring British standards closer to what were believed to be higher educational levels in other developed countries. However, questions about trends in educational attainment over time are fraught with methodological difficulties. International comparisons are just as problematic. It is not easy to establish whether standards are improving when those standards are themselves changing in content over time. Nor is it easy to compare educational performance across countries when there are so many differences in the way educational systems are organized, and in the way attainments are assessed. In other words, it is difficult to talk about absolute differences and about absolute change. Yet there can be little doubt that there are, and have always been, substantial differences in the average educational attainments of different groups *within* the British educational system. Pupils from working-class backgrounds do less well than pupils from middle- and upper-class backgrounds; pupils from most minority ethnic groups do less well than white pupils; and, increasingly, boys are doing less well than girls, although the picture of gender differences is not entirely clear, appearing to vary both by subject and by age. We are able to discuss relative differences, and relative change, even though the measurement of absolute change is methodologically more problematic.

Despite these well-documented inequalities (see, for example, Tizard *et al.*, 1988, Chapter 1), the Education Reform Act was silent not only about how they might be reduced, but indeed whether it was desirable to try to reduce them. It is possible for the reforms to be successful in their own terms, by raising standards generally, while at the same time increasing inequalities. This is illustrated in Figure 7.1 for two hypothetical groups measured on two occasions; the average member of each group scores higher at the second occasion but the average gap between the groups has widened. A more detailed analysis of this situation would need to take account not only of changing averages but also of changing variabilities over time. It is, for example, possible for the average gap between the two groups to widen over time but for the overlap between the groups to increase. Some educational interven-

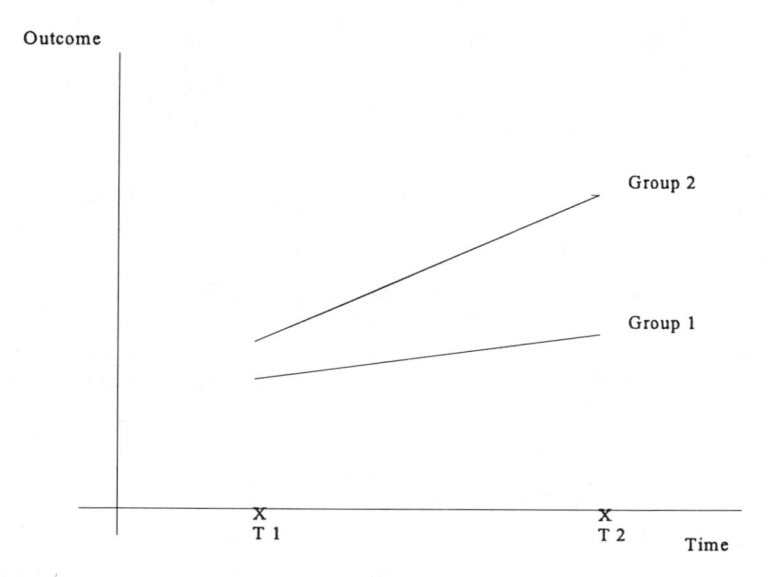

Figure 7.1 *Relative and absolute change over time*

tions may well serve to raise standards for everyone at the cost of greater inequality, while others may serve to reduce inequality, perhaps, although not necessarily, at the cost of not raising average standards. The choice between which of the two strategies to adopt is a political one.

It was against these twin backdrops – the research in the 1980s and the Education Reform Act 1988 – that a new research project started in 1992. Known affectionately as CECIL, and more long-windedly as 'Changes in the Classroom Experiences of Children in Inner London', it was essentially concerned with whether, and how, the legislative changes might have affected young pupils' school lives. This chapter presents evidence from this research on one aspect of inequality; differences in some of the school experiences of African–Caribbean and white boys and girls, and how these differences might relate to group differences in attainment.

The CECIL research

In CECIL, we studied around 500 year one pupils aged six, who were at twenty-two of the thirty-three ILEA schools in the original Infant School Project sample. These pupils were followed into their year two classrooms, and hence to the end of Key Stage One. About one-third of the sample were white and about one-quarter were African–Caribbean. By African–Caribbean I mean British children of African origin with at least one parent or grandparent born in the Caribbean; by white I mean children of two white parents born in the UK. The sample was fairly homogeneous in socioeconomic terms in the sense that all the schools in the sample were serving rather poor inner city areas.

We set out to answer two main questions, both of which were addressed to all the pupils in the sample, regardless of their ethnic background. The first question was whether there had been a change in the amount of *time* spent by pupils in year two in different activities at school since the introduction of the National Curriculum. To this end, we systematically observed a sub-sample of 173 year two pupils in their classrooms throughout the school day. We found that there are differences in time use although the changes are not dramatic. They can be summarized by saying that year two pupils in the mid-1990s are experiencing a more academic day than they were a decade earlier. For example, they do more science but much less art and craft. Our detailed findings related to this question can be found in Plewis and Veltman (1996a).

The second main question was whether there had been a change in *curriculum coverage* in maths for pupils in years one and two. These data were obtained by asking teachers to complete a checklist about each of the pupils in their class. This checklist consisted of separate maths items, put into groups such as addition, money, capacity, etc. which the teachers ticked if they had covered that item during the year with that pupil. The data were collected towards the end of years one and two but spanned the whole year. Our results suggested a change over the decade towards greater uniformity in coverage of the maths curriculum across classrooms in year two although not in year one. In other words, in year two, the differences between teachers in the extent of that coverage, although still marked, are nevertheless smaller than they were a decade earlier. However, we did not find any change over the decade in the variability of maths coverage between pupils within classrooms for either year one or year two. This part of the research is reported in detail in Plewis and Veltman (1996b).

The previous research has told us that there is a gender gap in the attainment of African–Caribbean pupils but not whether this gender gap is increasing. Our evidence on change comes from year two pupils, in 1985 and 1993. During 1985, for the TCRU cohort, relative to the white group, African–Caribbean boys fell behind African–Caribbean girls during year two by one-sixth of a standard deviation unit. During 1993, for the CECIL cohort, this relative decline had grown to one-third of a standard deviation unit. So we have some reason to suppose, at least from the boys' point of view, not only that there is a problem, but also that it appears to be getting worse. We can also call on evidence from a pilot study for the SATs at Key Stage One (NFER, 1991) which shows that 75 per cent of African–Caribbean boys are below the target level – level two – for number, compared with 57 per cent of African–Caribbean girls and only about 40 per cent of the white pupils. We now need to consider whether other aspects of the CECIL data can shed light on why inequality in the shape of this gender gap might be widening.

Inequalities and the National Curriculum

Time use, curriculum coverage and attainment

Two of the possible explanations as to why African–Caribbean boys are falling behind in maths are, first, that they spend less time doing maths in the classroom and, second, that they cover less of the maths curriculum. We would expect progress to be positively associated both with the amount of time spent on a subject, and with the amount covered of that subject's curriculum.

Let us first look at our results on time use. We did find that African–Caribbean pupils as a group spent less time doing maths in the classroom than white pupils. The proportions of classroom time were 15 per cent for African–Caribbean pupils compared with 19 per cent for white pupils, and this difference was consistent across the schools in the sample. (The numbers of white and African–Caribbean pupils in each school were about the same for the observation sub-sample.) However, we did not have enough data reliably to look at boys and girls separately within the two ethnic groups. Moreover, we had found a difference of a similar magnitude between the two groups in time use in 1985. As Plewis and Veltman (1996a) explain, the ethnic group difference in time given to maths is a cause for concern, but it does not appear to be able to account for the *widening* gender gap in attainment.

Our data on curriculum coverage are, however, more enlightening. Plewis and Veltman (1996b) show that the association between pupils' attainments at the end of year one and the amount of the maths curriculum covered by these pupils in year two was stronger in 1993 than it was in 1985. In other words, teachers appear to have become more strongly influenced by what their pupils can do in maths at the beginning of the year when deciding how much of the maths curriculum to cover with each of them. Also, there was less variability, or more uniformity, between teachers in this association, meaning that teachers had become somewhat more consistent in matching coverage to attainment. These findings generate the hypothesis that the widening gender gap in African–Caribbean pupils' attainment might be explained by changes in the way the maths curriculum is now covered. This leads us on to a model for explaining increasing inequality.

An explanatory model

If we are to establish a connection between changes in the way pupils cover the maths curriculum and a widening gap in attainment, then each of the following propositions should, ideally, hold. First, we would expect to find a link between ethnic group and gender on the one hand, and the level of curriculum coverage on the other. Moreover, this link should be stronger now than it was in 1985. Thus, we would expect African–Caribbean boys now to be covering less of the maths curriculum than the other three groups. (This is equivalent to saying that we expect to find a statistical interaction between ethnic group and gender, and curriculum coverage.) Also, we would expect African–Caribbean boys to be covering *relatively* less of the maths curriculum now than they were in 1985. It is important to remember that we are concerned with relative differences here. We do have evidence to suggest that, overall, pupils are covering more of the maths curriculum now than they were in 1985, although the amount of classroom time doing maths has not changed.

The second proposition is that African–Caribbean boys are behind in maths at the end of year one. This would then account, at least in part, for the fact that they cover relatively less of the curriculum in year two, because we know that curriculum coverage during year two is now more strongly associated with attainment at the end of year one.

Third, curriculum coverage should be associated with progress in maths during year two. Also, this association should be stronger now than it was in 1985. We would expect pupils who cover more of the curriculum to make greater progress. If inequality is increasing, we would also expect curriculum coverage now to be a more important predictor of progress.

Finally, ethnic group gender differences in progress should be smaller *after* allowing for the effect of curriculum coverage on progress. In other words, we hypothesize that some of the group differences in maths progress can be explained by group differences in maths coverage.

These four propositions are shown diagramatically in Figure 7.2. The arrowed lines indicate postulated causal influences, the curves indicate associations, with the double curve indicating a stronger association than a single curve. Our second and third propositions imply that the association between ethnic group and gender, and attainment at the end of year two, should be higher than the corresponding association at the end of year one. We now look at the evidence for each of these propositions in turn.

Is there support for the first proposition: do African–Caribbean boys cover less of the maths curriculum than the other three groups? Yes, they do.

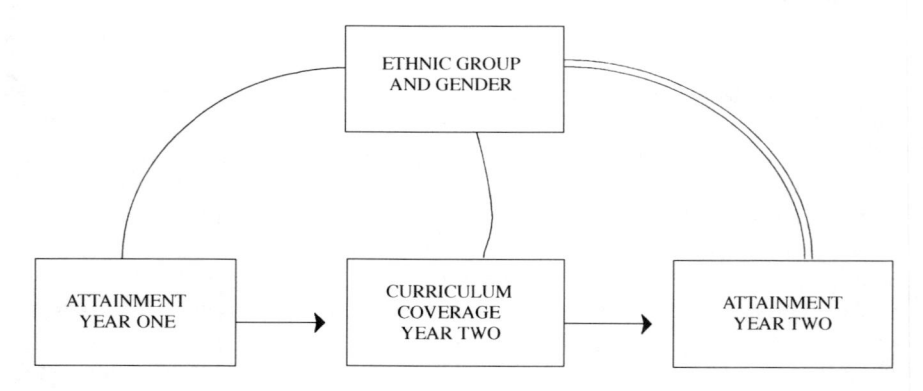

Figure 7.2 *Causal links over time*

They cover a little less than African–Caribbean girls whereas white boys cover a quarter of a standard deviation *more* than white girls. Thus, the relative gender gap in curriculum coverage is about one-third of a standard deviation. However, the interaction is not statistically significant although there is an overall effect of ethnic group of about half a standard deviation.

However, the ethnic group effect operates in a rather complicated way. Rather than explaining much of the variation in curriculum coverage *within* classrooms, it accounts for some of the variability in coverage *between* classrooms. The greater the proportion of African–Caribbean pupils in a classroom, the lower the level of curriculum coverage in that classroom, or by that teacher. A 10 per cent rise in the proportion of African–Caribbean pupils in a classroom predicts 0.14 standard deviation units less curriculum coverage on average. In other words, African–Caribbean pupils as a group cover less of the maths curriculum in year two because many of them attend those schools where less of the curriculum is covered. On the other hand, in any one classroom containing both African–Caribbean and white pupils, there is no systematic ethnic difference in the amount of the curriculum covered.

In 1985, the relative gender gap in curriculum coverage was 0.40 standard deviation units, which was a little greater in magnitude than that found in 1993, and which was also statistically significant. However, in 1985, the effect appeared to operate within schools rather than between schools. Thus, our first proposition is only partially supported by the data. African–Caribbean boys do have lower levels of curriculum coverage than the other groups, although no more so than in 1985. Also, there appears to have been a change in the way in which ethnic group is associated with curriculum coverage. In 1985, the effect applied mostly within classrooms whereas in 1993 it applied more between classrooms.

Are African–Caribbean boys behind the other three groups in maths at the end of year one? Our evidence does tend to support this second proposition. White boys score higher than white girls on the maths test at the end of year one whereas African–Caribbean boys are a little behind African–Caribbean girls; the relative gender gap is about a quarter of a standard deviation unit. Again, however, the statistical interaction between ethnic group and gender on maths is not statistically significant and so the differences could be due to chance.

We now move on to the third proposition: is curriculum coverage related to progress in maths? We find that it is. We base this on a regression model for educational progress widely used in educational research, with maths attainment at the end of year two as the response, and attainment at the end of year one and curriculum coverage as the explanatory variables. The effect size for curriculum coverage is 0.34. This means that for every standard deviation unit increase in curriculum coverage, pupils make one-third of a standard deviation unit more maths progress on average. However, the effect of curriculum coverage operates more to reduce between classroom differences in progress rather than to reduce within classroom differences. In 1985, the effect size was only one-sixth of a standard deviation unit, or half the size of the effect in 1993. So our third proposition is supported by the data. And, combining the second and third propositions, we do find, as we noted earlier, a more substantial gender gap in African–Caribbean maths attainment in 1993 than in 1985: up from a quarter to half a standard deviation unit.

Turning to the final proposition, was it the case that the inclusion of curriculum coverage in a statistical model for progress narrowed the gap between African–Caribbean boys and girls? The difference is indeed reduced – from 0.35 to 0.25 standard deviation units of progress – and, after allowing for curriculum coverage, the interaction between ethnic group and gender on maths progress is no longer statistically significant. On the other hand, the size of the reduction is rather modest.

If we put together the four pieces of the jigsaw, representing the four propositions, we do not get a perfect fit. This is hardly surprising, given the nature of non-experimental data with all the attendant lack of control, allied to sampling and measurement errors. Sampling errors are particularly important here, because the sizes of the two African–Caribbean groups were generally rather small. Hence, the power of our analyses to pick up statistically significant interactions is rather low. Nevertheless, there is a measure of support for each proposition. We now consider the implications of these findings.

Implications of the findings

The evidence presented in the previous section is consistent with what has been described in the literature as a 'Matthew' effect (Walberg and Tsai, 1983). This term, with its origins in the Gospel according to Matthew (Ch. 25, v. 29), is also referred to as cumulative advantage, or as a 'rich get richer' effect. Here, it is the obverse which is relevant: African–Caribbean boys appear to be cumulatively disadvantaged. We can conclude, albeit tentatively, that because African–Caribbean boys are behind in maths at the end of year one, they therefore cover less of the maths curriculum during year two, which in turn means that they have therefore fallen further behind by the end of year two. In other words, they suffer from a process which, if repeated every school year, is bound to lead to them falling further and further behind other groups. But our analyses do raise some questions.

First, we need to consider why African–Caribbean boys are behind in maths at the end of year one. It is possible that we have observed one frame of a film which started at the beginning of compulsory schooling. It could be that African–Caribbean boys have covered less of the maths curriculum in their reception year and during year one, and this accounts for their attainment position at the end of year one. We have no data for the reception year from the CECIL project, but our data for year one do not provide a lot of support for this argument. The within-classroom differences in curriculum coverage between the four ethnic gender groups were small for year one just as they were for year two. The effect of the proportion of African–Caribbean pupils in the classroom on the between-classroom differences in coverage was smaller, and not statistically significant, for year one than it was for year two. These differences in the pattern of results for years one and two are in line with other findings for curriculum coverage reported in Plewis and Veltman (1996b). It is possible that we have hit the beginning of the Matthew effect, in which case we have to look elsewhere for explanations of African–Caribbean boys' relatively poor performance at the end of year one. As Tizard et al. (1988) discovered, such explanations are not easy to find.

Second, our results suggest that the Matthew effect as it operates here for this early stage of schooling is more a between-classroom phenomenon than a within-classroom one. We find that African–Caribbean boys are disadvantaged because more of them are to be found in classrooms where less of the maths curriculum is covered by their teachers. They do not cover less of the curriculum than their white peer group in the same classrooms. It is important to stress that there is no reason to suppose that the relatively high proportion of African–Caribbean pupils in a classroom is in itself a *cause* of low coverage; these classrooms could well have a preponderance of socially and economically disadvantaged pupils, *regardless* of their ethnic background. However, it is also possible that teachers have lower expectations of their pupils in classrooms of this kind, and this leads to less of the curriculum being covered, to the detriment of *all* the pupils. Blatchford et al. (1989) found that teachers covered less of the curriculum with pupils where their expectations were low. Our data do lend further support to the possibility that the cumulative disadvantage is being created by a between-classroom process, because we find that some of the between-classroom differences in maths progress in year two can also be explained by variations in the proportion of African–Caribbean pupils in the classroom. One of the most commonly expressed fears about the 1988 Act was that it would lead to two groups of state schools: a popular, successful and relatively well-funded group, and an 'underclass' of unpopular 'sink' schools in poor areas. The results in this chapter do suggest that the demands of the National Curriculum could be leading to differences between schools in the extent to which the curriculum is being covered, which in turn reinforce inequality. Some schools are able to cope with these demands; others, with a more disadvantaged intake of pupils, are less able to.

Third, and very importantly, the emphasis of these results is on the relative failure of the African–Caribbean boys, whereas they might well have been interpreted as pointing to the relative success of African–Caribbean girls. As with a lot of data of this kind, the way in which we choose to discuss findings can vary, and I do not address the complex issue of gender and maths in this chapter. Nevertheless, the data do not point to African–Caribbean girls doing especially well. Both at the end of year one, and at the end of year two, their maths attainments are lower than those of the white girls: it is just that the ethnic gap for the girls is smaller than the corresponding gap for the boys. At least some of the ethnic gap is likely to be attributable to socioeconomic variables, even though our sample was relatively homogeneous in that way. Socioeconomic variables cannot explain a gender gap, and so we need to look elsewhere – to processes within the classroom or at home – for an explanation.

Implications for research

The separation of within-classroom from between-classroom processes is important in quantitative educational research of this kind. Most of the results reported earlier were obtained by using some relatively straightforward applications of multilevel modelling (Goldstein, 1995). This recently developed set of statistical techniques which, in this case, are an extension of multiple regression, enable the variation at different levels of an hierarchically structured system to be partitioned and explained. In this example, we work with just two levels: the classroom (or teacher) and the pupil. We seek to explain the between-classroom variation in, for example, curriculum coverage by variables defined at the pupil level, such as prior attainment, and variables defined at the classroom level such as the proportion of pupils in a particular ethnic group. Multilevel models have found wide acceptance in studies of school and teacher effectiveness and are routinely used in other areas of educational research. A set of applications of multilevel modelling, covering examples from health and geography as well as from education, can be found in Woodhouse (1995).

The logic of the method of analysis described earlier could be applied to other situations. In particular, rather than focus on ethnic and gender differences, it would be possible to look at social class differences in the same way. (We were not able to collect social class data in CECIL.) We know there are social class differences in attainment but we do not know whether these differences are widening as children get older, nor a great deal about whether they are widening across generations.

Conclusions

The evidence presented in this chapter is only a part of the evidence which would be required before it could be concluded with confidence that the changes wrought by the 1988 Act have led to an increase in educational inequality. We would need data for other ethnic and social groups from other parts of the country and for attainments other than maths. And we must recognize that we cannot necessarily attribute observed changes to the Act; they might have happened anyway or could have been brought about by other educational and social changes. Moreover, the Act did not produce just one major set of changes at a single point in time. Rather, the way in which the Act was put into operation has regularly been contested and revised, most recently as a result of the Dearing Review. What this chapter does do is to suggest a need for concern, at least about one aspect of inequality. It also indicates how data of a similar nature could be analysed in the future. Regrettably, it is not easy to monitor and to analyse the workings and effects of our system of state education. Official education statistics are not designed to evaluate the effects of major changes such as the Education Reform Act, either in terms of absolute change or in terms of the kinds of relative changes discussed here. Data on socioeconomic variables are not routinely collected, so we have to rely on occasional research studies, often with relatively small samples, to try to document and explain change.

This chapter has focused on the relatively poor performance of African–Caribbean pupils, especially boys, in maths. We do not know whether or not their average attainment is improving, but it is likely that African–Caribbean boys are falling further behind African–Caribbean girls, and even further behind white pupils. It is unlikely that this situation can be explained by just one factor and I do not purport to give a complete account of all the reasons. However, I do give some evidence which indicates that it is differences in the way in which teachers are now covering the curriculum which could, quite unwittingly, be leading to increasing inequality. I suggest that the effects of the major changes of the last few years could be generating more widespread inequalities than those described here, but that evidence for this will remain elusive for as long as so few resources are devoted to monitoring the education system.

Acknowledgments

This work was supported by the Economic and Social Research Council, as part of its 'Innovation and Change in Education' programme (grant L208252004). I acknowledge the contribution of Marijcke Veltman to the research and thank Charlie Owen for comments on an earlier version of this chapter.

References

BLATCHFORD, P., BURKE, J., FARQUHAR, C., PLEWIS, I. and TIZARD, B. (1989) 'Teacher expectations in infant school: associations with attainment and progress, curriculum coverage and classroom interaction', *British Journal of Educational Psychology*, **59**, pp. 19–30.

GOLDSTEIN, H. (1995) *Multilevel Statistical Models* (2nd Edn.), London, Edward Arnold.

MORTIMORE, P., SAMMONS, P., STOLL, L., LEWIS, D. and ECOB, R. (1988) *School Matters*, Wells, Open Books.

NFER (1991) *An Evaluation of the 1991 National Curriculum Assessment*, London, SEAC.

PLEWIS, I. (1991) 'Pupils' progress in reading and mathematics during primary school: associations with ethnic group and sex', *Educational Research*, **33**, pp. 133–40.

PLEWIS, I. and VELTMAN, M. (1996a) 'Where does all the time go? Changes in pupils' experiences in year two classrooms', in HUGHES, M. (Ed.) *Teaching and Learning in Changing Times*, Oxford, Blackwell, pp. 1–16.

PLEWIS, I. and VELTMAN, M. (1996b) 'Opportunity to learn maths at Key Stage One: Changes in curriculum coverage 1984–1993', *Research Papers in Education*, **11**, pp. 201–218.

SAMMONS, P. (1995) 'Gender, ethnic and socioeconomic differences in attainment and progress: A longitudinal analysis of student achievement over nine years', *British Educational Research Journal*, **21**, pp. 465–86.

TIZARD, B., BLATCHFORD, P., BURKE, J., FARQUHAR, C. and PLEWIS, I. (1988) *Young Children at School in the Inner City*, Hove, Erlbaum.

WALBERG, H. J. and TSAI, S. (1983) 'Matthew effects in education', *American Educational Research Journal*, **20**, pp. 359–73.

WOODHOUSE, G. (Ed.) (1995) *A Guide to MLn for New Users*, London, Institute of Education.

Part II

Research and Policy

Chapter 8

Staffing Innovations in City Technology Colleges: Policy into Practice

Jo Mortimore and Peter Mortimore

Introduction

A key policy question faced by governments in many countries today is how best to encourage professionals to innovate, within a cost-effectiveness framework, so as to increase the effectiveness of publicly funded institutions. In the realm of educational policies, a number of governments of different political persuasions have opted for large-scale restructuring. In the decentralized systems of the USA, for example, different states have interpreted the requirement for higher standards and better value for money in a host of ways, ranging from minor curriculum adjustments to the wholesale privatization of the system by commercial companies.

In the UK there have been numerous changes since the Education Reform Act (ERA) became law in 1988. One such change concerns the creation of fifteen City Technology Colleges (CTCs) designed to provide, for inner-city areas, high quality, innovative schools, offering a scientific and technologically led curriculum. The CTCs have been described as 'innovations of value and interest to all secondary schools' (CTC Trust, 1991). Innovations are, therefore, intrinsic to the nature of the colleges and not to innovate would be to fail in their mission. The funding, sponsorship, staffing arrangements and curriculum of this new type of school have provided scope for innovations in the role of and deployment of staff. Governing bodies of CTCs, for instance, although generally required to employ as teachers those who have qualified teacher status, can recommend exceptions to be made 'for individuals with other relevant background and experience' (DES, 1986, p. 7). Considerable opportunities exist, therefore, for flexible staffing practices and it would be surprising if governing bodies had not tried to use them to the full.

We have been studying the innovative nature of staffing practices in eight such colleges through an ESRC-funded project (R000 234807). Six of the eight are completely new colleges ('greenfield sites' in the colleges' argot) though not necessarily in new, purpose-built premises: two are 'new-from-old' colleges created out of existing local authority schools with premises and some staff inherited. We chose to focus, in each college, on four posts which we considered sufficiently innovative to be of wider interest and applicability but not so unusual or college-specific that they would be difficult to replicate. In the main, the posts provided:

- support for management and administration (ten posts including parent liaison and managers of finance, personnel, networks and premises);
- support for the curriculum (thirteen posts including tutor/technicians, instructors, managers of learning resources and technicians);
- support for both management and curriculum (nine posts including development/income-generation, graphics design and joint IT curriculum/network posts).

Since, however, almost every postholder made some input into the mainstream or enrichment curriculum, for the purposes of this chapter we have treated all these postholders as one category of respondents. The thirty-two postholders included fifteen women and seventeen men.

We are identifying in detail the benefits and disbenefits of the thirty-two posts, drawing on methods from a similar study in maintained primary and secondary schools (Mortimore and Mortimore, 1994). We are using cost-effectiveness analyses to judge the value of the posts to the overall missions of the institutions (Thomas, 1990; Thomas and Martin, 1996). In an earlier study we suggested that staff who were not teachers but who supported – or in some cases managed – the administration or curriculum be referred to as 'associate staff' rather than as 'non-teachers'. Associate staff is the terminology used throughout this chapter.

Our methodology is described in Mortimore and Mortimore (1995). Briefly, in the first year of the study we carried out 125 interviews with staff and with governors (including trustees and sponsors) using a semi-structured framework. All the interviews were tape-recorded and responses were post-coded. This chapter draws on preliminary analysis of our data from the early sections of the interviews. Further analyses will focus in more detail on the thirty-two posts chosen for study.

In this chapter we address four questions designed to probe the innovative nature of the staffing practices in these colleges:

- whether the relative freedom of CTCs has resulted in more innovative posts;
- whether the relative freedom has resulted in the recruitment of people from industry and commerce;
- whether people without formal teaching qualifications are engaged in teaching; and
- whether there are clear boundaries between teachers and the thirty-two associate staff postholders and, if so, how permeable these are.

The responses, by group of respondents, to these questions are presented in Tables 8.1 to 8.4. The groups are made up of: governors; senior management teams – or SMT (principals, vice-principals and other senior staff); teachers

Staffing Innovations in City Technology Colleges

(including the line-managers of the thirty-two 'focus' posts); and associate staff. Where there are pronounced differences in responses *within* the groups, for example, between principals and other SMT members or between line-managers and teachers, we discuss the significance of this intragroup variation.

Has the relative freedom of CTCs resulted in more innovative posts?

Eighty per cent of the responses to this question were in the affirmative. Examples were cited of directors of finance and administration; managers of information technology (IT), premises, catering, lettings and marketing; dual posts of tutor- or teacher-technicians; and staff development, quality assurance and parent-liaison posts. A small group of governors, senior staff and teachers, however, thought that the added freedom had not led to any significant innovation. A similar number were uncertain. Sixty-six of the 'Yes' respondents could identify factors which had helped in the creation of the innovative posts. See Table 8.1.

Emphasis on a CTC-specific curriculum

Over a third of respondents considered that the colleges had the freedom to create new posts or to extend the scope of existing posts in order to support a curriculum weighted towards their specialist subjects of science and technology. In the words of one principal, 'some innovations are related to necessity'. Staff took seriously the challenge to be at the cutting edge of curriculum innovations. Moreover, all colleges had relatively sophisticated IT systems.

Table 8.1 Factors associated with relative freedom of CTCs to create innovative posts

Response	Governors	SMT*	Teachers	Associate staff	Total	% responses
1 CTC curriculum	–	5	9	10	24	36.4
2 Culture of innovation	1	2	9	5	17	25.8
3 Easier from scratch	1	3	5	–	9	13.6
4 Financial autonomy	1	3	2	2	8	12.2
5 *In loco* LEA	–	1	2	1	4	6.0
5 Role of Principal	1	1	2	–	4	6.0
Total	4	15	29	18	66	100
N = 66						

*Principals, vice-principals & other senior staff who make up Senior Management Teams.

Both factors called for high levels of staff knowledge and expertise. Those who commented on the use of associate staff in supporting and, in some cases, shaping the CTC curriculum, noted the opportunity given to postholders to draw on previously acquired skills. The slant towards technology forced staff to think about the vocational aspects of a range of courses. Thus, a senior manager reported, 'Here we are able to look at how languages are used in industry and talk to people in industry about it.'

Culture of innovation

The development of a culture of innovation was noted in a quarter of the responses, mainly from those of teachers and postholders. Respondents commented on the need for a college ethos which welcomed and fostered innovation. As one governor said, 'We push innovation hard. We think it is important. We *want* innovative staff and are nudging the college to look for more. We are stretching them all the time.' Managers spoke of conscious attempts to emulate a *business* rather than a school environment and culture. These attempts included a longer school day, staff having business-sounding job titles, the design of the buildings (for example, a commercial-looking reception area) and, in at least one college, expecting post-sixteen students to dress as if they were going to work in a company. Teachers and postholders mainly drew attention to the need for all to pull together for the good of a high profile enterprise which, in some cases, was the subject of considerable local hostility.

Allied to innovation is risk-taking and, in some colleges, there was conscious encouragement and support for staff prepared to take a chance. Thus, one teacher reported that, before coming to work in the college, he had tried to promote some of his ideas but the people he was working with had been unable to change, roles were overspecific and expectations of the way staff did their jobs were based on traditional views. In the CTC, he found, 'If you have new ideas you can try them out. If they don't succeed you can work out why and abandon or modify them, and try again. Here it is so open to change.'

Easier from scratch

A minority of responses promoted the view that it was easier to grasp the opportunity to be innovative when one was starting with a blank page – with no history, no traditions, no 'baggage'. 'Greenfield sites' did not have long-established staff who might be set in their ways and hinder attempts at innovation. Thus, two principals and a vice-principal stressed the advantage of staff knowing – and accepting – that their roles were likely to change.

Financial autonomy

The considerable freedom in the new colleges over how financial resources were deployed and the greater financial expertise needed (to manage large budgets and deal with complex staff payrolls) were acknowledged by respondents to be factors in permitting freer staffing policies than normally existed in schools ('Certainly without that degree of freedom there would not be the posts there are'). This freedom provided the opportunity for the development of innovatory *cost-effective* posts. In the words of one postholder,

> There are more people controlling the budget here. Therefore I think the money is better spent. In the old days, money came from a trough. You just asked for more if it was needed. Now people are aware that it is *their* budget, they spend wisely, they protect it.

In loco local education authority

The new colleges receive their funding direct from central government and have had to take on many of the tasks previously undertaken by a local authority. They have therefore recruited staff able to handle large budgets, to hire staff, to manage sites and premises, and to deal with buying, catering and, in some cases, the transporting of students. As one vice-principal pointed out, initially the college had needed a much greater proportion of associate staff than a comparable school in a local authority since, without the supporting framework of an LEA, 'everything had to be home-produced, paperwork and procedures all had to be devised'. Although the ratio of associate staff to teachers had evened out, this early experience had resulted in more whole-college use of associate staff than the respondent had encountered in the maintained sector.

Role of the principal

A small number of respondents commented on the importance of the principal in promoting innovation. One principal was described as 'a highly innovative manager who creates innovative posts, who sees people's strengths and plays to that'. In another college the principal reported:

> We've not asked 'How innovative can we be?' I see our staff as our greatest resource. It's my job to use their potential to the benefit of the college and to the individual . . . staff are asked what they have done, what they would like to do, what untapped abilities they have. Maybe we are able to foster ambition.

Some respondents qualified their remarks about innovation. Two governors considered that, although the CTC was probably more innovative than many schools, the maintained sector contained enormous variations such that 'I expect there are a substantial number of maintained schools whose record would be similar to ours,' and 'The LEA system is rather good and the best LEA schools are super.' For some respondents, progress had been slow ('less than I would like but not necessarily less than I would expect').

Thus there was general agreement that the relative freedom of CTCs had indeed resulted in the creation of innovative posts. There was also reasonable agreement on the ways in which this had come about, with most respondents emphasizing the specific *technological* nature of the colleges themselves as being the principal influence. Interestingly, it was teachers and postholders rather than governors and senior managers who invoked the notion of the 'culture of innovation' in answer to this question. This may be due to the prior involvement of the latter groups in the establishment and early organization of the colleges eliciting more instrumental reasons for the creation of posts.

The second question focuses on the type of people recruited to become postholders and on the way their skills have been used.

Has the relative freedom resulted in the recruitment of people from industry and commerce?

Respondents were asked about the effects on staffing of the business and enterprise ethos of the colleges and their active and positive links with industrial sponsors. The responses are set out in Table 8.2.

It is clear from Table 8.2 that more than three-quarters of respondents supported the view that a broader range of appointments had been made,

Table 8.2 Effect of business ethos on CTC recruitment policy

Response	Governors	SMT	Teachers	Associate staff	Total	% response
Yes, direct from industry	10	9	39	19	77	62.7
Yes, ex-industry and qualified teacher	2	6	6	2	16	13.0
No, efforts failed	4	–	2	4	10	8.1
No conscious policy	–	5	4	1	10	8.1
Don't know	2	–	2	6	10	8.1
Total	18	20	53	32	123	100

N = 125
Missing = 2

although groups of respondents differed in how much they knew about the recruitment process. This is not surprising since many governors were not directly involved in staff appointments below the most senior level. Furthermore, associate staff and teachers were not usually directly involved in recruitment procedures, unless they were line-managers. Their clear impression, however, that recruitment had been made from a wider group than would be normal for a school, is a good indication of the perceptions that are common in the colleges.

Direct from industry

Almost two-thirds of the respondents believed that colleges recruited directly from industry those who were not qualified teachers. Attempts to recruit staff from outside education tended to be concentrated in specific subject areas (IT, technology, science) or in developing areas (business and marketing enterprises or quality control). This was considered necessary in order to develop or maintain the technological thrust of the colleges and the links with industry and commerce. Thus, a governor stated that, 'In maths, science and technology we've looked for people with industrial expertise and possibly put in the advertisement that we would take someone... without a teaching qualification.' One experienced teacher commented that she had:

> Never known such a concentration of staff with at least short, or even lengthy, periods in industry. The principal would never say about a job 'you must have such and such a qualification' but goes for those people who have the added weight of experience.

Respondents stressed that associate staff with practical skills and first-hand knowledge of industry brought technological expertise into the classroom. A teacher and a manager commented, respectively, 'Associate staff and breadth and depth. They bring their experiences in industry and enhance the quality of the students' experience.' 'We hope to open students' eyes to the business world, to link the business experience of associate staff to parts of the curriculum.'

This innovative practice, however, was not unproblematic. While welcoming such recruits for their skills and first-hand experience, several respondents expressed reservations. Some drew attention to the management time needed to support and train such staff for work in an educational setting. Moreover, the pay differential between teaching and industry made it hard to attract into education those who had been successful in industry. Thus, a governor commented, 'Teachers, by and large, are not paid well. If you take people from industry and pay them a teacher's salary they are under par.' Senior managers, too, noted the care needed in making such appointments. They were wary of undervaluing teaching expertise and warned of the risk of recruiting from industry candidates of insufficient calibre. However great their industrial expertise, staff needed to be able to communicate with, and cope with, the young people of today and to understand and use modern methods. As one principal put it, 'They need to be able to teach and communicate, not just lecture. We have recruited a few from industry but they have not coped well with new assessments, discipline and investigative methods.' One vice-principal cautioned, 'We want a positive experience of industry, not those running away. We want those with breadth, not those looking for an easy ride. We've had a few of them.'

Ex-industry and qualified teacher status

Given the *caveats* noted above, surprisingly few responses reported that colleges looked for industrial experience *but only if* allied with a recognized teaching qualification. Respondents who maintained that experience *and* qualified teacher status were the ideal had sometimes arrived at that conclusion after earlier mistakes in appointments or after fruitless efforts to recruit suitable candidates. One of the line-managers stated, 'There is a glibness about thinking you can bring in people from industry as teachers. Nearly everyone now is a qualified teacher.' Another reported that, if a teacher is appointed, he – as a manager – needed to spend much less time discussing strategies in the classroom but much more time pushing the teacher to be innovative. If a professional with expertise was brought in, the reverse was usually the case.

Efforts failed

A small group of respondents reported that, although the will was there, efforts to recruit from industry, with or without qualified status, had failed. Though few in number, most of these responses came from the governors and from the associate staff themselves – the two groups of respondents most likely to have business or industry experience. One governor lamented:

> I hope it would work but I don't think it has. There has been an attempt to go out and find engineers but they are not there. It's sad. I've worked all my life to get cross-fertilization between the two sides. I think there needs to be a transitional course, making good engineers and technical people into good teachers. It is difficult to recruit and keep people from industry.

Others commented, 'Our expectations have not been fulfilled – we have not found the right people.' 'We had no preconceptions – we advertised in different arenas but drew a total blank.' Part of this failure, noted by the associate staff respondents, was the pay differential: despite the resources available to them, some colleges still could not afford salaries which took account of substantial levels of industrial or commercial experience.

No conscious policy

A few responses came from principals who saw it as their priority to find the best person to do the job regardless of their background ('We always go for the best teacher – if they have industrial experience, that's a bonus.') Only in cases where it was obvious that the broad experience of the world of work would be a particularly valuable qualification for a specific post, or where someone had the skills required and, moreover, outweighed an applicant in the teaching profession, would they depart from their usual practice. One principal reported that, in his view, CTCs had 'Gone for youth and flash ... (but) when one is starting up a new institution ... you have to build up with a lot of experienced people.' He had tended to go for demonstrable capability in whatever candidates had done previously. Other respondents reported that the staffing balance was probably no different to any other secondary school, but that attitudes were more business-like in the CTC culture.

The answer to this question, therefore, is complex: it seems there has been a clear intention to broaden the recruitment policies of the colleges in an innovative way – especially in the technological and business areas of the curriculum – but that, for a variety of reasons including relative levels of pay and suitability, these intentions have not always resulted in an innovative outcome. Where appointments have been made from outside education, this has been because of what such postholders have been able to bring to the administration and curriculum of the colleges.

Our third question shifts the focus from recruitment into the colleges to the roles that staff played within them.

Are people without teaching qualifications engaged in teaching?

Table 8.3 shows that almost three-quarters of the respondents, particularly SMT and even more so teachers, considered that people other than qualified teachers were engaged in teaching activities. (Many governors were not close to the day-to-day work of the colleges, so were unable to comment.) Some respondents noted that, in line with official guidelines, unqualified people taught solely or mainly in IT, or in other technological areas where advanced levels of skills were scarce. As one governor put it, 'for this kind of school you need experts *and* teachers'. The reasons why associate staff were involved in teaching included stepping in to fill a temporary gap which then became part of their normal role; having an idea for an 'enrichment' or extra-curricular course which was taken up and, in some cases, became part of the mainstream

Table 8.3 Are people without teaching qualifications engaged in teaching?

Response	Governors	SMT	Teachers	Total	% responses
Yes	8	14	40	62	72.94
No	2	5	4	11	12.94
Don't know	8	–	4	12	14.12
Total	18	19	48	85	100

N = 93
Missing = 8

curriculum; or demonstrating skills or talents on which managers were able to capitalize in the mainstream or enrichment timetable.

Postholders sometimes taught alongside qualified teachers but did not have full control of a group or class. In other instances, associate staff initially supported or worked with qualified teachers in order to get used to discipline, standards and expectations, but then taught – in some cases – whole class groups and played a full role within the curriculum ('they are mature, experienced people with a lot to offer').

Some associate staff took the lead in areas such as IT where they had greater expertise than the teacher. Some passed on their skills and knowledge to teachers in staff-training sessions. A fairly typical scenario was described by one principal who reported that the way the teaching was organized in the college, with team teaching and supported self-study, meant there were several opportunities for small group activities when associate staff could work with students. This principal gave examples of a video technician who possessed specific skills superior to any of the qualified teachers and who worked both with an examination and an enrichment group; and of technicians who worked both formally (with timetabled groups) and informally (in the lunch hour) with students. In the principal's words, 'All that starts off by not compartmentalizing people. I look at them – let them develop – facilitate – enable – that's my role.'

In the eyes of some governors and two principals, some of the associate staff were better prepared and had better schemes of work than their qualified teacher colleagues. One principal claimed:

> We've got some super unqualified people now and we've got some teachers not coming up to scratch ... what matters is the ability to motivate students and to switch them on. You can either do it or not.

Six respondents qualified their remarks with comments on the need for caution ('It needs care and support ... you need to make sure the associate staff feel confident with the material'), and on the management needed ('It's never been the college view that associate staff could go straight into a teaching environment with no line-management aspects, counselling, etc.'). Four respondents commented that managers had to take account of the legal situation with regard to staff responsibility for students.

We questioned the eleven respondents who had answered 'No' to this question. Only one appeared to be opposed to the *idea* of unqualified people teaching, the others were simply unaware of it happening to any great extent in their college. An interesting development was that six of the thirty-two associate staff, having been drawn into the teaching role, were training part-time as teachers, often with some support for their fees from the colleges.

So in answer to this question, it appears that a significant number of the associate staff postholders were engaged in teaching. The kind of teaching, however, varied: only a minority were engaged with whole groups or classes and the majority were working with small groups or individuals. The fact that a sizeable minority (drawn from SMT as well as from teachers) did not agree that this was happening suggests that, in some cases, definitions of what constitutes teaching were not clear. In our fourth question, therefore, we sought to investigate whether there were clear lines of demarcation between the associate staff and teaching staff, what flexibility or overlap in roles existed, and what were respondents' views on these issues.

Are there clear boundaries between what teachers and associate staff do and, if so, how permeable are they?

It is clear from Table 8.4 that just over half the respondents did *not* perceive clear boundaries, although there were differences between the responses of different groups. SMT members were more likely than teachers *not* to perceive boundaries. Some respondents referred to ambiguity over the definition of teaching activities, asking 'When does supporting a teacher in the classroom

Table 8.4 *Are there clear boundaries between what teachers and other staff do?*

Response	Governors	SMT	Teachers	Associate Staff	Total	% responses
No	5	12	30	14	61	53.1
Yes	4	4	15	16	39	33.9
Don't know	5	–	1	–	6	5.2
Other	–	1	6	2	9	7.8
Total	14	17	52	32	115	100

N = 125
Missing = 10

become teaching?' Thus, a governor commented that, if he were to go into a classroom he would not necessarily know if the staff member was a qualified teacher or not, 'but I would know if the teaching was lacklustre'. Other respondents argued for a pragmatic approach to students' and curriculum needs and who best could meet them: an approach which sometimes involved 'loosening the boundaries'. The responses from the associate staff themselves were fairly evenly divided.

These comments refer to the *teaching roles* of associate staff. Respondents also spoke about associate staff in other roles and of the 'determined efforts made to involve staff as a whole' in the curriculum. Indeed, as noted, almost all the thirty-two postholders had some involvement in the mainstream or enrichment curriculum. Premises managers contributed to science modules on heating systems and electrical circuits; technician managers helped to design science experiments and devise and teach modules on health and safety and first aid; financial administrators were invited to students' business-studies seminars.

One-third of respondents thought that there *were* clear boundaries between the two groups. Proportionately more teachers and associate staff than governors or SMT perceived boundaries, perhaps reflecting greater knowledge of the detailed day-to-day working practices and relationships on the part of the first two groups. Where boundaries existed, they were established and maintained by means of job descriptions (which enabled people to say 'it's not my job, therefore I won't do it'); the intractable demands of the timetable; students' needs; 'custom and practice'; and teachers' resistance to change and the desire to preserve their territory. Governors of two colleges spoke of 'the arrogance of the staff common room which is alive and well' and of 'a cosy teaching profession which fixed things because it did not want interference'.

Half the associate staff perceived clear boundaries. Eight who were not primarily involved in teaching, but working in administration, finance or premises-related posts, stated there were boundaries to their work with regard to disciplining students, expenditure, recruitment, pastoral work and the organization of teaching spaces. Eight whose role involved some teaching also perceived boundaries relating to disciplining students; constraints on the contact they could make with other departments or external agencies; setting, marking, and assessing students' work; recruitment; and health and safety legislation governing the use or servicing of certain equipment.

Nine respondents (coded as 'Other') were equivocal. They reported that the maintenance of boundaries partly depended on the personalities of the associate staff involved and of the teachers with whom they worked. For example, some associate staff were reported as having a personality which made them ideal for a particular post, or which meant their post had been moulded accordingly, but it was recognized that if and when that postholder left, a new *modus vivendi* would probably have to be negotiated with a successor.

The permeability of boundaries

We were interested in whether the boundaries – where they existed – were permeable or impenetrable. In practice, it appeared that most people considered that permeability existed and that extensive 'grey areas' existed around the roles of associate staff in relation to the work of teachers. Governors and SMT were almost evenly divided on this issue. Teachers and, particularly, associate staff were more likely to consider boundaries to be permeable. Again these differences could reflect the more detailed knowledge of individual roles held by staff who worked closely together. ('She is not expected to cover lessons – but she does.' 'The boundaries are clear on paper. She does not take a class – but on occasions she has.')

Respondents noted that if associate staff were working in teams with teachers, boundaries tended to be more blurred and to weaken as associate staff's skills improved or as, in the course of the school year, new groups and new staff got to know each other and to judge each other's capabilities. Grey areas were also reported where associate staff had greater expertise than teachers. Speaking of a member of the associate staff with considerable technological knowledge, one teacher told us: 'When the postholder is timetabled to be with a member of the teaching staff and that teacher has not got the expertise, the postholder takes the lead instead of a support role.' When asked for their views on the *value* of boundaries, the replies showed that almost one-third preferred clear boundaries, two-fifths favoured 'grey areas' and one-fifth wanted there to be a mixture of the two. The distribution of replies, however, showed some differences between groups.

Grey areas preferred

Principals and vice-principals were considerably more likely to favour grey areas and permeable boundaries than were other groups. They reported not liking restrictive job descriptions 'because situations change and people need to be flexible', wishing to increase the delegation to associate staff; and making efforts to reduce existing boundaries. One vice-principal reported, 'The culture of the college is such that people work together, they are not status oriented . . . there is no definite divide.'

Only a minority of line-managers (six out of twenty-eight) actually favoured grey areas. The six stressed the increased flexibility they gained and the greater job satisfaction postholders enjoyed. Ten out of twenty-seven non-line-manager teachers also welcomed grey areas. Typical comments were 'I don't like people in boxes: that's not what education is about,' and 'We need to be versatile and cross boundaries. If boundaries are up, it leads to confrontation and unwillingness to budge.'

Associate staff, again, was the sub-group most evenly divided in its response. The third preferring grey areas welcomed the flexibility and variety these added to their roles, the value of working as a team and the opportunity to try out new ideas and support each other as well as having the satisfaction of seeing their specific skills recognized and used for the benefit of students and the college.

Boundaries preferred

A third of respondents were critical of the idea of permeability and preferred the existence of clear boundaries. Those principals who shared this view considered that boundaries reduced the likelihood of confusion and possible tension over who was in charge of whom and what. However, most such responses came from line-managers and teachers. This may have been because line-managers, in particular, had to deal with tensions or confusions arising as a consequence of slack boundaries and teachers were the sub-group most likely to be threatened by what they might perceive as associate staff encroaching on their territory.

Line-managers (the largest group in favour) reported that clear boundaries reduced the risk of tension. They raised the issue of teachers being forced to take on some associate staff tasks as a result of postholders being so busy with the innovative aspects of their roles that they neglected their more mundane but essential activities. For example:

> She is not a teacher. She is employed for a reason. If she gets too involved with teaching she would not be free to do the technician tasks for which she is employed. She likes elements of the teaching and gets dissatisfied when I want routine tasks done.

Some line-managers commented that boundaries 'saved time because people knew where they were and what was expected of them'. They also raised another issue when they commented that boundaries 'reduced the chances of managers exploiting willing staff'. An example of this came from one respondent who had greater technical expertise than the qualified teacher alongside whom she was working and had taken time to explain to the latter what needed to be taught. The postholder reported, 'It was an odd situation. I felt I was being drained of my knowledge so that she could go on and earn two and a half times my salary.'

In similar vein, some teachers reported that boundaries protected everyone's interests. As one put it:

> It's important to have boundaries as clearly defined as possible ... to be fair to people on both sides. It avoids in-between areas where associate staff would be too stretched and where people in

the department would expect too much or – at the other extreme – undue time being devoted to one aspect of a job.

Associate staff who favoured boundaries tended to do so to avoid being given too much responsibility ('I feel the responsibility in the end is the teachers'. They are in charge. I don't want to be seen as a teacher'); and to avoid confusion ('People can go off in different directions . . . there can be a conflict of interests').

Both grey areas and boundaries needed

One-fifth of respondents thought the situation was not clear-cut: boundaries but also some flexibility were needed in order 'to get the best out of everybody'. Line-managers spoke of the need to be able to negotiate boundaries: 'If they are set in concrete they militate against change and expansion.' 'There has to be boundaries but we need grey areas for creativity and innovation, to allow ideas to flower.' One line-manager stated that boundaries were better for individuals because staff knew what was expected and were able to measure their achievement against the expectations of their responsibilities. However, for the college as a whole, she thought grey areas were more useful since 'they enable you to ask a lot more of staff'. Teachers also spoke of the need for flexibility and teamwork *within* boundaries. Associate staff reported how they valued both clear boundaries allied with an open management style which fostered good communications and allowed them some scope. 'You need boundaries but you also need a working arrangement. Clear black and white can be dangerous.'

The answer to our fourth question, therefore, has proved to be the most complex of all. Although the majority of our total respondents expressed the view that there were no clear boundaries, nor should there be, sizeable minorities of each of the different groups of staff believed that there were and – in many cases – that there should be some demarcation. To put these feelings down simply to protectionism or self-interest would be unfair; the reality appears to be a web of mixed feelings.

Conclusions

These findings raise a number of issues for policy and practice. The policy of allowing greater freedom to CTCs has resulted in new posts being created, although it is possible that the creation of technology schools and the increase in grant-maintained schools has led to some of these institutions following suit. The policy has undoubtedly helped to promote the CTCs' aim of being leaders in curriculum development in science and technology. It has been aided by the initially generous resource levels but also by senior managers' pragmatism.

The colleges have attracted principals who bring a wealth of experience (usually from the maintained sector) but also some frustrations at what they have found to be unhelpful constraints in many LEAs. The colleges have attracted staff, often young and with few fixed notions, drawn by the appeal of being part of something new, who expect and are willing to be challenged by change. The colleges generate an excitement, a commitment, a determination to make the new, high profile enterprises succeed. Such sentiments foster the cohesion of staff groups with often adverse local reactions to their presence. All this creates fertile ground for pragmatic use of the skills of all staff and reinforces an ethos or culture among staff generally in which innovation is expected and even encouraged.

There has clearly been considerable investment in seeking to recruit candidates from outside education. The bringing in of new blood from industry and commerce can lessen what Goodson and Hargreaves (in press) call 'the local institutional preoccupations of teachers' and may extend the body of specialist knowledge available to staff and students. Where such recruitment has happened, this innovative practice has sometimes brought into colleges people who lack formal teaching qualifications, although even at a time of recession it has not proved easy to recruit good candidates from industry and commerce. In many instances the practice has worked well for both the colleges and the individuals concerned. In some cases, however, those recruited have not proved suitable and have needed considerable management support.

Moreover, while some principals and governors set out to recruit *as teachers* people without formal teaching qualifications, there has also been an extension of the roles of some associate staff who had been recruited for support posts in the colleges but who ended up in quasi or actual teaching roles. Pragmatism and serendipity have played a major part in this aspect of staffing. Skills and talents have been recognized and capitalized upon. Roles have been extended and boundaries weakened, out of necessity to meet opening-date deadlines, as part of conscious attempts to break new ground or develop a new college culture, or for hard-nosed reasons of economy: associate staff can take some tasks from teachers and are usually paid less.

Some of those associate staff whose jobs have altered have performed well in the teaching role. Others have been expected to act only in a supporting capacity, either because they did not have the desire, skills or confidence to do otherwise or because teachers, for legal or other reasons, were not happy for them to take responsibility. This situation poses questions about the definition of what constitutes 'teaching' and about how weak or strong its boundaries are or should be. Undoubtedly some associate staff have been given scope and sometimes the training to develop new career opportunities. This raises the issue, however, of who then carries out the tasks the associate staff were recruited to undertake. If these tasks should revert to teachers, the purpose of many of the posts – and some of the innovations – would be lost. Furthermore, associate staff, initially pleased at the opportunities offered, may come to resent what they then perceive to be exploitation.

Our analyses indicate some consistent differences in views between the different categories of respondents. In some cases, these differences could be attributed to varying degrees of access to information about, for example, the genesis of some decisions or the organization of some innovations. In other cases, however, the differences were likely to be a consequence of one group having a closer working knowledge of a situation and having to deal with problems arising from the introduction of changes which may be perceived differently by, and which may have differential implications for, management, teachers and associate staff.

The analyses are not yet complete. We hope findings on the benefits, disbenefits and cost-effectiveness of the thirty-two associate staff posts and the relationship of our findings to relevant theories of change will shed further light on these issues and prove useful to those involved, as managers, practitioners or researchers, in innovation and change in educational settings.

Acknowledgments

We wish to thank the numerous people in the eight City Technology Colleges who made this study possible. We include not only those who agreed to be interviewed and, accordingly, proved so generous with their precious time – governors, principals, managers, other teachers and postholders – but also those staff members whose organization and co-operation facilitated our visits: their patience and courtesy were greatly appreciated. We also wish to acknowledge the support of the CTC Trust. Thanks are due to Denise Walker-Hutchinson and Ranjna Patel for their assistance with word-processing. The study was funded by the Economic and Social Research Council (Grant R000 234807).

References

CITY TECHNOLOGY TRUST (1991) *A Good Education with Vocational Relevance*, London, CTC Trust.
DEPARTMENT OF EDUCATION AND SCIENCE (1986) *City Technology Colleges: a New Choice of School*, London, DES.
GOODSON, I. and HARGREAVES, A. (in press) *Teachers' Professional Lives: Aspirations and Actualities*.
MORTIMORE, J. and MORTIMORE, P. (1995) 'Innovatory staffing practices in City Technology Colleges', *School Organisation*, **15**, 2, pp. 145–53.

MORTIMORE, P. and MORTIMORE, J. with THOMAS, H. (1994) *Managing Associate Staff: Innovation in Primary and Secondary Schools*, London, Paul Chapman Publishing.
THOMAS, H. (1990) *Education Costs and Performance*, London, Cassell.
THOMAS, H. and MARTIN, J. (1996) *Managing Resources for School Improvement: Creating the Cost-effective School*, London, Routledge.

Chapter 9

The Thirty Year Contribution of Research in Child Mental Health to Clinical Practice and Public Policy in the UK

Philip Graham

Introduction

As a psychologist studying developmental issues in their social context, Barbara Tizard turned her attention to a remarkable variety of research issues with significance for clinicians dealing with children and their families as well as for public policy. These include the importance of play, the development of language, the outcome of children adopted after infancy, and the identity of children of mixed race. In all these areas, she has carefully considered the way in which her findings might influence practice and policy and has often entered public debate on the issues. At the same time, there has been a very considerable expansion of research activity relevant to the management and prevention of child psychiatric disorders. In this chapter I consider evidence for the impact of this work.

Within the last thirty years, about fourteen chairs of child psychiatry and a Medical Research Council Unit have been established in the UK. The two leading journals in the field of child psychiatry (the *Journal of Child Psychology and Psychiatry* and the *Journal of the American Academy of Child and Adolescent Psychiatry*) quadrupled the number of papers they published each year, and two new journals, *European Child and Adolescent Psychiatry*, and the *Journal of Clinical Child Psychology and Psychiatry*, both have healthy submission rates. To what degree have research findings changed clinical practice – the way clinicians think and act? What has this research contributed to the development of public policy?

A truly satisfactory answer to the first of these questions would require a great deal more information than is available about clinical practice thirty years ago. Nevertheless some information is available, both from the recollections of those practising at the time, from the content of publications about clinical work and from accounts of the development of child psychiatry more generally over that period (Hersov, 1986).

Clinical practice thirty years ago

In the mid-1960s great changes began to take place in the way child mental health professionals practised in hospital departments and in child guidance clinics. For the previous thirty years, since the early 1930s, the leading London departments responsible for training many of the UK social workers, psychologists and psychiatrists practising in the child mental health field had been The Maudsley, The Tavistock, The Child Guidance Training Centre, and Great Ormond Street Children's Hospital. In all these centres of excellence, despite considerable theoretical differences, the assessment and treatment procedures were similar, with slight variation at the Maudsley, where the doctors took a more active role in assessment. At first attendance, the social worker saw the mother (only occasionally the father) to take a history. The psychiatrist saw the child to assess especially the child's fantasy life. Psychologists tested the child using standard procedures. The team then met to discuss their formulation. The theoretical basis of child guidance work is well described by Maclay (1970), a child psychiatrist towards the end of his career in the child guidance service.

If a child was 'taken on' for treatment, and this was usually the case, therapy would consist of the social worker seeing the mother and the psychiatrist and, except at The Maudsley, a non-medical psychotherapist seeing the child. Remedial teaching might be undertaken by the psychologist. Treatment was based on the assumption that problems arose from unconscious processes in mother and child that needed to be made conscious. So-called 'psychodynamic' treatment would enable both mother and child to function more effectively together. Clinics that regarded themselves as in the van of progress advertised they were 'dynamically orientated' in contrast to the clinics, though these were few in number, that focused on biological factors.

It should be explained that the stated theoretical basis of leading child psychiatrists over this period was much more eclectic than one might have imagined from the nature of clinical practice in child guidance clinics. Thus, for example, in a book edited by Gordon (1939) to which many of the most prominent child psychiatrists of the day, including John Bowlby, Mildred Creak, William Gillespie, Emmanuel Miller, William Moodie and Donald Winnicott contributed, there is strong emphasis in many of the chapters on the importance of constitutional and organic factors. Cameron (1956), reviewing past and present trends in child psychiatry, pleaded for a Meyerian socio-psycho-biological position in child psychiatry, but appeared to concede that therapeutic approaches were, in fact, largely dictated by psychoanalytic concepts at that time.

Round about the late 1960s, practice gradually changed, not in all centres, but certainly at The Maudsley and Great Ormond Street. The change did not, it must be made clear, come about because of new research findings. Indeed it is not at all clear why it did come about. There was a feeling of disenchantment with existing methods among some child psychologists and psychiatrists. This was reinforced by meta-analyses of clinical outcome studies indicating weak effectiveness of existing treatments (Levitt, 1963). Somewhat later, mild disenchantment was sometimes replaced by scathing criticism, such as that expressed by J. Tizard (1973). Two major figures, one British – John Bowlby

– and one American – Nathan Ackerman – were pointing to the importance of looking at interpersonal rather than intrapsychic processes and Ackerman, in particular, demonstrated it was possible to gain insights and effect change by seeing whole families together, rather than individual family members separately. Even in the early 1960s, it was regarded as pioneering even to see mothers and fathers together (Martin and Knight, 1962). The therapeutic potential of other theories, especially behavioural approaches, began to be seriously considered (Rachman, 1962). As family therapies developed, other theoretical formulations, especially different versions of systems theory, were increasingly applied. Finally, and this might be more important than the scientific influences I have mentioned, the cultural zeitgeist, reflected in the writings of Ronald Laing, was hostile to constricting aspects of conventional family life.

Although the change in practice did not come about because of research findings (there was no evidence that the new methods were any more effective than those they replaced), there was, all the same, a real change in attitude towards the possibility that hypothesis-testing research investigations could and should be undertaken in the clinical field, and in related fields that might contribute to clinical effectiveness. In the mid-1960s, a government report (Department of Education and Science, 1964) reviewing the working of the clinics, concluded that it was difficult, perhaps impossible, to produce good statistical evidence for effectiveness. Those who worked in the clinics thought they were doing a good job, and there was greater demand for their services than they could meet. That would have to be enough.

Ten years later, the attitude to research had significantly changed. The findings from epidemiological research, especially the Isle of Wight studies, made it clear that psychiatric disorders could be reliably measured and reliably diagnosed (Rutter, Tizard and Whitmore, 1970). Further, follow-up studies of both clinic samples (Robins, 1966) and community samples (Graham and Rutter, 1973) demonstrated some regularity of outcome depending on diagnosis. This paved the way for a considerable expansion of hypothesis-testing research in a whole range of areas relevant to the child mental health field.

If change in the late 1960s did not come about as a result of research endeavour, how has the greatly expanded volume of relevant research affected subsequent developments in clinical practice?

Aetiological research

Research findings concerning the causation of psychiatric disorders influence practice in a variety of ways. The clinician, knowing that a disorder suspected in a child has been found to have a strong genetic or constitutional component and a weak environmental component, will ask different questions, take a different attitude to parents, and plan treatment differently from when the reverse is the case.

Philip Graham

Genetic factors

The last twenty-five years and particularly the last ten years have seen a surge of interest in the role of genetic and constitutional factors in child psychiatric disorders (Rutter *et al.*, 1989). Two main findings have influenced clinical practice. The strongly genetic basis of autism has now been so firmly established (Le Couteur *et al.*, 1989) that the previous widely held clinical view that autism was a result of parental behaviour, reported by Stone (1965) has been firmly discarded. Parental behaviour is no longer held responsible for autism and this has led to a considerable lightening of the load borne by parents of such children. Parenting an autistic child is burden enough without carrying the extra load of guilt brought on by the implication from professionals that one has produced the condition oneself.

The second main group of findings relates to the role of genetic factors in the causation of more common childhood behaviour and emotional disorders. The hyperkinetic syndrome (attention deficit disorder) probably has a strong genetic component (Goodman and Stevenson, 1989). The role that temperament plays in the genesis of conduct disorders, anxiety and depressive states and the non-specific emotional disorders of childhood has also been clarified (Chess and Thomas, 1991). Again clinicians faced with these common disorders are now likely to take a different attitude to the possible constitutional elements present than would formerly have been the case, and parents can expect management more accepting of the personality of their children.

Family relationships

Research into the role of marital disharmony and the quality of parental relationships with children as reflected, for example, in the levels of warmth, criticism and hostility shown towards children has, in general, confirmed existing views held by clinicians. Disturbances of relationships and negative relationships have a powerful influence on the development of conduct disorders (Kazdin, 1995). The impact on clinical practice of these findings has, however, probably not been very great. In large part, the findings have confirmed existing beliefs. Nevertheless, the greater precision of information now available can exert an influence on practice. For example, the finding that children of divorced parents have two or three times the rate of conduct disorders than do children in the general population or than those who have lost a parent through death (Rutter, 1971) can have a variety of effects on management. When seeing a child of divorced parents, the clinician may pay particular attention to the relationship between the parents before and since the divorce. She may also bear in mind the fact that the research findings indicate that 70–80 per cent of children of divorced parents are *not* disturbed and therefore note particularly the protective factors and coping mechanisms that characterize the clinical situation she faces. She may take a more optimistic view of the outcome than would otherwise have been the case. Finally, knowing that, in studies of children of divorced parents, only a relatively small amount of the variance is explained by family variables, she may keep a more open mind on other factors that might be causing the disturbance she is assessing.

Life events

It is common sense to assume that upsetting events influence the behaviour and emotions shown by children. How far have research findings taken clinicians beyond this common-sense viewpoint? Goodyer (1991) has reviewed the evidence of a body of work which is much less substantial than life events research in adulthood. It is clear that the common sense view can be supported, at least in relation to childhood depression, but it cannot be claimed, at least at this stage, that specific negative life events have been identified or that life events have specific effects in terms of the types of disorder they cause. Nevertheless clinicians are likely to have been influenced by the work of Brown and Harris (1978) and Richman, Stevenson and Graham (1982) pointing to the stressful nature of parenthood, especially in adverse social circumstances, and the high prevalence of maternal depression with negative impact on children's lives and behaviour.

School effects

Thirty years ago, clinical practice took little account of differences between schools or even differences between teachers. It was broadly assumed by professionals in their clinical practice (though it is doubtful if they took this view in relation to their own children!) that one school was very like another and one teacher very like another. It followed that school factors were regarded as of little importance in the causation or outcome of child psychiatric disorders. This view has been firmly refuted by research findings, both with children with very special needs such as autism (Rutter and Bartak, 1973) and for children with much more common problems (Rutter et al., 1979). The study of school effectiveness is now a central feature of educational research, and one of the criteria for an effective school is the degree to which its standards are more or less likely to promote mental health (Mortimore, 1995). Further, it has been demonstrated that planned and concerted action within schools can have a measurable effect on behaviour problems such as bullying and being a victim of bullying (Olweus, 1991). These findings have resulted in clinicians paying more attention to what is going on in school. School-based mental health services, advocated by J. Tizard (1973) are unusual, but clinical practice that did not involve obtaining information from school about a referred child would now be regarded as of doubtful clinical value.

Other epidemiological research

One of the important findings of the Isle of Wight Studies (Rutter, 1989), carried out at the beginning of the period under consideration, is the degree of overlap between psychiatric disorders, physical disorders (especially those involving brain dysfunction) and educational problems such as academic under-achievement. This has probably had rather little clinical impact, but the effect of these findings on policies for the education of children with special needs has been considerable (see below).

A further, perhaps more significant, contribution made by epidemiological research to clinical assessment, has arisen as a result of the investigation of 'normal' children in the general population. The description of parents of children without emotional and behaviour problems and the self-description of such children when asked questions about their everyday lives, their worries and fantasies, has provided clinicians with a valuable additional clinical perspective.

Psychological processes

The last thirty years have seen at least a beginning in the closing of a gap between empirical research into developmental psychological processes and developmental psychopathology. The paramount influence of psychoanalysis on clinical practice at the beginning of the period under consideration has diminished, allowing other psychological theories to be tested and applied. The growth of cognitive psychology (Eysenck and Keane, 1990) is beginning to bear fruit in terms of clinical practice (Kaplan, Thompson and Searson, 1995) though links in the childhood field between cognitive psychology and cognitive therapy remain somewhat tenuous. The study of cognitive processes in children with autism (Frith, 1989) and of attributional processes in children with conduct disorders (Lochman and Lenhart, 1995) is beginning to have implications for therapeutic interventions in children with both these problems.

Clinical assessment

The research contribution to clinical assessment is particularly difficult to gauge. Although the information obtained from the development of reliable and valid measures has been found useful clinically, the interview measures were in fact largely derived from long-established clinical practice. Thus the content of now well-tried measures to assess the mental state of the child (Rutter and Graham, 1968) take an account of a child's psychiatric state from parents (Graham and Rutter, 1968) and evaluate the quality of family relationships (Rutter and Brown, 1966; Brown and Rutter, 1966) owes a great deal to clinical practice current at the time. However, findings derived from the use of these measures to assess 'normal' comparison groups in turn informed clinicians, in a way that had not previously been possible, about the clinical significance of responses to their questions. Further, research such as that carried out by Cox, Holbrook and Rutter (1981) enables clinicians to identify styles of history-taking more informative than others.

The development of checklists to assess a child's behaviour at home (e.g. Rutter, Tizard and Whitmore, 1970) and at school (e.g. Rutter, 1967) has also had some clinical value in that it has enabled clinicians to screen children referred to them to highlight particular problematic areas. Especially in the United States, there is increasing clinical use of structured interviews derived from research investigations. Hodges (1993) has reviewed various measures used in this way. The advantages and disadvantages of structured interviews purely for clinical purposes have not yet been adequately explored.

Finally, the recent use of psychoanalytic concepts in the development of research assessment procedures should be mentioned. Thus Hodges, Lanyardo and Baghurst (1994) have been exploring the fantasies of teenage boys both at risk of perpetrating sexual abuse and actual perpetrators, in order to develop better prediction of outcome and better treatment measures. While in the UK over the last thirty years empirical research and development of psychoanalytic ideas have gone along parallel paths, in this field and in clinical trials (see below) there is now some evidence of convergence.

Classification

The last thirty years have seen major revisions of the classification systems used to delineate child psychiatric disorders. The International Classification of Disease has undergone two major revisions (ICD-IX and ICD-X) and the *American Diagnostic and Statistical Manual for the Classification of Mental Disorders* has undergone three revisions (DSM III, DSM III-R, and DSM IV). Increasingly research findings have been used to underpin the classification systems now both published in versions designed to serve both research and clinical purposes. It would be pointless to try to disentangle within the field of classification to what degree research has influenced clinical practice and vice versa. There is clearly a mutually symbiotic relationship between the two. Given the limited state of knowledge available, it is inevitable that there are imperfections in the present classification systems (Graham, 1995) and that they are still of limited value. Nevertheless, their development has enabled clinicians to think more logically about their work and this is perhaps especially true of the development of multi-axial systems clearly delineating behavioural, developmental, intellectual, physical and social aspects of a child's functioning and background (Rutter, Shaffer and Sturge, 1975).

Clinical trials

The conduct of controlled clinical trials is the research activity that might be expected to have greatest impact on clinical practice. Evidence for the effectiveness of child psychiatric treatment available from such trials has been summarized by Graham (1993). Briefly, there is now available some evidence from controlled trials for the effectiveness of family therapy in psychosomatic disorders and anorexia nervosa, school-based group treatments in mixed emotional and conduct disorders, medication in the hyperkinetic syndrome, Tourette syndrome and obsessional disorder, psychoanalytically orientated psychotherapy in difficult-to-control diabetes, and behavioural treatments in enuresis and school refusal. In contrast, there is evidence from such trials of a lack of support for the notion that tricyclic medication is helpful in childhood depression and there is a lack of information from controlled trials of dynamically orientated medium- and long-term treatment, although some pointers in this direction have recently been published (Target and Fonagy, 1994).

Many treatment research findings are therefore relevant to clinical practice. This does not, however, mean that most or even perhaps the majority of clinicians modify their practice to take research findings into account. There is really no good evidence currently available on the way child psychiatrists and clinical child psychologists operate in practice, but there are some pointers. It seems likely that tricyclic antidepressant medication is overused (Bramble, 1995) bearing in mind the lack of evidence for its effectiveness, and it also seems likely that stimulant medication is underused. Epidemiological studies suggest the rate of hyperkinetic disorder in the population of seven to ten-year-old children is around 1 per cent and, if all such children in England and Wales received medication, there would be about 15,000 children on such treatment. The exact figure for children receiving stimulant medication is not available, but it must be a tiny fraction of that number. Most clinicians mainly practise different types of unevaluated psychotherapy – family therapy, individual psychotherapy, counselling and behavioural, especially cognitive behavioural therapy.

Evidence-based clinical approaches

Bearing in mind the very reasonable calls for the increasing use of evidence-based medicine, and the recent establishment at the Institute of Child Health, London, of a centre for evidence-based paediatrics, it is reasonable to ask why a relatively small proportion of clinical activity in the child mental health field has been evaluated, and why clinicians may, in any case, fail to incorporate research findings into their practice where they do exist.

Failure by clinicians to use methods that have been validated by research evidence is by no means specific to child psychologists and psychiatrists. It is widespread in medical and surgical practice (*Lancet* Editorial, 1993). Various reasons have been suggested (Greco and Eisenberg, 1993). These include the fact that clinicians may not have read the relevant material, they may be isolated and out of touch with recent developments or there may be a lack of rewards for clinicians incorporating effective methods into their practice. Medical student and postgraduate teaching is often over-didactic and fails to train the clinician in critical reflection or to appraise new material critically. This inevitably leads to resistance to new approaches. Finally, clinicians will perhaps appropriately resist new approaches to assessment and treatment if there are inadequate opportunities for supervision while new techniques are being learned.

These impediments to incorporating new, valid clinical methods are daunting enough, but there may be additional reasons for the late development of evidence-based clinical child psychiatry and psychology. One problem, shared with general psychiatry, is that the effective assessment and treatment of psychiatric disorders involves the use of the personality of the clinician to a considerably greater degree than is the case in other specialties. Of course, the effectiveness of general physicians and surgeons is also influenced by their personalities, but the degree to which personal factors play a part is likely to be much smaller. The personality of a psychotherapist dealing with a child with an anxiety state is surely of greater significance than the personality of a paediatrician treating a diabetic child. Second, the treatment of psychiatric disorders involves more complex variables than is the case with physical disorders. In planning treatment for a ten-year-old boy with a conduct disorder, at the very least, the nature and severity of the problem behaviour, the presence of co-morbid anxiety or depression, the circumstances in which the undesirable behaviour occurs, the behaviour and motivation of parents for treatment, and the willingness of the school to continue to tolerate difficult behaviour are all relevant. While a controlled trial of treatment of conduct disorder may point to useful methods of dealing with such problems, it is unlikely that research results will be readily translatable to more than a minority of children showing such disorders. In general, controlled trials of treatment are carried out with groups of motivated parents and children showing rather pure forms of the disorder in question. But many children do not show disorders in such pure form. As Kanner (1969) picturesquely put it, 'They have not read the books,' and this leads to difficulties in the implementation of research findings. Finally, research findings in the child mental health field, whether derived from clinical or epidemiological studies, produce results of a probabilistic rather than a definitive nature. Using one form of psychotherapy, a satisfactory outcome may be achieved in 60 per cent of patients rather than 40 per cent with another form of psychotherapy, but the value of such information to a clinician is inevitably rather limited. Some patients may in fact respond to the less generally successful form of therapy, but not to the other one. In addition, there are usually few indicators to help predict which patients will respond and which will not.

This is not to suggest that clinical research in the field of child mental health is futile or that clinicians should ignore research findings. However, it is only realistic to point out that there are special problems in the mental health field which make the application of research findings much more difficult.

Impact of research on public policy

The reasons for changes in public policy in matters relating to children, or indeed in any other field, are always complex, and it would be very unusual to be able to point to research findings as the mainspring for political action in a particular case. To begin with, the direction of applied research enquiry arises in the first place, at least to some degree, from political considerations. Social science researchers are influenced by political ideas current at the time, and research requiring grant support will have a greater chance of funding if it is in line with existing political thinking. Research findings are often open to a variety of interpretations and even if researchers themselves fail to draw politically acceptable conclusions from their work, journalists, politicians and public servants will do it for them.

Further, there are likely to be more important influences than research findings in determining much public policy. Politicians are strongly influenced by the need for electorally popular policies, by the need to deal with problems revealed by one or two highly publicized scandals or tragedies, by single-issue campaigns that have gained public attention and by the existing political ideology, whatever that may be. The decision to remove lead from petrol may, for example, be seen as much more closely linked to a well-co-ordinated single-issue campaign than to rather weak support from research findings that low-level lead was affecting the mental development of children (Pocock and Smith, 1994).

All the same, it would be quite misleading to suggest that research findings have no effect. All government reports concerning children and families published over the last thirty years have cited research studies to support their conclusions and, in some cases, it is likely that research played a significant part in altering policy. The fact that epidemiological studies produce probabilistic results is much less a limiting factor in public policy decisions than it is in clinical decision-making. If a change in policy would benefit the majority of children, then the fact that many would be unaffected is no bar to political action providing there is no evidence that some children would be harmed.

Numerous examples may be cited where, over the last three decades, research probably played some part, sometimes quite small but sometimes quite significant, in determining public policy. These include:

- The establishment of unlimited visiting by parents of children in hospital. Research evidence derived from studies of the outcome of separated children (Douglas, 1975).

- Legislation requiring the multidisciplinary assessment of children with special needs. Research evidence based on epidemiological findings demonstrating the overlap between physical and psychiatric disorders, and educational difficulties (Rutter, Tizard and Whitmore, 1970).
- Government guidance on anti-bullying policies. Evidence derived from controlled studies of the effectiveness of anti-bullying programmes in reducing this problem (Olweus, 1991).
- Legislation making it a duty on local authorities to take reasonable steps to identify the extent to which there are children in need in their areas. Evidence from epidemiological studies on the extent to which disabled children are not identified in school health registers (Rutter, Graham and Yule, 1970).
- Legislation replacing the concepts of parental rights and duties with the concept of parental responsibility. Evidence derived from family studies pointing to the deleterious influence on children of parents involved in physical and emotional abuse (Egeland, Sroufe and Erickson, 1983).
- Legislation making it mandatory for children's views to be taken into account when parental care breaks down and their future is being considered. Evidence derived from studies demonstrating that even young children can articulate a valuable, independent opinion on those looking after them (Madge and Fassam, 1982).
- The establishment of a National Curriculum and regular testing of schoolchildren. Evidence of very variable educational standards after the quality of home care has been taken into account (Rutter *et al.*, 1979).
- Considerable expansion of child mental health services over the last thirty years. Evidence derived from epidemiological studies showing unmet child mental health needs (Rutter, Tizard and Whitmore, 1970).
- Increasing emphasis on community treatment of delinquency. Evidence derived from studies showing the generally poor outcome of delinquents in residential care. (On a small scale, this policy is now being reversed without any support from research findings.) (Sheldrick, 1994).
- Legislation leading to the greater involvement of parents in school management. Evidence from studies demonstrating improved standards when parents are encouraged to co-operate with teachers in educating their children (Hewison and Tizard, 1980).
- Emphasis on conciliation proceedings in parents wishing to divorce. Evidence derived from studies showing the ill-effects of parental disharmony and disagreement on children's psychological development (Jenkins and Smith, 1990).

It is arguable, and it is indeed argued, for example, in Chapter 7 by Ian Plewis in relation to the National Curriculum, that some of these policy developments have had undesirable effects. Inevitably, when policy change takes place, even where such change is strongly influenced by research findings, it becomes clear at some point that new research and different policies are required. Further, it can be argued, with some justice, that many research findings have been ignored by policy-makers; the lack of preschool provision in the UK is a case in point. But it also seems likely from the above examples that the increase in research activity in this field over the last thirty years, though very variable in quantity, has led to a significant if unquantifiable effect on policy change.

Conclusions

Consideration of the impact of research in the child mental health field has revealed that many findings have emerged from clinical research relevant to clinical activity, though the degree to which these findings have been incorporated into clinical practice is uncertain and may be quite limited. But the main reason why clinicians do not act in accord with research findings is that the relevant research has just not been done, partly because of lack of resources, but also, and very importantly, because of the inherent complexity of the questions that require consideration. There is still a long way to go before clinical psychologists and psychiatrists can claim their practice is evidence-based, but there is a definite move in this direction.

The effects of research findings in this field on changes in public policy over the period in question, while impossible to quantify, are nevertheless detectable. Findings derived from epidemiological studies have been particularly influential, though not as significant in their impact as they might have been. When preventive measures compete for resources with treatment services, it is usually the latter which are seen as having the greater priority. Further, in considering preventive approaches, there are still many unanswered questions, not least why rates of virtually all psychosocial disorders in the young have continued to rise over the whole of the period since the Second World War (Rutter and Smith, 1995). The situation poses important challenges to those who continue to work in this complex and demanding field.

Finally, let me consider how research findings in the future might be more rapidly and effectively acted upon than has been the case in the past. Perhaps the most important barrier to implementation has been a lack of understanding among politicians, civil servants, professionals and parents of the ways in which treatment and practitioner issues can be usefully addressed. Many hold expectations of research and research workers that are confused. They expect both too much in the way of quick answers to complex questions, and too little, as typified by the government minister recently quoted as saying research was useless – it either told you what you knew already, or what you didn't want to know. There is a clear need for greater understanding of the strengths and limitations of the research process at all levels of society, and research workers themselves must take some responsibility for ensuring this happens. The material in this chapter surely reveals that both treatment strategies and public policies with respect to children's mental health are likely to be greatly improved if they are informed by sound research findings.

Acknowledgments

I am grateful to Lionel Hersov for a helpful discussion of developments in clinical practice.

References

BRAMBLE, D. (1995) 'Antidepressant prescription by British child psychiatrists: practice and safety issues', *Journal of the American Academy of Child and Adolescent Psychiatry*, **34**, pp. 327–31.
BROWN, G. and HARRIS, T. (1978) *Social Origins of Depression*, London, Tavistock Publications.
BROWN, G. W. and RUTTER, M. (1966) 'The measurement of family activities and family relationships: a methodological study', *Human Relations*, **19**, pp. 241–63.
CAMERON, K. (1956) 'Past and present trends in child psychiatry', *Journal of Mental Science*, **102**, pp. 599–603.
CHESS, S. and THOMAS, A. (1991) 'Temperament', in LEWIS, M. (Ed.) *Child and Adolescent Psychiatry: A Comprehensive Textbook*, Baltimore, Williams and Wilkins, pp. 145–59.
COX, A., HOLBROOK, D. and RUTTER, M. (1981) 'Psychiatric interviewing techniques. V Experimental study: eliciting facts', *British Journal of Psychiatry*, **139**, pp. 29–37.
DEPARTMENT OF EDUCATION AND SCIENCE (1964) *The Health of the School Child*, London, HMSO.
DOUGLAS, J. W. B. (1975) 'Early hospital admissions and later disturbances of behaviour and learning', *Developmental Medicine and Child Neurology*, **17**, pp. 456–80.
EDITORIAL (1993) 'Clinical trials and clinical practice', *Lancet*, **342**, pp. 877–8.
EGELAND, B., SROUFE, L. A. and ERICKSON, M. F. (1983) 'Developmental consequences of different types of maltreatment', *Child Abuse and Neglect*, **7**, pp. 459–69.
EYSENCK, M. W. and KEANE, M. T. (1990) *Cognitive Psychology: A Student's Handbook*, Hove, Erlbaum.
FRITH, U. (1989) *Autism: Explaining the Enigma*, New York, Blackwell.
GOODMAN, R. and STEVENSON, J. (1989) 'A twin study of hyperactivity II. The aetiological role of genes, family relationships and perinatal adversity', *Journal of Child Psychology and Psychiatry*, **30**, pp. 691–709.
GOODYER, I. (1991) *Life Experiences, Development and Psychopathology*, Chichester, John Wiley.
GORDON, R. G. (1939) *A Survey of Child Psychiatry*, London, Oxford University Press.
GRAHAM, P. (1993) 'Treatment of child mental disorders: types and evidence for effectiveness', *International Journal of Mental Health*, **22**, pp. 67–82.

GRAHAM, P. (1995) 'ICD-10 and the clinician', *Association for Psychology and Psychiatry Newsletter*, **17**, pp. 127–31.
GRAHAM, P. and RUTTER, M. (1968) 'The reliability and validity of the psychiatric assessment of the child II, interview with the parent', *British Journal of Psychiatry*, **114**, pp. 581–92.
GRAHAM, P. and RUTTER, M. (1973) 'Psychiatric disorder in the young adolescent: a follow-up study', *Proceedings of the Royal Society of Medicine*, **66**, pp. 1226–9.
GRECO, P. and EISENBERG, J. M. (1993) 'Changing physician's practices', *New England Journal of Medicine*, **329**, pp. 1271–4.
HERSOV, L. (1986) 'Child psychiatry in Britain – the last thirty years', *Journal of Child Psychology and Psychiatry*, **27**, pp. 781–801.
HEWISON, J. and TIZARD, J. (1980) 'Parental involvement and reading attainment', *British Journal of Educational Psychology*, **50**, pp. 209–15.
HODGES, K. (1993) 'Structured interviews for assessing children', *Journal of Child Psychology and Psychiatry*, **34**, pp. 49–68.
HODGES, J., LANYARDO, M. and BAGHURST, P. (1994) 'Sexuality and violence: preliminary clinical hypotheses from psychotherapeutic assessments in a research programme on young sexual offenders', *Journal of Child Psychotherapy*, **20**, pp. 283–308.
JENKINS, J. and SMITH, M. (1990) 'Factors protecting children living in disharmonious homes: maternal reports', *Journal of the American Academy of Child and Adolescent Psychiatry*, **29**, pp. 60–9.
KANNER, L. (1969) 'The children haven't read those books: reflections on differential diagnosis', *Acta Paedopsychiatrica*, **36**, pp. 2–11.
KAPLAN, C. A., THOMPSON, A. E. and SEARSON, S. M. (1995) 'Cognitive behaviour therapy in children and adolescents', *Archives of Disease in Childhood*, **73**, pp. 472–5.
KAZDIN, A. (1995) *Conduct Disorders in Childhood and Adolescence*, New York, Sage.
LE COUTEUR, A., BAILEY, A., RUTTER, M. and GOTTESMAN, I. (1989) 'An epidemiologically based study of autism', Paper given at the First World Congress of Psychiatric Genetics, Churchill College, Cambridge, 3–5 August 1989.
LEVITT, E. E. (1963) 'Psychotherapy with children: a further evaluation', *Behavior, Research and Therapy*, **1**, pp. 45–52.
LOCHMAN, J. E. and LENHART, L. (1995) 'Cognitive behavioural therapy of aggressive children: effects of schemas', in VAN BILSEN, H., KENDALL, P. C. and SLAVENBURG, J. H. (Eds) *Behavioural Approaches for Children and Adolescents*, New York, Plenum Press.
MACLAY, D. T. (1970) *Treatment for Children*, London, Allen & Unwin.
MADGE, N. and FASSAM, M. (1982) *Ask the Children*, London, Batsford Academic.
MARTIN, F. and KNIGHT, J. (1962) 'Joint interviews as part of intake procedure

in a child psychiatric clinic', *Journal of Child Psychology and Psychiatry*, **3**, pp. 17–26.

MORTIMORE, P. (1995) 'The positive effects of schooling', in RUTTER, M. (Ed.) *Psychosocial Disturbances in Young People: Challenges for Prevention*, Cambridge, Cambridge University Press, pp. 333–63.

OLWEUS, D. (1991) 'Bully/victim problems among schoolchildren: basic facts and effects of a school-based intervention program', in PEPLER, D. and RUBIN, K. (Eds) *The Development and Treatment of Childhood Aggression*, Hillsdale, NJ, Erlbaum.

POCOCK, S. and SMITH, M. (1994) 'Environmental lead and children's intelligence: a systematic review of the epidemiological evidence', *British Medical Journal*, **309**, pp. 1189–97.

RACHMAN, S. R. (1962) 'Learning theory and child psychology: therapeutic possibilities', *Journal of Child Psychology and Psychiatry*, **3**, pp. 149–63.

RICHMAN, N., STEVENSON, J. and GRAHAM, P. (1982) *Preschool to School: A Behavioural Study*, London, Academic Press.

ROBINS, L. (1966) *Deviant Children Grown Up*, Baltimore, Williams & Wilkins.

RUTTER, M. (1967) 'A children's behavioural questionnaire for completion by teachers', *Journal of Child Psychology and Psychiatry*, **8**, pp. 1–11.

RUTTER, M. (1971) 'Parent-child separation: psychological effects on the children', *Journal of Child Psychology and Psychiatry*, **12**, pp. 233–60.

RUTTER, M. (1989) 'Isle of Wight revisited. Twenty-five years of child psychiatric epidemiology', *Journal of the American Academy of Child and Adolescent Psychiatry*, **28**, pp. 633–53.

RUTTER, M. and BARTAK, L. (1973) 'Special educational treatment of autistic children: a comparative study: II Follow-up findings and implications for services', *Journal of Child Psychology and Psychiatry*, **14**, pp. 241–70.

RUTTER, M., BOLTON, P., HARRINGTON, R., LE COUTEUR, A., MACDONALD, H. and SIMINOFF, E. (1989) 'Genetic factors in child psychiatric disorders I. A review of research strategies', *Journal of Child Psychology and Psychiatry*, **31**, pp. 3–37.

RUTTER, M. and BROWN, G. W. (1966) 'The reliability and validity of measures of family life and relationships in families containing a psychiatric patient', *Social Psychiatry*, **1**, pp. 38–53.

RUTTER, M. and GRAHAM, P. (1968) 'Reliability and validity of the psychiatric assessment of the child', *British Journal of Psychiatry*, **114**, pp. 563–79.

RUTTER, M., GRAHAM, P. and YULE, W. (1970) 'A neuropsychiatric study in childhood', *Clinics in Developmental Medicine, Nos 35/36*, London, S.I.M.P., Heinemann.

RUTTER, M., MACDONALD, H., LE COUTEUR, A., HARRINGTON, R., BOLTON, P. and BAILEY, A. (1990) 'Genetic factors in child psychiatric disorders II', *Journal of Child Psychology and Psychiatry*, **31**, pp. 39–83.

Rutter, M., Maughan, B., Mortimore, P. and Ouston, J. (1979) *Fifteen Thousand Hours*, London, Open Books.
Rutter, M., Shaffer, D. and Sturge, C. (1975) *A Guide to a Multi-Axial Classification Scheme for Psychiatric Disorders in Childhood and Adolescence*, London, Institute of Psychiatry.
Rutter, M. and Smith, D. (Eds) (1995) *Psychosocial Disorders in Young People: Time Trends and their Causes*, Chichester, John Wiley.
Rutter, M., Tizard, J. and Whitmore, K. (Eds) (1970) *Education, Health and Behaviour*, London, Longman.
Sheldrick, C. (1994) 'Treatments of delinquents', in Rutter, M., Hersov, L. and Taylor, E. (Eds) *Child and Adolescent Psychiatry: Modern Approaches*, Oxford, Blackwells Scientific Publications.
Stone, F. (1965) 'Child psychopathology', in Howells, J. (Ed.) *Modern Perspectives in Child Psychiatry*, Edinburgh, Oliver Boyd.
Target, M. and Fonagy, P. (1994) 'The efficacy of psychoanalysis for children', *Journal of the American Academy for Child and Adolescent Psychiatry*, **33**, pp. 1134–44.
Tizard, J. (1973) 'Maladjusted children in the child guidance service', *London Educational Review*, **1**, pp. 22–37.

Chapter 10

The Socio-legal Support for Divorcing Parents and their Children

Martin Richards

Introduction

The Family Law Bill currently before Parliament contains new provisions concerning divorce which continue the trend toward private ordering in family law matters. The proposals would remove any consideration of fault in granting of divorce. A spouse will simply record their wish to divorce and, in principle, this would be granted a year later, provided that matters concerning property and arrangements for the children are settled.[1] There is a strong emphasis in the proposals on using mediation to settle disputes and the intention is for adjudication in court to become a rare final step when all else fails, again underlining the continuing shift toward private ordering and away from formal public procedures.

In both the Green and White Papers (Lord Chancellor's Department, 1994, 1995) which preceded this Bill, there was a very strong emphasis minimizing harm to children, reflecting the now large body of research evidence indicating the difficulties that some children may face. However, in the Bill, the procedures that might do this are indirect, operating via the provision of information to parents and the encouragement to use mediation. It is expected that mediation will reduce conflict between parents, and so lead to a more co-operative approach toward making arrangements for children. As several commentators have pointed out (Piper, 1994; Richards, 1995a; Douglas, Murch and Perry, 1996) the Bill has no provisions which attempt to safeguard children's interests directly and, in this, it is weaker than earlier legislation. So how does it come about that a White Paper which states that 'the government is committed to promoting the best interests of children whose parents are involved in separation and divorce' (Lord Chancellor's Department, 1995, para 5.16) and which acknowledges the evidence of the difficulties that some children face, is followed by legislation which provides less protection for children than some of its predecessors? I argue that this situation arises through a conflict between, on one hand, a long-standing shift towards an emphasis on relationships in domestic life, rather than social institutions and, on the other hand, the growing acknowledgment of children's rights of protection which extend into the increasingly privatized domestic sphere. These rights are, for instance, expressed in the United Nations Convention on the

Rights of the Child which was adopted by the General Assembly in 1989 and subsequently ratified by the British government.

This chapter has three parts. First, I outline the historical shift away from the public regulation of domestic life toward private choice and the legislative changes which follow this trend. I then discuss the research evidence about children's wellbeing and parental divorce. The final section of the chapter will return to the current legislative proposals and the ways in which these might be modified to protect children more adequately and so provide some compromise between the thrust towards private ordering in domestic life and the rights of children in matters concerning their lives.

The trend toward the privatization of domestic life

There has been a very substantial increase in the rates of divorce since the dissolution of marriages first became a matter for the civil courts through the Matrimonial Causes Act 1857. There was a relatively slow rise in divorce numbers over the following century, though with sharp peaks following the First and Second World Wars. But then the rate accelerated significantly, with a steep increase from the late 1950s until the early 1970s, not just in Britain but more or less throughout the industrialized world (Goode, 1993). For the past two decades rates have stabilized: only a very slight increase has been recorded. There has been much academic debate about the reasons for this pattern of change. There is now a reasonable degree of support for a view which sees a long-term accelerating trend combined with a variety of short-term factors operating from time to time which modify underlying upward trends. The long-term rising trend has been associated with the development of companionate marriage and the shift from marriage as an institution to it being seen as a relationship (Phillips, 1988). Increasingly, marriage has come to be regarded as a matter of individual choice with high expectations of a shared emotional, social and sexual relationship (Gillis, 1985; Richards, 1993). Particularly in the period since the late 1950s, the belief has grown up that if a marriage relationship does not work out, it is appropriate to try again with a new partner. In economic and social terms divorce has come into the reach of the whole population in the period after the Second World War. The poorest came to afford it economically, while those in public life or with a social position to uphold could afford it socially as the stigma that had been attached to divorce has largely disappeared. This rising trend has been modified from time to time by other factors, such as the disruption to conjugal life that was brought about by the First and Second World Wars. In the late 1950s and 1960s, the increase was probably accelerated by the growing participation of married women in the labour force and the increased ability of women on their own with children to support themselves through employment and/or state benefits. Conversely, rates in the 1980s and 1990s may well have been depressed by difficulties for separating people in finding affordable housing and by an increasing acknowledgment of the difficulties faced by children at parental divorce. The self-help books of the 1960s which portrayed divorce as the optimistic beginning of the rest of your life are now replaced by others which emphasize the economic, social and emotional problems that divorce may bring for parents and their children.

The long-term trend of rising divorce rates has been accompanied by other demographic changes which are associated with the privatization of relationships. Sexual relationships before (and after) and outside marriage have become much more common (Reibstein and Richards, 1992; Johnson et al., 1994). Cohabitation has become more frequent and socially acceptable and increasingly involves childbearing (Kiernan and Wicks, 1990; Utting, 1995; Richards, 1995b).

These changes in norms and attitudes towards family life are reflected in successive reforms of divorce legislation. The first Matrimonial Causes Act 1857 embodied the principles that had been used in earlier divorces obtained through private Acts of Parliament. Divorce was only obtainable if a sexual offence could be proved, simple adultery in the case of women but adultery compounded by other offences in the case of men. The grounds were widened in the next major reform in 1937 to include cruelty, desertion and insanity. Then in 1969 came the introduction of a single basis for divorce – irretrievable breakdown of the marriage – but this still needed to be demonstrated by a list of marital offences which followed earlier legislation but now included the 'no fault' grounds of separation. This progression is completed by the 1996 Family Law Bill which abolishes all grounds and simply requires a spouse to register a wish to divorce without needing to provide any account at all of the history of the marriage (see Fine and Fine (1994) for some comparative discussion of these trends). Over the century and a half of divorce legislation the emphasis has changed from the question of whether or not there is sufficient evidence to justify a divorce to that of settling disputes about property and children under a system where the divorce itself is a foregone conclusion. In other words, the system has changed from one which has the primary concern of regulating exits from marriage[2] to one which adjudicates in disputes that may arise when relationships end.

The legal treatment of children of divorcing couples has a somewhat different history from that of divorce itself. Up to the Second World War, the courts regarded children in much the same way as property: as something to be divided between the spouses. In the last century the sexual double standard was extended to motherhood. A woman who committed adultery was considered to be an unfit mother and her children would be awarded to her husband who would then pass them on to servants or female relatives to bring them up. As we move into the present century, with ideas of (middle-class) marriage as shared domestic life with the women as home makers and mothers growing in strength, the pattern of custody of children after divorce shifted toward a presumption that the pattern in marriage of childcare by the mother will continue after a divorce. By the 1940s, the courts' role in deciding childcare arrangements in cases where there was a dispute was extended to one of exercising protection over children. As Douglas, Murch and Perry describe (1996), by 1947 the Committee on Procedures in Matrimonial Causes argued that divorcing parents have no right to determine the future of their children. Procedures were set up which, in theory at least, allowed the courts to check the welfare of children and the suitability of the arrangements for their care. However, after the Children Act 1989, the emphasis on the welfare of children changed once again with parental responsibility (rather than rights) becoming the central theme. In the period when privatization becomes significant in adult relationships, with cohabitation serving not simply as a prelude to marriage but increasingly as a substitute for it, the theme in family law is of a hands-off approach which minimizes intervention (Bainham, 1990). In other words, as relationships become more privatized, the law has privatized the public interest in children. In the Children Act there is a presumption that parents' responsibilities toward their children which existed within marriage will extend through divorce, so that there is no requirement for the court to make any order about the children (Roche, 1991; Hoggett, 1994). Divorcing parents simply provide the court with a written 'statement of arrangements'. Apart from the addition of an 'information appointment' at which the initiating spouse (in the great majority of cases the wife, if current patterns persist) is given information about the needs of children, these Children Act procedures will remain unchanged under the proposals of the Family Law Bill 1996.

It can be argued – and was – that the pre-Children Act 1989 divorce procedures were ineffective in achieving their aim of checking the welfare of children. However, it was also said that these procedures had an important symbolic function in that they indicated directly to parents that society recognizes that divorce can make difficulties for children and that there is a public interest in parental care and children's welfare. Such a public concern is in line with the UN Convention on the Rights of the Child which in article 9 says that 'states parties shall ensure that a child shall not be separated from his or her parents against their will' and further that 'states parties shall respect the right of the child who is separated from one or both parents to maintain personal relations and direct contact with both parents on a regular basis, except if it is contrary to the child's best interest' (see Children Rights Office 1995 for a discussion of implications of the Convention for children within the family).

So while procedures which allow divorcing parents to make arrangements for the children without any necessity of seeking court orders, or being subject to a direct welfare check, are very much in line with the process of the privatization of domestic relationships and private ordering (Bainham, 1990), they run counter to the movement, expressed in the UN Convention, that children have specific rights to relationships with their parents that the state has a duty to protect.

The wellbeing of children and parental divorce

Since divorce rates entered a phase of rapid increase in the 1960s (Goode, 1993) there has been a growing body of research on the wellbeing of children whose parents separate. The large body of research has been reviewed many times and the overall pattern of findings is now well-established (Rutter, 1981; Hetherington, Cox and Cox, 1982; Richards and Dyson, 1982; Burgoyne, Ormrod and Richards, 1987; Richards, 1987; Demo and Acock, 1988; Emery, 1988; Hetherington and Arasteh, 1988; Amato and Keith, 1991a; Hetherington and Clingempeel, 1992; Amato, 1993; Richards, 1996; see also Demo, 1995).

Parental separation is almost always very distressing for children. From the time when it becomes clear to children that their parents' marriage or cohabitation is in serious difficulty, most children will become distressed and upset and will express this in a variety of ways. For some children this point will come long before the separation itself takes place, while for a few, there will be little or no warning before the split occurs. Most children deeply resent their parents' separation, even when they may intellectually accept the reasons for it, as may be the case with older children. Parental separation makes children feel angry, sad, powerless and abandoned. Resentment often arises because children feel that their parents have chosen to do something which is against their own interests – interests which their parents ought to protect (Walzak and Burns, 1984; Mitchell, 1985).

Children's anger is not always expressed directly toward their parents: it may be redirected towards others or internalized. So around the time of separation children often become difficult and aggressive, or quiet, moody and withdrawn. School work may suffer (Elliott and Richards, 1991; Bhrolchain, Chappell and Diamond, 1994). Children may get into difficulties in their relationships with both adults and other children. While most children will show some signs of distress, reactions are varied in both their intensity and kind. Much will depend on the particular circumstances, the child's character, the quality of their relationship with each parent and their gender and age. Along with their distress, children may develop an earlier social maturity after separation which has both positive and negative aspects (Weiss, 1979). For most children the acute phase of upset and distress gradually resolves. The time course for this is variable, though evidence indicates that within a couple of years most children will have reached a new equilibrium. Much may depend on how supportive and consistent the living arrangements are after separation.

In the longer term, compared with those of similar social background whose parents remain married, children whose parents have divorced show consistent, but small, differences in their behaviour, as has been demonstrated in several longitudinal studies (e.g. Kiernan, 1986; Kalter, 1987; Maclean and Wadsworth, 1988; Kuh and Maclean, 1990; Elliott and Richards, 1991; Maclean and Kuh, 1991; Kiernan, 1992; Amato, 1994; Rodgers, 1994;

Bhrolchain, Chappell and Diamond, 1995; Chase-Lansdale, Cherlin and Kiernan, 1995; Cherlin, Kiernan and Chase-Lansdale, 1995). A number of transitions to adulthood are reached at earlier average ages, especially in girls. These include leaving home, beginning heterosexual relations and entering cohabitation, marriage and childbearing. Educational attainments may be reduced. In young adulthood there is a tendency towards more changes of job, lower socioeconomic status, a greater propensity to divorce and there are some indications of a higher incidence of depression and lower levels of psychological wellbeing. The relationships with parents and other kin may be more distant and complex (Richards, 1996).

The links between the degree of distress a child may exhibit around the time of separation and the longer term effects are complex. Assessments of behaviour problems around the time of separation have not been a good predictor of the likelihood of long-term problems. Indeed, there are some indications of a *negative* association suggesting that the children who express their distress at the time are more likely to do better in the long term (Elliott, Richards and Warwick, 1993).

There appears to be a secular trend in the findings for children and young adults with fewer and smaller differences being found in some of the most recent studies (e.g. Morrison and Cherlin, 1995; Sweeting and West, 1995). However, comparison between studies is difficult because of differences in the populations and the measures used. If there is indeed a change, it could be ascribed to a reduction in the stigma of divorce, a growing appreciation by both parents and professionals of the difficulties that children may face and the adoption of strategies to minimize the effects.

Processes that may affect children

At or before separation

There is abundant evidence that marital conflict has damaging effects for children (Grych and Fincham, 1990). Effects are most marked when conflict is intense, frequent and involves violence. When it directly involves children, because they are present, or even more so when they are the subject of the conflict, effects are most marked. On the other hand, when marital quarrels and anger are seen by children to be resolved, they are much less distressing.

Parents engaged in the emotional turmoil of a decaying marriage have been shown to have poorer psychological and physical health (Amato and Keith, 1991b). There may be a decline in household income, presumably because of difficulties that may follow at work. These sorts of stresses may also reduce the capacity to look after children adequately and consistently.

When a parent moves out, some of the immediate conflict and stress within the home may be reduced, but new factors enter the situation that may reduce or eliminate any benefit that the reduction in stress might bring. Most obviously, the child's relationship with the departing parent will take on a new intermittent pattern, or may end (Simpson, McCarthy and Walker, 1995). The remaining parent (most often, the mother) will face a series of emotional and practical problems. Preoccupation with these may reduce effective parenting and household routines may become, at least temporarily, disorganized and erratic. A child who is likely to be extremely distressed and anxious at the departure of the other parent and who is seeking comfort, stability and reassurance may find that the remaining parent is emotionally unavailable to them. While this acute phase may be short-lived, it can be particularly distressing, especially for children who do not have relatives or other adults, apart from their parents, who can offer support.

Research suggests that at the time a parent moves out a majority of children have not had a clear explanation of what is happening from either parent (Mitchell, 1985). Without such explanations children's fantasies and anxieties may grow and they may come to feel further neglected and rejected by their parents. Self-esteem, which may already have fallen because of preseparation conflict, may be further depressed by a lack of direct communication with parents. Matters can be made worse if children face an immediate move of home. This may mean a change of school and loss of friends. Stability of place and social networks are likely to be especially important at times of major emotional upheaval for children.

In most cases parents are in broad agreement about caretaking arrangements after separation. Within the marriage the mother is most likely to have been the major caretaker, and so it is after separation. Most couples assume that the children will remain with the mother and the relationship with the father will become intermittent. Immediately after separation, very frequent contact with the father (visits, phone calls, letters, etc.) seems especially important to reassure children that the relationship will persist. Not surprisingly, many children (especially younger ones) who have witnessed the breakdown in their parents' relationship, become anxious that their own relationship with either or both parents may end. Where there is disagreement about arrangements, continuing uncertainty may contribute to children's general feelings of anxiety. Dispute resolution through mediation has been shown to be beneficial to children. To quote the abstract of the Dillon and Emery (1996) study:

> In this follow-up study, separated parents who had been randomly assigned to the option of resolving disputes through traditional adversarial methods or through mediation were contacted nine years post-settlement. By parents' reports on phone surveys, mediation non-custodial parents currently had more frequent contact and were more involved in current decisions about the children. Mediation parents had communicated about the children on a more frequent basis in the time since the dispute was resolved.

The longer term

The key issues for the longer term appear to be the quality of the relationships with the residential and non-residential parents and economic factors, together with any residual effects of the disturbance experienced around the time of the separation. When post-separation arrangements are relatively stable, household income levels do not fall too far, and children maintain good relationships with their mother and their father and their wider kin, there seems to be the best chance of children recovering from behaviour and health problems or reduced self-esteem, if these have been a problem around the time of separation. Results of studies of step-parent households suggest that, in general, the mother's remarriage (or cohabitation) makes relatively little difference overall to the longer term wellbeing of the children compared with households where the mother remains on her own. Household incomes tend to rise with the advent of a new partner but such benefits that may follow from this may be offset by the difficulties that children sometimes face coping with their mother's new partner and the changes that may follow in their relationship with their mother (Ihinger-Tallman, 1988). Remarriage (or cohabitation) of either parent also tends to be associated with a decline in children's contact with the father (or the non-resident parent).

After separation regular contact with fathers (or the non-resident parent) tends to decline over time. We do not have good recent surveys but a reasonable guess might be that about one-third of children have lost regular contact with their father within a couple of years of separation. Such a guess assumes that levels of contact have improved over the past decade or so, as public attitudes and professional practice have become more supportive of post-separation father-child relationships (see Simpson, McCarthy and Walker, 1995). Conflict between parents which persists beyond separation is associated with reduced or an ending of contact with the non-residential parent. However, conflict seems to have less direct effect on the quality of parent-child relationships (provided these have the opportunity to continue) than conflict when the parents are still living together (Emery, 1988).

Some studies have shown that for a small minority of children, a separation is followed by a series of disruptions with several successive step-figures coming and going through their childhood. Continuing change seems to be particularly distressing for children and those who experience this are more likely to face significant longer term problems (Cockett and Tripp, 1994).

There are a growing number of studies which suggest that the style and consistency of parental care for children is a more significant indicator for future problems than the structure of the household a child is living in (Hetherington and Clingempeel, 1992; McFarlane, Bellissimo and Norman, 1995). Where caretaking is warm, consistent and authoritative (in that it sets clear and appropriate limits for children), children do best. However, we know that sometimes it may be very difficult to maintain such caretaking through the upheavals and emotional turmoil that are associated with many separations. But this research strongly suggests that we should not let all our attention be focused on conflict resolution at divorce; we also need to do all we can to support the parenting roles of both mothers and fathers after divorce.

Consequences persisting into adulthood are likely to be a combination of the residual effects of much earlier events (such as continued loss of self-esteem) and others that arise from weakened family relationships and ties (see Tasker and Richards, 1994). Effects seem to be particularly marked for women rather than men and for those from middle-class rather than working-class homes of origin (Elliott and Richards, 1991). The emotional and economic support from kin may be of great significance for young adults as they come to set up their own homes, seek employment, start businesses and so on. Kin ties may be lost as a consequence of the earlier parental divorce. Where parents form new households with further children after a separation, the children in these later households may get preferential treatment for continuing economic support for such things as education and the establishment of independent households (Amato, Rezac and Booth, 1995; Ganong, Coleman and Mistina, 1995).

Research and social policy

The research that has been outlined in this chapter provides associations between parental separation and divorce and a number of aspects of the lives of teenagers and young adults. If we are to devise policies which may reduce the negative association, the first step is to define the processes which may provide the link between the ending of the parental marriage and the lives of young adults. The three principal ones will be discussed in turn.

Relationships with mothers and fathers

Parental divorce and separation bring profound changes in the nature and quality of parental relationships. In most cases at separation, children remain with the mother while the father becomes, at best, a visitor in their lives. Relationships with both parents are likely to change. Initially at least, during the upheavals and emotional turmoil that usually accompany separation, relationships often deteriorate as parents are likely to be particularly preoccupied with their own lives and concerns. As new household patterns become established, there may well be some redrawing of the intergenerational boundaries, especially with older children. This may be associated with the advanced social maturity that has been described for children in single-parent households.

Research suggests that in itself, growing up in a single-parent household may not be of significant disadvantage to children (Ferri, 1976). It is the *change* from two parents to a single residential parent, especially when this is brought about by divorce (rather than the death of a parent) that is significant (Richards, 1987), coupled with the usual, but not inevitable, low income for households of separated mothers (see below).

It is widely assumed that, post-divorce, children do best if they maintain a good relationship with both parents. While this may be argued on general developmental grounds, the direct evidence to support this assumption is very sparse as much of the required research remains to be done. However, it is demonstrated that it is not simply a matter of the presence or absence of a parent in a child's life that is significant, but the style and patterning of parent-child relationships (Amato, 1993). Given the likelihood of a continuing relationship with the mother rather than the father, it is the quality of the mother-child relationship that has most salience for most children. However, the father-child relationship is also of significance (Amato, 1994). Children do not seem to do particularly well (or badly) if they grow up in a single-parent household with a parent of the same sex (Downey and Powell, 1993). What is obvious is that post-divorce, as within marriage, the great bulk of childcare is provided by women. Female-headed single-parent households tend to be poorer than those headed by men. Because of the difficulties in obtaining adequate childcare, many women leave the labour force when their marriages end.

The arrival of new partners may create further periods of family upheaval and times when parents' attention may be distracted from the children, although, overall, children who grow up in step-families do almost as well as those who stay with a single parent (Ihinger-Tallman, 1988). It may well be that the rise in household income that usually follows a remarriage (or cohabitation) may offset some of the social and psychological complications that a new partner usually brings. Teenagers, especially girls, tend to leave home earlier if there has been a parental divorce, especially if this is followed by a remarriage (Kiernan, 1992). This may lead young people to be removed from the direct influence of parents (and may, for example, be associated with an earlier entry into sexual relationships). The social, emotional and economic ties between parents and children, and with other kin (Simpson, 1994), may be changed by divorce with lifelong effects (White, 1992, 1994). As, for instance, a divorced father may provide less assistance to his young adult children (Amato, Rezac and Booth, 1995) while elderly divorced people may both offer and receive less help from their children (Eggebeen, 1992).

From this discussion two priorities for social policy emerge: encouragement for both mothers and fathers (and the wider kin) to remain in relationships with children, not simply during their childhood but throughout the life span; and support for the parenting role in the period around separation and divorce.

Conflict between parents

Conflict between parents who live together can have negative effects for children (Slater and Haber, 1984) and this has been suggested as a major source of difficulty for children of separated parents and, in particular, is associated with low self-esteem (Amato, 1993, but see Clark and Barber, 1994, for a contrary view). Low self-esteem may be a significant factor in the reduced educational attainment and some of the social and relationship problems which have been associated with parental divorce.

Marital conflict can be acted out in a variety of ways which may have differential effects on children (Katz and Gottman, 1993). The conflict will often persist after separation, but the ways it may affect children at that time may be rather different to when the two parents were living together. While parents are together it may be important whether or not they involve the children in their quarrels, either directly by using them as the subject of conflicts or more indirectly by conducting their rows in the presence of children. After separation a major effect of continued conflict is that it can reduce or end contact with the non-residential parent. This may be through the denial of contact or, more indirectly, by creating a situation in which a child feels that it is too emotionally dangerous and disloyal to the resident parent to visit the non-resident parent. Hearing one parent denigrating the other, to whom the child will feel attachment, is likely to be particularly damaging to the child's self-esteem.

The policy aim in this area would be to reduce conflict between parents both in marriage and after separation. Where that cannot be done, encouraging parents to play out their conflict in ways which do not involve their children is likely to be beneficial.

Economic factors

Divorce almost always brings a sharp decline in income for households headed by women (e.g. Everett, 1991; Maclean, 1991; Jackson *et al.*, 1993). For many women it may bring the first experience of living on state benefits. Poverty and low incomes damage the life chances of children (see Oppenheim, 1993). Research suggests that some of the differences between children associated with divorce and separation are mediated by the fall in income though this cannot account for all the associations. This is perhaps most obvious in cases where there is a remarriage (see Elliott and Richards, 1991). In general, remarriage restores incomes to something approaching the pre-divorce situation. However, outcomes for children are no better, and sometimes worse, than where mothers with children remain on their own. Presumably the advantages that an increased income may bring are offset by the upheaval and complex dynamics for children of the advent of a new partner for their mother.

The economic disadvantages of parental divorce may continue into adulthood not only because of the accumulated effects of deprivation in childhood but also because intergenerational transfers of money and support which could benefit adults may be disrupted by parental divorce and remarriage (White, 1992).

In recent years a number of jurisdictions have introduced child-support schemes which are intended to increase the support provided for children by non-resident parents, usually fathers (Maclean, 1994; Rhoades, 1995). Typically such schemes prioritize children in first relationships, while the previous practice as in England and Wales, which had been supported by the courts and the tax and benefit systems, has been for men to give priority to the children of their current relationship. While preliminary studies of the scheme in Britain suggest it makes little difference to the income of households of divorced and separated women and their children (Clarke, Glendinning and Craig, 1994; Garnham and Knights, 1994; Gillespie, 1996), the importance of these schemes in the longer term may be the way in which they aim to uphold the interests of the children of earlier relationships and their carers. In time, if these aims are achieved, there may be significant consequences in reducing the economic effects of parental divorce for children. However, under pressure from those parents directly affected, government changes are placing this aim in danger. Because rather different issues are involved in policy questions concerning the economic support of children and their mothers after separation which would take us away from the main themes of this chapter, these questions will not be pursued further here. However, it is important not to underplay the profound economic consequences of divorce for children or, indeed, to detach consideration of the economic ties of family and kin from the social relationships.

How do we regard children?

There is a general issue which needs to be raised at this point in the discussion. The research which has been described in this chapter is dominated by a conceptualization of children as vulnerable and consequently in need of protection when their parents' marriage runs into difficulties or ends. Children are seen as the *objects* rather than the subject in the research and not as social actors in their own right (see James, 1995a; Morrow and Richards, 1996). Thus the research on parental divorce and children is focused on later undesirable characteristics and life situations. Avoiding these 'outcomes' then becomes the objective of welfare and social policies. While desirable policies may receive support from this approach, it ignores other central issues. Welfare approaches to issues related to children at divorce have put increasing emphasis on the best interests of children in decision-making about them in the sociolegal process. However, given the conception of children as vulnerable, this decision-making is dominated by adults – parents and professionals – in processes which pay little or no attention to the voices of the children themselves. This exclusion of the children is further encouraged by debates which present decision-making about children at divorce as a power struggle between the genders – as represented by the two parents.

However, if children are seen as social actors, their own views and desires in the situation become a key concern (Landsdown, 1995). With a few honourable exceptions (e.g. Walzak and Burns, 1984; Mitchell, 1985), the research that has been described does not investigate children's views and experiences directly. This gap becomes particularly crucial if it is acknowledged – as the Children Act 1989 does, for example – that children should be consulted about important decisions concerning their lives. Where children have been directly consulted in research studies, it becomes clear that the failure to inform them about what is happening when the parents' marriage ends or to let them express their wishes is, in itself, a source of distress and may lead to feelings of rejection (e.g. Mitchell, 1985). While informing children is relatively straightforward given sensitivity from parents and others who are involved, it is a great deal more complicated to ensure that their voices are heard. This is especially so in a culture in which their opinions are not usually sought on matters that affect them. There are particular difficulties in determining the views of children over decisions that concern them when there is disagreement between the parents over these. The classic dilemma arises over decisions about where children should live. In a small minority of divorce cases, both mother and father want the children to live with them. If the dispute reaches the court a decision has to be taken about their place of residence. In this situation most children want their parents to stay together, so any direct question to them about where they want to live is unanswerable. The question is also potentially very distressing to children as it may seem to shift responsibility from their parents to them for actions in which they have had no part. I return to this point in the concluding section of the chapter, but here I want to make the point that the lack of relevant research makes discussion of how children could or should be involved in decision-making at divorce much more difficult than it should be.

Ways forward

In the first part of this chapter I argued that there has been a progressive privatization of family life which has been accompanied by a parallel shift from public ordering in the courts, towards private ordering by individuals. While private ordering may be acceptable or desirable for adults at divorce,[3] it conflicts with measures that may serve to protect the interests of children. More specifically, I have suggested the Children Act 1989 presumption of a continuation of parental responsibilities through divorce, without a requirement for the court to make orders concerning children, and in the absence of welfare checks, may not be in the best interests of children. I now return to these broader issues in the light of discussion of research on children and divorce.

In discussing the Children Act 1989 as related to divorce, one of its architects, Brenda Hoggett (1994), argues that the function of the law should be adjudication rather than welfare. She suggests that attempts at welfare, such as the old Section 41 hearing at which a parent would present their plans for the care of their children face-to-face in court for scrutiny, were ineffective. As a concession to those who argued that measures should be retained in the Children Act – not least for their symbolic value – a statement of arrangements was required to be submitted though the matter was dealt with by post rather than a face-to-face meeting in court. The proposal is for these arrangements to remain in the 1996 Family Law Bill. If the argument is accepted that the court should not or cannot undertake a welfare function in relation to children, there is no dispute, save to ask how the state can fulfil the obligation of the UN Convention to protect children's rights to a continuing relationship with both parents and to give them a voice in important decisions concerning their lives? But I suggest we should be slow to accept the argument that courts' functions should be limited to adjudication and should exclude any welfare function.

In a number of ways the Family Law Bill could fulfil some of the policy objectives I have highlighted in the last section. The abolition of fault and the current requirement to present a petition outlining the grounds on which a divorce is sought has long been argued to be a desirable step likely to reduce conflict between separating spouses (Burgoyne, Ormrod and Richards, 1987; Davis and Murch, 1988). So too is the acknowledgment that the granting of the divorce itself is an administrative matter, and that the core of the socio-legal process should be the settlement of issues concerning children, property and income. As the White Paper suggests, both the proposed initial information appointment and the emphasis on mediation are likely to serve these same policy objectives. American studies of mediation (Emery, 1994) suggest that, compared with lawyer-negotiated settlements or those decided in court, it encourages parents to agree on caretaking arrangements that preserve children's relationships with both parents. Both the provision of direct counselling for children when appropriate (Richards, 1994) and of a range of support services for parents under stress (Smith and Pugh, 1995) would follow in the spirit of the proposed legislation and, again, flow with the policy objectives I have outlined. It is to be hoped that such initiatives will receive government support in the wake of the Bill.

For cases where disputes about children are not resolved by mediation or other negotiations, court procedures will follow current arrangements. This means that a welfare report can be ordered by the court and that this will usually provide a recommendation to the court in the light of the particular parental circumstances and includes a view of the children's wishes. However, restriction of budgets and a shift in emphasis by court welfare officers from a welfare stance to one concerned more with mediation, may have reduced the role of these reports in protecting children's interests (James, 1995b). We should also note that while it is for the courts to decide whether to order these reports, there is no requirement to do so. However, under the new legislation it is hoped that fewer cases will reach the court for adjudication as more will be settled along the way by mediation and other means. So, given that the few cases that do reach court should be the most complicated and may often involve the most conflicted parents, there is a strong argument to make such reports mandatory (as already is the case in Northern Ireland) in all cases that reach the court for adjudication.

In most cases both parents assume that the children will remain with the mother – who will have been the major caretaker in the marriage – and the father will become a visitor in their lives. So there is no dispute about arrangements for the children, except perhaps about who will pay what toward their upkeep. The key issue in these cases is whether or not the state is justified in making any intervention at all. Under the new arrangements, the initiating spouse will be given information about the needs of children and presumably this will include encouragement for both parents to continue to maintain good relationships with their children. At the conclusion of the divorce process a statement of arrangements for the children will have to be filed in court. Are these procedures sufficient to ensure that the best possible arrangements are made for children and their voice has been heard in the decision-making? If we think not, how can procedures be made more effective? One route here is to follow Australia where the concept of a parenting plan has been introduced. Here parents are required to make a much more detailed statement to the court about their proposals for the children. They are provided with a kit of how to do this with suggestions of how the children may be included in the process. The aim is not so much to produce a document that could subsequently be used for enforcement, but rather to encourage parents to think about and address the relevant issues for children. This seems a very interesting experiment. If it works, it could provide an admirable compromise between procedures which effectively make no public attempt to provide a welfare function for children and others which could be overly intrusive and heavy handed.

While few cases of dispute concerning children may reach court, it should not be assumed that the remainder do not involve conflict. Many of them will involve disputes and disagreements between the parents about the children which are settled along the way. Under the new arrangements, parents will be encouraged to use mediation to settle such disputes. But, as at present, negotiations between solicitors will continue to remain important for many couples. How are children's interests represented in either of these dispute-resolution processes? In those cases which are settled by negotiations between solicitors there are no procedures which safeguard children or protect their interests. Children are very seldom seen by solicitors. And we should note that at divorce, solicitors are representing one or other of the parents, not their children. Arrangements about visits to the non-resident parent, for instance, may be as much a compromise between proposals from the two parents than any attempt to meet the needs of children. Here, as within marriage, it is the parents who are taken to represent the interests of children.

In mediation a similar issue arises (Garwood, 1992). It has been suggested that as part of the mediation process a mediator could see the children on their own to hear their views and then introduce these views into the session with parents. However, such a process runs the danger that it may destroy the neutral and independent role of the mediator who would then become a third party to the negotiations (Richards, 1994). A few mediators sometimes use a technique which at least gives children a degree of involvement in the proceedings while protecting them from having to carry any responsibility for parental decision-making. Here children are invited to a final mediation session when an agreement has been reached to hear directly from their parents what is proposed. Seeing the parents together describing the agreed arrangements may carry great symbolic significance for children – as well as ensuring that they also have a chance to clarify details and to have things which are unclear explained to them. This technique preserves the neutrality of the mediator and also the generation boundary between the adult business of negotiation of arrangements and the children. To a degree, children are being provided with a voice without having to carry the responsibility of being forced to make a decision which they could feel involves taking sides. It is at least arguable that such a procedure would satisfy Article 9 of the UN Convention on the Rights of the Child. Though I am not aware that it ever happens, such a children's meeting could be set up as part of a solicitor-negotiated settlement.

Conclusion

In this chapter I have drawn a connection between the privatization of domestic relationships and the shift in family-law matters from public to private ordering. I have suggested that these parallel historical developments present a problem if we wish to continue to have special procedures to protect the interests and welfare of children at divorce. However, I have suggested a number of ways in which this problem can at least be partially solved in the context of the proposed procedures for divorce embodied in the Family Law Bill currently before Parliament. However, if parents chose not to marry, they cannot divorce. In so far as procedures designed to protect the interests of children are linked to divorce, they cannot operate to protect children when cohabitations end. Given the increasing reluctance of the state to intervene in any family matters, it seems most unlikely that any measures to regulate the ending of cohabitation in the same way as divorce would be acceptable. This means that as childbearing within cohabitation becomes more common, we are being forced to give up any measures by the state to protect the interests and welfare of a growing proportion of children whose parents separate. Should this point persuade us to give up the apparently unequal struggle of trying to safeguard the welfare and interests of children at divorce through the legal system? We might then follow Douglas, Murch and Perry's (1996) suggestions that the welfare of children at divorce should become a matter for social and health services, not the law. In that way we could perhaps detach the issue of child welfare from the marital status of parents.

Acknowledgments

I should like to thank Jill Brown for her skilled technical assistance with this chapter. I should also like to thank Ginny Morrow and Ros Pickford for comments on a draft and for earlier discussion of some of the issues and Wanda Jackson and Kitty Wells for general encouragement.

Notes

1 That is the position as of March 1996. However, it is possible that amendments will be introduced which may alter the details of the legislation.
2 In this era divorce was extremely expensive and limited to the rich. Those less well-off could obtain separation orders in the magistrates courts which provided for arrangements for support and care of children but did not end the marriage, so barring remarriage.
3 It has been suggested that it may favour men rather than women, and the articulate and well-informed rather than the less articulate and ill-informed, but these issues will not be pursued here.

References

AMATO, P. R. (1993) 'Children's adjustment to divorce: theories, hypotheses, and empirical support', *Journal of Marriage and the Family*, **55**, pp. 23–38.
AMATO, P. R. (1994) 'Father-child relations, mother-child relations, and offspring psychological well-being in early adulthood', *Journal of Marriage and the Family*, **56**, pp. 1031–42.
AMATO, P. R. and KEITH, B. (1991a) 'Parental divorce and the well being of children: A meta-analysis', *Psychological Bulletin*, **110**, pp. 26–46.
AMATO, P. R. and KEITH, B. (1991b) 'Parental divorce and adult well being: A meta-analysis', *Journal of Marriage and the Family*, **55**, pp. 23–38.
AMATO, P. R., REZAC, S. J. and BOOTH, A. (1995) 'Helping between parents and young adult offspring: The role of parental marital quality, divorce and remarriage', *Journal of Marriage and the Family*, **57**, pp. 363–74.
BAINHAM, A. (1990) 'The privatisation of the public interest in children', *Modern Law Review*, **53**, pp. 206–21.

BHROLCHAIN, M. N., CHAPPELL, R. and DIAMOND, I. (1994) 'Scolarite et autres caracteristiques socio-demographiques des enfants de mariages rompus', *Population*, **49**, 1585–612.

BHROLCHAIN, M. N., CHAPPELL, R. and DIAMOND, I. (1995) '*How do the children of disrupted families fare in young adulthood?*', paper presented at 1995 Annual meeting of the Population Association of America, San Francisco.

BURGOYNE, J., ORMROD, R. and RICHARDS, M. (1987) *Divorce Matters*, Harmondsworth, Penguin Books.

CHASE-LANSDALE, P., CHERLIN, A. J. and KIERNAN, K. E. (1995) 'The long term effects of parental divorce on the mental health of young adults: A developmental perspective', *Child Development*, **66**, pp. 1614–34.

CHERLIN, A. J., KIERNAN, K. E. and CHASE-LANSDALE, P. L. (1995) 'Parental divorce in childhood and demographic outcomes in young adulthood', *Demography*, **32**, pp. 299–318.

CHILDREN'S RIGHTS OFFICE (1995) *Building Small Democracies*, London, CRO.

CLARK, J. and BARBER, B. L. (1994) 'Adolescents in post divorce and always-married families: Self esteem and perceptions of father's interest', *Journal of Marriage and the Family*, **56**, pp. 608–14.

CLARKE, K., GLENDINNING, L. and CRAIG, G. (1994) *Losing Support. Children and the Child Support Act*, London, The Children's Society.

COCKETT, M. and TRIPP, J. (1994) *The Exeter Family Study. Family Breakdown and its Impact on Children*, Exeter, University of Exeter Press.

DAVIS, G. and MURCH, M. (1988) *Grounds for Divorce*, Oxford, Clarendon Press.

DEMO, D. E. (1995) 'The relentless search for effects of divorce: Forging new trails or tumbling down the beaten path', *Journal of Marriage and the Family*, **55**, pp. 42–5.

DEMO, D. K. and ACOCK, A. C. (1988) 'The impact of divorce on children', *Journal of Marriage and the Family*, **50**, pp. 619–48.

DILLON, P. A. and EMERY, R. E. (1996) 'Long term effects of divorce mediation in a field study of child custody dispute resolution', *American Journal of Orthopsychiatry* (in press).

DOUGLAS, G., MURCH, M. and PERRY, A. (1996) 'Supporting children when parents separate – a neglected family justice or mental health issue?', *The Child and Family Law Quarterly* (in press).

DOWNEY, D. B. and POWELL, B. (1993) 'Do children in single parent households fare better living with same sex parents?', *Journal of Marriage and the Family*, **55**, pp. 65–71.

EGGEBEEN, D. J. (1992) 'Family structure and intergenerational exchanges', *Research on Ageing*, **14**, pp. 427–47.

ELLIOTT, B. J. and RICHARDS, M. P. M. (1991) 'Children and divorce: Educational performance and behaviour before and after parental separation', *International Journal of Law and the Family*, **5**, pp. 258–76.

ELLIOTT, B. J., RICHARDS, M. and WARWICK, H. (1993) *The Consequences of Divorce for the Health and Well Being of Adults and Children. Vol. 2. Children*, Cambridge, Centre for Family Research, University of Cambridge, unpublished.

EMERY, R. E. (1988) *Marriage, Divorce and Children's Adjustment*, California, Sage.

EMERY, R. E. (1994) *Renegotiating Family Relationships. Divorce, Child Custody and Mediation*, New York, Guilford Press.

EVERETT, C. A. (1991) *The Consequences of Divorce. Economic and Custodial Impact on Children and Adults*, New York, Haworth Press.

FERRI, E. (1976) *Growing Up in a One-Parent Family*, Slough, National Foundation for Educational Research Publishing Company.

FINE, M. A. and FINE, D. R. (1994) 'An examination and evaluation of recent changes in divorce laws in five Western countries. The critical role of values', *Journal of Marriage and the Family*, **56**, pp. 249–63.

GANONG, L. H., COLEMAN, M. and MISTINA, D. (1995) 'Normative beliefs about parents' and stepparents' financial obligations to children following divorce and remarriage', *Family Relations*, **44**, pp. 306–15.

GARNHAM, A. and KNIGHTS, E. (1994) *Putting the Treasury First: The Truth about Child Support*, London, Child Poverty Action Group.

GARWOOD, F. (1992) 'Conciliation: A forum for children's views?' *Children and Society*, **6**, pp. 353–63.

GILLESPIE, G. (1996) 'Child support – the hand that rocks the cradle', *Family Law*, **26**, pp. 162–4.

GILLIS, J. R. (1985) *For Better, For Worse: British Marriages 1600 to the Present*, New York, Oxford University Press.

GOODE, W. J. (1993) *World Changes in Divorce Patterns*, New Haven, Conn., New Haven.

GRYCH, J. H. and FINCHAM, F. D. (1990) 'Marital conflict and children's adjustment: A cognitive-contextual framework', *Psychological Bulletin*, **108**, pp. 267–90.

HETHERINGTON, E. M. and ARASTEH, J. D. (1988) *Impact of Divorce, Single Parenting, and Stepparenting on Children*, Hillsdale, NJ, Erlbaum.

HETHERINGTON, E. M. and CLINGEMPEEL, W. G. (1992) 'Coping with marital transitions', *Monograph of the Society for Research in Child Development*, **57**, Nos. 2–3.

HETHERINGTON, E. M., COX, M. and COX, R. (1982) 'Effects of divorce on parents and children', in LAMB, M. E. (Ed.) *Non-Traditional Families: Parenting and Child Development*, Hillsdale, NJ, Erlbaum.

HOGGETT, B. (1994) 'Joint parenting systems: The English experiment', *Journal of Child Law*, **6**, pp. 8–12.

IHINGER-TALLMAN, M. (1988) 'Research on stepfamilies', *Annual Review of Sociology*, **14**, pp. 25–48.

JACKSON, E., WASOFF, F., MACLEAN, M. and DOBASH, R. E. (1993) 'Financial support and divorce: The right mixture of rules and discretion', *International Journal of Law and the Family*, **7**, 230–54.

JAMES, A. (1995a) '*Methodologies of competence for a competent methodology?*', paper given at the 'Children and Social Competence' conference. Guildford, Surrey, July.

JAMES, A. L. (1995b) 'Social work in divorce: welfare, mediation and justice', *International Journal of Law and the Family*, **9**, pp. 256–74.

JOHNSON, A. M., WADSWORTH, J., WELLINGS, R. and FIELD, J. (1994) *Sexual Attitudes and Life Styles*, Oxford, Blackwell Scientific Publications.

KALTER, N. (1987) 'Long-term effects of divorce on children: A developmental vulnerability model', *American Journal of Orthopsychiatry*, **59**, pp. 587–600.

KATZ, L. F. and GOTTMAN, J. M. (1993) 'Patterns of marital conflict predict children's internalizing and externalizing behaviors', *Developmental Psychology*, **29**, pp. 940–50.

KIERNAN, K. (1986) 'Teenage marriage and marital breakdown', *Population Studies*, **37**, pp. 368–80.

KIERNAN, K. E. (1992) 'The impact of family disruption in childhood on transitions made in young adult life', *Population Studies*, **46**, pp. 213–21.

KIERNAN, K. and WICKS, M. (1990) *Family Change and Future Policy*, York, Joseph Rowntree Memorial Trust.

KUH, D. and MACLEAN, M. (1990) 'Women's childhood experience of parental separation and their subsequent health and socio-economic status in adulthood', *Journal of Biosocial Science*, **22**, pp. 1–15.

LANDSDOWN, G. (1995) *Taking Part. Children's Participation in Decision Making*, London, Institute for Public Policy Research.

LORD CHANCELLOR'S DEPARTMENT (1994) *Looking to the Future. Mediation and the Grounds for Divorce. A Consultation Paper*, CM. 2424, London, HMSO.

LORD CHANCELLOR'S DEPARTMENT (1995) *Looking to the Future. Mediation and the Grounds for Divorce*, CM. 2799, London, HMSO.

MACLEAN, M. (1991) *Surviving Divorce. Women's Resources after Separation*, London, Macmillan.

MACLEAN, M. (1994) 'Delegalizing child support', in MACLEAN, M. and KURCZEWSKI (Eds) *Families, Politics and the Law*, Oxford, Clarendon Press.

MACLEAN, M. and KUH, D. (1991) 'The long term effects for girls of parental divorce', in MACLEAN, M. and GROVES, D. (Eds) *Women's Issues in Social Policy*, London, Routledge.

MACLEAN, M. and WADSWORTH, M. E. J. (1988) 'The interests of children after parental divorce: A long term perspective', *International Journal of Law and the Family*, **2**, pp. 155–66.

MCFARLANE, A. H., BELLISSIMO, A. and NORMAN, G. R. (1995) 'Family structure, family functioning and adolescent well-being: The transcendent influence of parental style', *Journal of Child Psychology and Psychiatry*, **36**, pp. 847–64.

MITCHELL, A. (1985) *Children in the Middle*, London, Tavistock Publications.

MORRISON, D. R. and CHERLIN, A. J. (1995) 'The divorce process and young children's well-being: A prospective analysis', *Journal of Marriage and the Family*, **57**, pp. 800–12.

MORROW, V. and RICHARDS, M. P. M. (1996) 'The ethics of social research with children: An overview', *Children and Society* (in press).

OPPENHEIM, C. (1993) *Parenting: The Facts*, London, Child Poverty Action Group.

PHILLIPS, R. (1988) *Putting Asunder. A History of Divorce in Western Society*, Cambridge, Cambridge University Press.

PIPER, C. (1994) 'Looking to the future for children', *Journal of Child Law*, **6**, pp. 98–102.

REIBSTEIN, J. and RICHARDS, M. P. M. (1992) *Sexual Arrangements: Marriage and Affairs*, London, Heinemann.

RHOADES, H. (1995) 'Australians' child support scheme – is it working?', *Journal of Child Law*, **7**, pp. 26–37.

RICHARDS, M. P. M. (1987) 'Children, parents and families: Developmental psychology and the re-ordering of relationships at divorce', *International Journal of Law and the Family*, **1**, pp. 295–317.

RICHARDS, M. P. M. (1993) 'Learning from divorce', in CLULOW, C. (Ed.) *Does Marriage Matter?*, London, Karnac Books.

RICHARDS, M. P. M. (1994) 'Children: Giving a voice or addressing needs?' *Family Mediation*, **4**, p. 13.

RICHARDS, M. P. M. (1995a) 'But what about the children? Some reflections on the divorce White Paper', *Child and Family Law Quarterly*, **7**, pp. 223–7.

RICHARDS, M. P. M. (1995b) 'Changing family life', in HILL, M., KIRK, R. and PART, D. (Eds) *Supporting Families*, Edinburgh, HMSO.

RICHARDS, M. P. M. (1996) 'The interests of children at divorce', *Brussels, Edition Bruylant* (in press).

RICHARDS, M. P. M. and DYSON, M. (1982) *Separation, Divorce and the Development of Children: A Review*, London, DHSS.

ROCHE, J. (1991) 'The Children Act 1989: Once a parent always a parent', *Journal of Social Welfare and Family Law*, pp. 344–61.

RODGERS, B. (1994) 'Pathways between parental divorce and adult depression', *Journal of Child Psychology and Psychiatry*, **35**, pp. 1289–308.

RUTTER, M. (1981) *Maternal Deprivation Reassessed* (2nd Edn), Harmondsworth, Penguin Books.

SIMPSON, B. (1994) 'Bringing the "unclear" family into focus: Divorce and remarriage in contemporary Britain', *Man (N.S.)*, **29**, pp. 831–51.

SIMPSON, B., MCCARTHY, P. and WALKER, J. (1995) *Being There: Fathers after Divorce*, Newcastle, Relate Centre for Family Studies.

SLATER, E. J. and HABER, J. D. (1984) 'Adolescent adjustment following divorce as a function of familial conflict', *Journal of Consultancy and Clinical Psychology*, **52**, pp. 920–1.

SMITH, C. and PUGH, G. (1995) *Learning to be a Parent: a Survey of Group-Based Parenting Programmes*, London, Family Policy Studies Centre.

SWEETING, H. and WEST, P. (1995) '*Young people and their families: analyses of data from the Twenty-07 Study Youth Cohort*'. Working Paper No. 49, Glasgow, MRC Medical Sociology Unit.

TASKER, F. L. and RICHARDS, M. P. M. (1994) 'Adolescents' attitudes towards marriage and marital prospects after parental divorce: A review', *Journal of Adolescence Research*, **9**, pp. 340–62.

UTTING, D. (1995) *Supporting Families, Preventing Breakdown: A Guide to the Debate about Family and Parenthood*, York, Joseph Rowntree Foundation.

WALZAK, Y. and BURNS, S. (1984) *Divorce, The Child's Point of View*, London, Harper.

WEISS, R. S. (1979) 'Growing up a little faster: The experience of growing up in a single parent household', *Journal of Social Issues*, **35**, pp. 97–111.

WHITE, L. (1992) 'The effect of parental divorce and remarriage on parental support for adult children', *Journal of Family Issues*, **13**, pp. 234–50.

WHITE, L. (1994) 'Growing up with single parents and stepparents: long-term effects on family solidarity', *Journal of Marriage and the Family*, **56**, pp. 935–48.

Chapter 11

The Institute of Public Policy Research: A Case Study of a Think Tank

Tessa Blackstone

Throughout her career, Barbara Tizard has focused her research on problems with important policy implications. Not content simply to describe and analyse the factors that shape the way in which children develop in their early years, she has always tried to find solutions to the many problems of caring for children in contemporary societies. She has engaged with vigour in a wide range of policy debates. It is therefore appropriate in a volume honouring her work to include a contribution on the relationship between research and policy from the perspective of a think tank. Since the history of the Institute of Public Policy Research (IPPR) has not yet been written, it provides me with a welcome opportunity to tell the story of its origins, its way of operating and the work it has done over its first seven years.

The 1980s were depressing years for the left in Britain and particularly for those who espoused progressive, interventionist policies and a commitment to the provision of high quality public services. In 1983 the Labour Party suffered its worst electoral defeat since the Second World War. Bolstered by a huge majority in Parliament, the Conservative government embarked on a programme of privatization, tax cuts for the wealthy and the well-heeled, cuts in benefits and reductions in the role of local authorities in the provision of local services. It aimed to cut public expenditure, but failed as a result of the continuing high levels of unemployment. Its policies were supported and sustained by the work of a number of right-wing think tanks, which fed ideas to ministers and their political advisers. The Institute of Economic Affairs had been in existence for many years but it received a new boost to its influence as a result of the ideological climate at Westminster. The Centre for Policy Studies, founded in the late-1970s by Keith Joseph and others, was the Conservative Party's main source of radical right-wing ideas. The Adam Smith Institute and the Social Affairs Unit also fed in right-of-centre prescriptions for social and economic policy. The focus of these think tanks varied slightly but they all had in common a free market approach and strong hostility to almost all forms of collectivism.

The pamphlets they produced did not sell in very large numbers, with the exception of the IEA in its early years, but they received a certain amount of publicity in the broadsheet newspapers. The ideas they peddled fitted well with the values of the Thatcherite right. Their solutions to the policy problems they posed did not always prove acceptable to Conservative politicians. For example, although apparently attracted to the idea of private medicine through an insurance scheme, Thatcher saw the political cost of any radical dismantling of the National Health Service, and pulled back from it. This was a privatization too far. However, in many areas the think tanks helped to shape the agenda, even though none of them would claim they determined it.

The intellectual left was thought to be in hiding, sidelined and demoralized. Uncertainty and even confusion about the meaning of socialism was combined with serious doubts about whether the democratic left could ever recapture the voters' confidence. Psephologists were arguing that the changing class structure of post-industrial societies spelt the end of democratic socialist parties; in Britain the Labour Party would be reduced to a small rump of left-wing ideologues and the SDP would replace it as the opposition to the Conservatives. Academics identified with Labour were teased by political columnists for being in retreat and asked why we thought so few social scientists working in universities were engaged in debates about policy in the 1980s. This was certainly my experience and I suspect others like me had similar telephone calls from journalists.

The 1983 Labour Manifesto had been aptly described by Gerald Kaufman as the longest suicide note in history. The 1987 Manifesto was a much more succinct and circumspect document. However, it was still bogged down with 1970s thinking, even though it had shed some of the more extreme policies being espoused in the early 1980s. Even if it had been bouncing with new and exciting proposals for the reform of Britain, it would probably have failed to win the 1987 election for the Labour Party. With hindsight, it is obvious that Labour had little chance of recovering so soon from the internal conflicts following the 1979 defeat, from the lurch to the left in the early-1980s, and from the SDP split. But worthy as the 1987 Manifesto was, it failed to inspire and there was too little new thinking behind it.

As Thatcher started her third term it had nevertheless become apparent that she and her government's agenda were taking the ideas of the new right beyond the tolerance of the electorate. The idea that markets should be introduced in health and in education did not catch on. Removing the eligibility of young people for benefit was linked in many people's minds with youngsters sleeping rough on the streets of London and other big cities. The poll tax, espoused by at least one of the right-wing think tanks and picked up by the Number Ten policy unit was the biggest political disaster since 1945. There were encouraging signs for those of us interested in new policies on the left that the electorate was beginning to reject the right's agenda and was disillusioned with some of the effects of their policies. The time was ripe to fill the lacunae in left-of-centre policy thinking that then existed.

The particular provenance of the founding of the IPPR has not been described before. Clive Hollick, one of a small number of Labour Party supporters in the City, had been impressed by the influence of some of the American think tanks he had observed while working in the USA in the mid-

The Institute of Public Policy Research

1980s and thought it would be worth trying to gain support for a new left-of-centre think tank in Britain. Robert Albury, a television producer and long-time Labour Party supporter, put him in touch with John Eatwell, Neil Kinnock's economic adviser. Eatwell was enthusiastic and, together with Hollick, raised the idea with the Leader of the Opposition. He in turn was positive, recognizing the need for new thinking and painfully aware of the limitations of the Party's resources and structures for providing it. These discussions took place in late-1986 and early-1987 before the election that year. Nothing much happened until after it, apart from some preliminary work on fund-raising.

Meanwhile, quite independently, Clive Brooke, the then Assistant General Secretary of the Inland Revenue Staff Federation, had written a paper for the TUC, which proposed the establishment of an independnet think tank to fill what he also perceived as a gap on the left. This was then taken to the TUC by Tony Christopher, General Secretary of the Inland Revenue Staff Federation, and endorsed by the General Council. Clive Hollick and John Eatwell met with Clive Brooke and agreed that the two initiatives should be combined.

Once the election was over, Hollick and Eatwell began to push strongly for the project, backed by Christopher and Brooke. One of the first questions which had to be resolved was how to pay for it. Party funds were short, and in any case from early on it was agreed the new body ought to be independent of the Labour Party, so Clive Hollick and John Eatwell continued to approach possible donors, work they had started before the election. My own involvement began when, at a party Neil Kinnock gave to thank those who had worked for him personally during the election campaign, John Eatwell asked me whether I would consider becoming the first chairman. A little later I met Neil Kinnock to discuss the chairmanship, and the kind of organization he thought was needed. We agreed that it should be small, independent, wide-ranging in the policy areas and issues it covered and that it could challenge conventional Party thinking where its staff and trustees believed this was needed. From the beginning he backed the idea and gave it his full support without interfering in any way in its construction. On several occasions he also helped with fund-raising, going to see key potential donors to ask for their support.

By the spring of 1988, £250,000 had been raised – enough to launch the think tank. The Trustees included distinguished academics, left-leaning business men, people from the private sector and senior trade unionists. The launch press conference in July 1988 was well-attended and the coverage was extensive and positive. Across the political spectrum the newspapers recognized that there was a good case for a counter to the right-of-centre groups. For the most part they conceded that 'the case for an approach which emphasizes the mutual responsibility of the individual and the Community has gone by default', as the press release put it. They welcomed the fact that it would be politically independent and as such aimed to be a catalyst for radical thinking.

Some were a little sceptical and queried just how independent it would be. Indeed, throughout its history the press has frequently referred to the IPPR as the Labour Party's think tank. The Trustees, however, were determined from the outset that it should be independent and this has been not only accepted but preferred by three Labour Party leaders, all of whom have welcomed independent advice. From the outset it has had Trustees who are not Labour Party members.

What united them was not Party membership, but the belief that a free market approach was not the solution to every social or economic problem. Instead they took the view that there was also an important role for public investment in the social and economic infrastructure, including education and training, research and development and transport. They shared a commitment to the importance of full employment policies and rejected Thatcherite claims that this was something for which the government had no responsibility. They strongly objected to the view that efficiency requires inequality.

It was apparent from the outset that the IPPR would have to rely on the work of volunteers as well as the efforts of its own paid staff. Indeed, we hoped that it would encourage and promote policy-orientated research in the universities and elsewhere and help to dispel the perception of some journalists that even in academia the right was dominating the policy-research agenda. Above all, we hoped to promote new thinking and debate about policy, whether in private seminars or more publicly in Parliament and the press. The press release at the launch committed the IPPR to publishing 'a wide range of reports and consultation papers which reflect a broad spectrum of opinion'. It also made a commitment to 'provide a forum for political and trade union leaders, academic experts, those working at a senior level in business, finance, government and social administration, as well as the press and broadcasting media'. As what follows shows, the IPPR has fulfilled its original objectives and done so admirably.

Credit for this rests with its staff, not with the Trustees. The first director was James Cornford who, after an academic career at Cambridge and Edinburgh, where he was Professor of Politics, had spent eight years as Director of the Nuffield Foundation. He had nearly all the necessary characterisitics to run a new think tank: high intelligence; open-mindedness and independence; a wide-ranging knowledge of public policy; good contacts; the ability to write and edit well; and extraordinarily good social skills in dealing with both staff and the many outsiders with whom an organization of this kind would need to be in contact. His deputy was Patricia Hewitt, who complemented him perfectly. After running the National Council for Civil Liberties and just failing to be elected to Parliament, Patricia had been Neil Kinnock's press secretary and a senior policy adviser. She knew how Westminster worked and had a wealth of experience in dealing with the press and media. Like James Cornford, she brought to the IPPR high intelligence and extensive knowledge of public policy. She also had excellent organizational skills and a rare dynamism and energy, which made her immensely productive. Jane Frankin was appointed as the Institute's administrator. Not long afterwards, David Miliband, a young Oxford graduate who had recently returned from a Kennedy scholarship at MIT, and Irene Brunskill were appointed as the first researchers. Thus IPPR began with only three members of staff rising to five some months later.

From the outset the IPPR was able to attract good staff from strong fields, a sign perhaps that the intellectual left was not quite so depleted as some right-wing commentators had assumed. It was also able to acquire commitment and loyalty from people who had the courage to join a risky new organization that was under-capitalized and might easily collapse. They believed in the venture and they saw it as an exciting challenge in spite of the risks involved. Any rewards they have had, have certainly not been financial. Financing the right-wing think tanks was undoubtedly easier throughout the 1980s because of the backing they received from Conservative businessmen. The recent decline in business support for the Conservative Party may or may not be reflected in support for right-of-centre think tanks. The new one recently launched by John Redwood appears to have raised the necessary funds from individual backers. The IPPR has always had to struggle to survive financially and after initial backing from some of the big unions and from wealthy critics of the Tories, it has had to rely more and more on funding for specific projects from foundations and others, leaving it with a serious problem in raising enough core funding to cover its overheads.

A little slow to get off the ground and start publishing, it was soon producing a regular stream of monographs and pamphlets. Its very first publication was a paper on road-pricing (Hewitt, 1989). It was a good start, proposing a mixture of market solutions (pricing cars out of the centre of cities) and public investment (better bus services on roads less choked by traffic). It did not find favour with the Labour Shadow Secretary of State for Transport. One reason may have been that it challenged traditional Labour thinking. While arguing that road transport could not be left to market forces, it suggested at the same time that market mechanisms could be used to help improve traffic congestion and protect the environment. It certainly stimulated a good debate on the issues and provided a basis for further work on the complex technical problems involved.

This was followed by more work on the environment, including proposals for green taxes, and by a number of publications in economic and industrial policy. Papers came out on European Monetary Union, regional policy, technology transfer and the interface between economic and housing policies. The IPPR also started a substantial programme of work on the future of education, producing in July 1990 what has turned out to be one of its most successful and influential publications, *A British 'Baccalaureat'* (Feingold et al., 1990). Its proposals for a radical reform of the examination system, in particular the replacement of A levels with a scheme which would require broader-based study with less specialization and would integrate theoretical and more practical study, were quickly taken up and developed by the Labour Party and have influenced others such as the National Commission on Education.

Tessa Blackstone

By the summer of 1990, sixteen months after starting work, the IPPR had brought out thirteen publications. By then it had increased its full-time staff to seven and had several others working on a part-time basis. From the outset, however, it relied on building networks of outside experts who came to its seminars and produced papers, which might be considered for publication. It also received a certain amount of unsolicited material. As might be expected, much of this was not publishable; some of it was barmy. Every think tank must have a nut-case file. However, by bringing in reputable outsiders, the IPPR has been able to cover an astonishingly wide range of policy questions. In its second annual report it described new work on social policy and the future of welfare (which had led to half a dozen publications), on broadcasting, labour market policy, defence and security and family policy to add to what it was already doing on economic and industrial policy, the environment and education. To coincide with Britain assuming the Presidency of the European Union in 1992, new work was initiated on European issues. As well as continuing to analyse questions of economic integration and European defence, work was initiated on the home affairs area of migration, immigration and refugees.

Probably the most ambitious project in the IPPR's early years was the construction of a written Constitution of the United Kingdom. There had been increasing numbers of complaints about the way the Constitution worked, some going as far as to argue that it was a major block to the modernization of Britain, contributing to the nation's relative decline. Specific criticism ranged from indequate protection of civil rights by Parliament and the Common Law to the failure to give adequate political expression to the separate nations of the UK. Many experts were consulted before the Constitution was drafted. What emerged was not a brand new Constitution remade from scratch – on the principle of if it works don't fix it – but a fairly radical set of solutions to the many concerns that had been expressed (IPPR, 1991). It did, however, retain a constitutional monarchy, though with prerogative powers removed, a bicameral legislature with the executive based in the legislature and the ultimate authority of Parliament. Republicans would have thought it insufficiently radical. Some of its recommendations, such as a Bill of Rights and Scottish and Welsh assemblies, have been adopted by the Labour Party. Others, such as fixed-term elections and proportional representation, have not, as yet.

After the disappointment of a fourth Conservative victory in 1992, the IPPR reconsidered its programme and pattern of work and decided to shift a little away from individual reports on specific policy problems with recommendations which a new Labour government might have wanted to adopt. It decided to focus rather more on larger and longer term undertakings. The first of these was a project to examine the future of the welfare state. Instigated by John Smith, who had just become Leader of the Opposition (1992), the IPPR set up the Commission on Social Justice. It aimed to be a root-and-branch rethink of the welfare state in Britain, ranging beyond issues of social security and taxation to issues of education and training, housing and flexible working.

Chaired by Sir Gordon Borrie, QC, formerly the Director-General of Fair Trading, the Commission aimed to produce a programme of change for social reform and economic renewal that would catch on. It hoped to have the kind of impact that the Beveridge Report had had fifty years earlier.

Sadly, John Smith did not live to see the outcome. Launched in September 1994 it received enormous media coverage both on radio and television and in the quality press. It had operated a little like a Royal Commission, its sixteen members hearing oral evidence as well as receiving a great deal of written evidence. It produced fifteen publications, some by members of staff of the Commission, others by outside experts, *en route* to its final report. Its recommendations are too wide-ranging and complex to summarize adequately here (The Report of the Commission on Social Justice, 1994). Above all, it sought ways of linking employment policy to social welfare, arguing that the welfare state should be transformed from a safety net in times of trouble to a springboard for economic opportunity. This meant investing in people by radically improving access to education and training, particularly for those suffering from the poverty associated with dependency such as single mothers and the long-term unemployed. Eschewing both the market solutions of what it called deregulators' Britain and the old left's reliance on a tax and benefit system to create social justice – Levellers' Britain – it went for an Investors' Britain in which 'the ethics of community' were to be combined with 'the dynamics of a market economy'.

The Commission on Social Justice was the most prominent of the IPPR's attempts to look beyond the resolution of clearly defined policy problems in specific areas to broader questions of what the centre-left's response should be to political, economic and social change. One of the most strongly held convictions of the right in recent years has been that equality and efficiency are incompatible. In a project bringing together economists and social policy experts to challenge this assumption, David Miliband and Andrew Glyn, an Oxford economist, edited their work for a volume on the relationship between equality and efficiency in ten policy areas (Glyn and Miliband, 1994). Their eye-catching starting point was that the gap between the highest and the lowest paid is greater than at any time since 1886 and the richest 1 per cent of the population own 129 times as much per head as the 50 per cent least wealthy. Their conclusions were first, that such inequality and its manifestations – poverty, exclusion and disadvantage – is immensely costly, particularly because of the waste of human potential entailed; second, that the disincentive effects of high taxation to fund generous social security benefits have been greatly exaggerated; and third, that cross-national macroeconomic data does not support the alleged trade-off between inequality and efficiency.

Findings of this sort ought to have some effect on the political agenda. What that agenda should be for the Left was the subject of a number of IPPR seminars during 1993. This is a big topic and a difficult one about which to reach a consensus when traditional definitions of left and right are no longer accepted. In *Reinventing the Left* the IPPR brought together a number of essays by British and continental European thinkers and politicians on how social and economic change is shaping the agenda and on what that agenda should contain (Miliband, 1994). Utopias and blueprints (Robert Owen and the Webbs for example) are out of favour. Instead, many of the contributors wanted a more open-ended set of commitments in which process is as important as end states; and in which the left responds to the failures of existing economic and social systems, not with rigid top-down prescriptions but through a more adaptive form of policy-making. Thus in tackling the inequalities Glyn and Miliband recorded, the left needs to consider how to do so without sacrificing personal autonomy and diversity. Indeed, it needs actively to promote greater personal autonomy. There was broad consensus about this and the need to regulate rather than abolish markets. The traditional view of the left that all market solutions are undesirable is being replaced by the view that public actions and market decisions need integrating. The way power is distributed used to be criticized by the left mainly in the context of the workplace. It is necessary to look at power relations beyond the workplace as well as in it, just as it is important to think creatively about new forms of political process. Democracy is an end as well as a means.

These principles are increasingly being accepted as a general framework within which the IPPR works in the more specific studies it is doing of various sectors. They are more discernible in some studies than others, but a careful analysis of the Institute's output would show that many of the recommendations that emerge are consistent with them or apply them to particular areas of policy. The recommendations of the Commission on Social Justice exemplify this particularly well. So does the general editorial stance of *New Economy*, a quarterly journal on economic policy that the IPPR has been publishing since the autumn of 1993. The same is true of the IPPR's work in extending democracy and human rights. Work has been done on minority rights in the context of the European union and concepts of European citizenship, on immigration policy, on the rights of children and young people, for example, in the context of decisions taken about them by agencies outside the home, such as local authorities or hospitals.

In the autumn of 1994 the three original research staff at IPPR left: James Cornford departed to run the Hamlyn Foundation; Patricia Hewitt to take charge of Andersen Consulting's Research Department and David Miliband to be senior policy adviser to Tony Blair. This last appointment meant there was a direct link between the work the IPPR had undertaken in its first five years, to which David Miliband's contribution was central, and policy-thinking in the office of the Leader of the Opposition – without the IPPR losing its much-valued independence from the Labour Party. The new director of the IPPR, Gerald Holtham, came from the City where he was chief economist at Lehman Brothers. He had contributed to some of the IPPR's earlier work on economic policy and was familiar with its method of working and its political approach. Earlier in his career he had worked at the Brookings Institution and

The Institute of Public Policy Research

at OECD and had briefly been an academic at Oxford. Bringing with him considerable knowledge about the UK economy in an international context, about the workings of financial institutions and about economic policy more generally as well as a remarkable commitment to explore new ideas on the centre left, as evidenced by his willingness to take a huge cut in his salary, the IPPR was extremely fortunate in being able to recruit him. Anna Coote, a long-standing member of the IPPR staff, became his deputy. As in the original appointment of Cornford and Hewitt to their posts, the new Deputy Director complemented the new Director well. One of the IPPR's most prolific authors, a superb fund-raiser for the projects for which she has had responsibility, Anna Coote is an expert on health and social policy, taking the lead in the IPPR's substantial programme of work in this area.

The most important new project since Gerry Holtham's arrival is the Commission on British Business and Public Policy. In some ways this complements the work of the Social Justice Commission in the 'softer' areas of social and employment policy in the 'tough' areas of industrial and economic policy. It is about wealth creation and will focus on how Britain can improve its competitive postion in an increasingly competitive world. It aims to make new recommendations to this end, examining policies in several key areas: taxation and subsidies; training and education; infrastructure; competition and corporate governance; social policy and regulation; finance; and research in innovation. Chaired by George Bain, Principal of the London Business School, its members include a number of leading business men and women, the General Secretary of the TUC and several academic experts. This work will be undertaken by a secretariat based at the IPPR, but will be unconstrained by previous IPPR positions. It will focus, quite independently of Party position, on how to improve the government's performance in creating the conditions in which a market economy can be dynamic and successful. Whichever Party wins the next general election, it is hoped that the government will be influenced by the Commission's recommendations, which will emerge prior to the election.

As well as work for the Commission, the IPPR is now focusing much of its activity on the interface between the public and private sectors. It is asking questions about who should provide public services never previously asked by the left, which automatically assumed that only government, with some contribution from voluntary organizations, could do. It is also challenging the right's assumption that choice and competitiveness are the 'be all and end all' of good public services. Quality is central and what is necessary is to try to identify in what kind of mix for which services private and public provision are needed. These are difficult questions. Answering them requires careful research which examines the evidence objectively, minimizing preconceived ideological stances.

The IPPR is trying to address these issues across the spectrum of public policy. For example it is studying how community care purchasing affects quality in local government. It is looking at how far a Learning Bank, providing private finance for students set up at arms' length from government, might work. It is challenging old conceptions of the welfare state with new ones in which self-help and mutual aid might have a more important role, granting the individual more personal autonomy. Given the dramatic changes in the media, the IPPR is considering what forms of regulation are possible in a world of global megacompanies. On a smaller scale, it has come up with proposals for allowing the BBC more commercial freedom at the same time as serving the public interest. It is undertaking further work on how to regulate the public utilities.

Another part of IPPR's work is concerned with empowerment and democracy. This includes work on open government, on young people's rights, as well as further work on constitutional reform, including devolution. In yet another field, it is examining the UK's current and prospective defence-spending requirements, and the implications for British industry of a post-cold war defence policy.

The catalogue is an impressive one and the studies I have cited are only a small fraction of what the IPPR has produced so far. Since its first publication in 1989 it has brought out books, monographs and pamphlets. There can be no question about its productivity. However, quality is more important than quantity when evaluating the work of a think tank. Does the IPPR pass the quality test too?

The answer to this question will depend on what the criteria for success in a think tank are. Should quality be judged in a largely academic way or is something more required? High academic standards mean well-conducted research with a proper regard for the evidence, rigorous analysis, accuracy and attention to detail, clarity of exposition and originality. Think tanks with a political mission such as the IPPR do not, however, usually undertake much research themselves, particularly research that requires the collection of empirical data. Instead they draw on others' research, looking at the implications of their findings for policy. In so far as they do research of their own, it is what has sometimes been called strategic research, in which they act as intermediaries between the academic world and decision-makers (James, 1993). There can be little doubt that the IPPR's pamphlets and books have drawn on academic research a great deal and reported it with meticulous care, bringing it to the attention of people who would not otherwise have seen it. Criticism of the IPPR has to my knowledge never been about shoddy analysis or a failure to exploit existing research findings.

A think tank must also be selective in what it does and tackle problems that have some relevance to political debate and the policy agenda. The IPPR has been less selective in its coverage than some think tanks: it has chosen to cover virtually the whole range of public policy. It has not yet done anything much on policies towards the arts or development aid. But apart from these notable exceptions, every department of government should have at least one IPPR study on its shelves that relates to some aspect of its work. Taking a broad approach does not relieve a think tank from the need to be relevant within the policy areas it covers. For example a paper calling for the renationalization of British Airways, Thomas Cook and the pubs of Carlisle may raise a few eyebrows but is not likely to attract much interest from serious politicians. It is too far off the agenda.

Choosing to be relevant is common sense. Yet if it is taken too literally it may mean playing unnecessarily safe and defining the politically possible too narrowly. It is a difficult tightrope to walk. It might be said that the IPPR has erred on the cautious side. In doing so it has been earnest, reliable and worthy rather than zany, exciting or mischievous. It has sought to impress by its seriousness, by its pragmatic approach to what can be achieved in the foreseeable future, and by its awareness of the political constraints on more radical solutions. It rarely comes out with anything silly or ill thought-out. On the other hand some might accuse it of being a bit too careful, a little dessicated, even passionless in its approach. More passion, more vision, even the occasional lapse into something wild and provocative might be appreciated. This appears to be the view of the *Independent on Sunday* (Pepinster, 1995). In a chart showing the political think tanks on the 'Pzazz factor' the IPPR was rated one out of ten; on the 'barmy quotient' it was given the same score with the added comment, 'if only it were barmy'. Journalists like to be entertained (so do many of their readers) and reporting daft ideas is more fun than having to cover the nuts and bolts of detailed policy-making.

In spite of Tony Benn's claim that politicians can do their own thinking and don't require think tanks to help them, the pressures on modern politicians are such that without denying that they can think (or at least some of them can), few can do *all* their own thinking. Politicians are constantly on the look-out for new policies and this is especially true when they are in opposition. They do not have the back-up of a large civil service to come up with new ideas about policy or to help develop ideas from elsewhere. And they want new policies to help them get elected.

Indeed, it might be argued that the existence of a number of think tanks with a variety of positions on the political spectrum is an important aid to the proper working of democracy. In the 1950s the role played by the Social Democrat Friederich Ebert Stiftung and similar bodies for the Christian Democrats and Liberals were important forces in helping to re-establish German democratic institutions. In the USA, think tanks have flourished for longer and in larger numbers than in Britain, feeding into the political and policy debate. Pluralism in the ideas industry is certainly desirable and the IPPR has always welcomed the creation of new think tanks such as Demos and the European Forum. Those who worry about being crowded-out are mistaken. Moreover, in a context where the civil service has been substantially slimmed down at senior levels with an increasing emphasis on their role as managers rather than policy-makers, the need for policy analysis outside Whitehall increases. Vigorous and well-informed policy debate is the essence of effective democracy. Think tanks have a crucial role in contributing to such debate.

Much of the IPPR's influence and, indeed, some of its credibility, comes from being reasonably close to mainstream Labour Party thinking while remaining independent. To do so, its approach has to be instrumental and politically aware rather than visionary and a-political. Perhaps it could be a little more adventurous. A successful think tank must, however, be an effective problem-solver and its output must be capable of being picked up and used by the politicians and civil servants who have to solve these problems. At the same time it must never be craven. If Labour wins the next election, the IPPR will in fact be freer to take a more critical and more adventurous stance than it has during a period in which the centre-left has been in opposition for many years. As ministers, Labour politicians should have the support of their officials in working out the nuts and bolts of new policies and how to implement them, reducing the IPPR's obligations in this respect. Its role as a gadfly or, as James Cornford put it, as one of 'the performing fleas of the body politic constantly seeking that critical moment when a small sting may goad the beast in the right direction' (Cornford, 1990) may be easier to play once the left is at last back in power.

A little goading will be beneficial and ought to be tolerated by Tony Blair. He should certainly avoid reacting in the way President Nixon did to Brookings' criticism about US involvement in Vietnam (Higgott and Stone, 1994). The President sought to use the Internal Revenue Service to put pressure on Brookings and his aides even toyed with the idea of exploding a firebomb in Brookings!

References

CORNFORD, J. (1990) 'Performing fleas: Reflections from a think tank', *Policy Studies*, **10**, 4, pp. 22–30.
FEINGOLD, D., KEEP, E., MILIBAND, D. and RAFFE, D. (1990) *A British 'Baccalaureat': Ending the Division between Education and Training*, London, IPPR, July.
GLYN, A. and MILIBAND, D. (Eds) (1994) *Paying for Inequality: The Economic Cost of Social Injustice*, London, IPPR/Rivers Oram Press, April.
HEWITT, P. (1989) *A Cleaner, Faster London: Road Pricing, Transport Policy and the Environment*, London, IPPR, September.
HIGGOTT, R. and STONE, D. (1994) 'The limits of influence: Foreign policy think tanks in Britain and the USA', *Review of International Studies*, **20**, pp. 15–34.
IPPR (1991) *The Constitution of the United Kingdom*, London, IPPR, September.
JAMES, S. (1993) 'The idea brokers: The impact of think tanks on British government', *Public Administration*, **71**, Winter, pp. 491–506.
MILIBAND, D. (Ed.) (1994) *Reinventing the Left*, Oxford, Polity Press.

PEPINSTER, C. (1995) 'Redwood raises stakes in the fight for ideas', *Independent on Sunday*, 23 July.
THE REPORT OF THE COMMISSION ON SOCIAL JUSTICE (1994) *Social Justice Strategies for National Renewal*, London, Vintage, October.

A complete list of the IPPR's publications, including work on family policy, the education of young children and young people's rights, all of which would be of special interest to Barbara Tizard and some of which would have drawn on her work, can be obtained from IPPR, 30–32 Southampton Street, London WC2E 7RA (Tel. 0171 379 9400; Fax 0171 497 0373).

Chapter 12

School-age Childcare and the School: Recent European Developments

Pat Petrie

Introduction

This chapter draws on a survey of school-age childcare in the member states of the European Union (Meijvogel and Petrie, 1996), undertaken by the author, who is coordinator and founder of the European Network for School-age Childcare (ENSAC). ENSAC is a network which operates throughout Europe and is not confined to the EU.

School-age childcare is a new coinage and has, perhaps, a clumsy ring. It links together complex concepts and refers to a variety of service types which, for the European children who use them, go under more homely names: clubs, free-time homes, shelters, out-of-school and so on. These services are developing in different ways and at different rates. In some Member States of the European Union, for example, they have a twenty-year history and a well-defined place in social policy towards families. In others, while there is currently some development, services are not in any way systematic. In still others they do not yet figure on the social agenda.

School-age childcare services take responsibility for children outside normal school hours and when parents are not available. This is time which children in earlier decades of this century used to spend at home, looked after by their mothers, or playing with friends in the neighbourhood. School-age childcare services operate on the basis of an agreement between parents and staff, which includes the hours when children attend. That children are not allowed to come and go as they please is important for the definition of school-age childcare services. They are unlike so-called 'open door' or 'open access' services, which are supervised play provision, where there is no understanding between parents and staff that children will remain for a set time, and where they leave at will.

In Europe and elsewhere these services are increasing and developing, hence their interest. Their recent growth arises, largely, in response to the increasing rates of female employment, although child protection, in the context of hazards to be met in the local neighbourhood, also plays a part. The services represent a reorganization of children's time and an increase in the hours they spend supervised by non-family adults. They develop within specific social contexts, responsive to, and having an effect on, various social

School-age Childcare and the School

phenomena: the education system, employment, the status of women, the status of children, and the state's role in providing for the welfare of its members – to name the most salient.

The subject of this chapter is the relationship between the school and school-age childcare services as this has developed in different countries. In some countries, the recently perceived need for services has caused a radical redefinition of the school and its function; elsewhere, school-age childcare is, or has become, formally linked to the school and subordinate to it, while in yet other countries there is an arms-length relationship, or none at all. First, however, some background and history may be helpful.

Why school-age childcare?

Once they go to school, the organization of children's time revolves around the school's daily timetable and yearly calendar. And just as the school imposes its structures on *children*, simultaneously employment exacts its own requirements and consequent organization on the routines of *working parents*. These parallel requirements would pose no problem if schools and employment shared a common timetable. However, full-time working hours are longer than school hours and, to compound the problem, the annual leave of adult workers is less than their children's school holidays. Services for school-age childcare intervene to reconcile these differences, accommodating to the organization of both school and work. In this dual accommodation they are subordinate to the requirements of both employment and education, and more complex than services for preschool children. Before children start school, parents make childcare arrangements to suit their own working hours. They do not have to take into account a shifting school calendar.

The history of school-age childcare lies in the last century, in universal education and child-protection legislation. Working-class children, who might earlier have been gainfully occupied for a full working week, now had their days reorganized by the school. Not only did they have to spend time in school, they also had free time out-of-school. It was their free time that was seen as problematic. Beyond the control of either school or work, they were sometimes construed as a nuisance to society at large or a danger to themselves. During the nineteenth century there was some movement towards 'getting children off the streets' in many countries, by providing centres where they could go after school, perhaps have some food and take part in various 'worthwhile' activities. (Interestingly, in the UK, the establishment of Sunday schools in the eighteenth century had a similar motivation: to occupy young workers and keep them out of mischief on their one free day.) These centres were sometimes known as *day shelters* (compare the modern usage *daycare*) and may be seen as analogous to the *residential care* for homeless children – street children – set up by people like Barnardo. Examples of nineteenth-century day shelters for poor urban children are to be found, for example, in Germany, Austria, Sweden and the UK.

221

Janet Trevelyan, herself a campaigner for children's play and the daughter of Mary Ward, wrote of the child-protection basis to her mother's work, campaigning for children's recreational facilities:

> Every evening there were those lonely hours *when school and tea were over*, when children used to wander forth into the streets, out of the way of the hard-worked mother, and had nothing better to do than play in the gutter or run off to the well-lighted thorough-fares some distance away, there to gaze in the shop windows and to form small gangs on the look out for accidents or fights. (Trevelyan, 1919; my italics)

Nevertheless, despite a history which goes back to the early decades of the nineteenth century, the growth of day shelters was often slow; their more rapid development is quite recent and coincides with increasing female employment. In the hours immediately after school, mothers are less available for their children, whether to provide tea or to carry out those tasks which have become their customary duties, such as supervising children's homework, facilitating their social lives by driving them to the houses of friends, or taking them to educational, recreational and sporting activities. School-age childcare services step in to take over these tasks – or to supply their equivalent – where the alternative, that children be left to fend for themselves, is unacceptable to individual parents or to the state. Since the 1970s, they have started to increase in parts of Europe, Canada, the USA, South East Asia, Australia and New Zealand – in some regions rapidly, but elsewhere patchily or not all.

The European context for services

Maternal employment

Both maternal and paternal employment form part of the context for childcare. If neither parent is available, then other care must be sought – at least to the extent that a society places a high value on child protection. The growth in mothers' employment outside the home is recent for many countries, and any development in childcare – both preschool and school-age – is a reaction to it. In the EU the proportion of employed mothers increased rapidly between 1985 and 1993: from 42 per cent to 51 per cent (for mothers with a child under the age of ten) overall (Meijvogel & Petrie, 1996). There are clear differences in employment rates in different countries. Where there is a child under the age of fifteen, while 34 per cent of mothers are employed in Ireland and Spain, the rate rises to 70 per cent in Portugal and 76 per cent in Denmark. Part-time employment also differs. The prevalence of part-time work is relevant because it can be easier for part-time workers to accommodate to the school's daily timetable, although holidays may still present a problem. Part-time work among mothers is particularly high in The Netherlands, where 88 per cent of working mothers are part-timers, in the UK with 64 per cent part-timers and in Germany with 60% per cent. In contrast, the proportion working part-time is very low in Southern European countries (less than 20 per cent in Italy, Greece, Portugal and Spain). The reasons for all these differences are complex and include the general economic background, types of industry and the implementation of any equal opportunities policies.

The influence of the school

The school plays an important role in determining the need for school-age childcare services and in shaping their organization and curricula. This is the case where there is explicit educational policy to this end *and* where no policy links have been made between the two sets of services. Factors having an effect include the age for staring school, school holidays and school hours.

Compulsory schooling

The age at which schooling begins is decreasing in many European countries. It is compulsory for children between six and seven years in most member states of the EU, and for younger children in Greece, Luxembourg, The Netherlands and the UK. However, before compulsory schooling, most countries are moving towards extensive or universal provision of nursery schooling for children from at least three upwards.[1] Thus schooling comes to play an increasingly large part in the lives of children and parents, taking over time and functions which were once domestic, or which belonged to childcare services which were not part of any formal educational system. In most countries the nursery school has similar hours and holidays to primary schools. So even before children reach the age of compulsory schooling, many working parents need childcare compatible with school hours and holidays.

Holidays and leave

Once they start school the children's year is punctuated by regularly recurring holidays. Within the EU, annual school holidays last from twelve weeks (for children in Italy, Denmark and The Netherlands) to eighteen weeks (for secondary school children in both Ireland and Spain) (Eurydice, 1993). Working part-time, where it is a freely chosen option rather than the only possibility, may be useful during term-time, but even for parents employed part-time, problems remain when it comes to school holidays – which may cover more than a third of the year.[2] In most Member States, workers are entitled to annual leave ranging from fifteen to thirty days.³ Actual annual leave may exceed this entitlement, but everywhere the average leave taken by adults is far less than children's holidays.⁴ The result is that childcare is needed for holidays as well as for the beginning and end of the school day.

Organization of school time

School hours vary considerably between Member States, as to the length of the school day and in the following ways, whether:

- there are two main sessions (morning and afternoon) or only one;
- children stay at school during a midday break (if any) – and, related to this, whether lunch is provided;
- children attend for the same number of hours on each school day, and whether these hours have a regular pattern;
- children have a free day (or half-day) Wednesdays.

School-age childcare must respond to all of these organizational differences in the school.

Different policies towards provision

There are many policy options for school-age childcare – including that of 'no policy' – and great differences between national and regional policies. Some countries have a strong proactive policy and high levels of provision, notably Denmark, France, Sweden and some German and Austrian states. There is a small recent increase, and developing policy, in publicly funded provision in Luxembourg, Portugal and Finland, and experimental programmes in Greece. Flanders, The Netherlands and the UK have all had short-term government initiatives promoting school-age childcare. As yet there is little development and/or no articulated policy towards school-age childcare in Greece, Ireland, Italy, Spain and some of the Austrian and German states, especially the more rural. Where there is no national policy, private voluntary organizations may make some provision and so may some individual schools, within state systems. Private services run on a commercial basis are not common in the EU.

Differences also lie at many levels of service provision and practice: whether they are the responsibility of education or of social services; the part played by the voluntary sector; and issues to do with programme content and quality including the requirement for staff qualification. There are also the differences which this chapter mainly addresses: the relationship between school-age childcare services and the school.

School-age Childcare and the School

Examples of national policies

In order to illustrate policy differences, three EU Member States provide case studies: Sweden and Germany, each of which has, traditionally, a short school day, with irregular hours, and France with a long school day and regular hours. Each will begin with some details about mother' employment and the organization of schooling.

School-age childcare in Sweden

We start with Sweden, because here school-age childcare is well established. It presents a particular model of integration between school and childcare. There is a high level of maternal employment and school-age childcare services form one part of the Swedish policy to allow parents to reconcile the responsibilities of work and family life. Other elements of this policy are parental leave[5] and childcare services for pre-school children.

Box 12.1 Work, school and school-age services in Sweden

- In 1993, 78 per cent of women with a child aged seven to ten were employed.
- The difference between school holidays for children and the average annual leave for employed adults is nine and a half weeks each year.
- Education is compulsory from the age of seven, but most children receive a year of part-time nursery schooling when they are six, either in a primary school or a childcare centre.
- Until recently children have attended between thirteen and nineteen hours a week in school in the first three years (changes are covered below). In the first year, children went into class between 08.00 am and 10.00 am while brothers or sisters could start earlier or later. The irregular school day, with its short hours, proved difficult for working parents.
- The development of services arose from a concern for child protection when, in the 1970s, surveys showed that one in five children aged seven to twelve years had no contact with adults between the end of the school day and parents' return from work (The Swedish Institute, 1994). Since 1975, local authorities have been obliged to provide some school-age childcare and there has been a concomitant growth in services which take children up to twelve years – although they are used mostly by under-tens.[6] In 1993, about 40 per cent of seven to nine-year-olds attended a *fritidshem* – a free-time home – and a further 12 per cent were in family daycare, organized by local authorities. There are places for up to 90 per cent of children in some urban authorities. This increase continues and from

Continued

> 1995 local authorities must provide childcare before and after school for children aged six to twelve years, if their parents are studying or are gainfully employed.
> - In response to what was a short and irregular school day, the *fritidshem* has opened both before and after school and in school holidays, for example from 6.30 am until about 18.00 pm. Light meals are served, including breakfast.
> - The staff who carry out this work are mostly qualified as a *fritids pedagog*, which literally means a free-time child leader. It has also been translated as a recreation teacher, but perhaps 'free-time educator' suggests more closely what it signifies for Swedish people. The *pedagog* training comprises a three-year university course.[7]

Currently Swedish educational and childcare services are in rapid transition, evolving a new relationship between school and free-time and greater integration between them. This development started in 1985, with the recommendations of a Parliamentary committee and was taken up by the National Board of Health and Social Welfare with an 'educational programme' (*pedagogiskt program*).

The earlier organization of services – many features of which survive – is shown in Box 12.1. Before giving an account of more recent developments, it is interesting to consider the name given to school-age childcare in Sweden: the 'free-time home'. This contains the domestic connotations of the word *home* – counterbalancing the school which children are obliged to attend for the rest of the day. Similarly with *free-time*, the notion is that the time which children spend in the free-time home is their own, to do what they want with – unlike the time spent at school or even, perhaps, at home.

Nevertheless, free-time or not, the *fritidshem* provides a programme of educational activity, but one which is linked to general rather than those more specific goals which are more typical of the school curriculum. During the 1980s the National Board of Health and Welfare recommended child-centred educational programmes for both preschool and school-age childcare. The recommendations said that the *fritidshem* should present children with a general, holistic introduction to nature, culture and society, using thematic approaches. Children should have the opportunity to learn in many different ways: by reading and listening to stories, through drama, dance and movement, and in various kinds of creative activity. Group play is also emphasized as important for children's learning and development. In short, the *fritidshem* curriculum contains many of the elements recommended in the 1960s, by the Plowden Report, for British primary schools to provide child-centred education; but it must be seen in contrast to the Swedish school and its more formal and subject-centred curriculum. A video produced by the Swedish National Board of Health and Welfare (Socialstyrelsen, 1992) illustrates vividly the differences between the school and the *fritidshem* and the way in which their two sorts of staff approach their work with children. The video's treatment is light and perhaps exaggerated; nevertheless the contrasts are marked. The teachers are stern and authoritarian; they make the children line up to enter a classroom and teach in a formal style. (Remember that formal schooling begins at seven and the school day is short, so that there is much work to get through in a short time, compared with, say the French or British systems.) A *pedagog*, who comes to work in the same school in a teacher's absence, encourages the children to talk, to offer suggestions, to be 'creative', to learn through experience. Her approach to the children and their behaviour is portrayed as relaxed and informal.

Thus the *fritidshem* has been like a jigsaw piece, filling the gaps left by the school in the child's day. Not only did it fill the irregular gaps between parents' working hours and the school's starting and finishing hours, it also accommodated to the formal school curriculum in that the *fritids pedagog* have complemented the work of the teacher. They have facilitated expressive activities, play and informal learning, and emphasized the interpersonal and collective dimensions of children's activities in the comparatively long hours which surrounded the short school day.

The complementarity of school and 'free-time' was not always perceived as problem-free (Harmer, 1991, pp. 16–17). Separate childcare services were seen as expensive at a time of expansion. In addition some felt that the children were leading a very 'bitty' life: going from home to *fritidshem*, to school, to *fritidshem* and back home each day.

However, perceived inadequacies in the previous system have been confronted in recent, speedy developments. The aim of these is a formal integration of the *fritidshem*, which are often situated on or near school premises, with the school. In order to achieve this they now fall within the remit of the local education authority – a move away from a child-protection basis that is evidenced in other ways. Children may still go to the *fritidshem* very early in the morning, after school and in the holidays, but the school day and its curriculum has now changed, as has the role of the *pedagog*. Now all children must attend school for five hours a day, between about 8.00 am and 13.00 pm. The *pedagog* and the teacher for the first and second years (seven and eight-year-olds, the group which makes most use of the *fritidshem*) co-ordinate their activities, with the *pedagog* working for eight to nine hours per week within school, alongside the teacher.[8] Groups of children also leave school to go to the *fritidshem* – located in the school or separately – for set periods during the day and then return to class. During this time the *pedagog* may continue, in a less formal way, a subject tackled at an academic level in class. For example, the children may bake bread in the *fritidshem* having had a lesson about cereals in class (Harmer, 1991, p. 20). On the other hand he or she may decide that the children would benefit more, at any particular moment, from games or free play.

This co-operation aims to create greater continuity for the children, since they meet the *pedagog* before, during and after school. Another objective is to give the *pedagog*, and through the *pedagog* the teacher, an overall view of the child's day. What happens in school might affect their feelings and behaviour in the *fritidshem* and vice versa, and under the new system this can be taken into account. It is as though a therapeutic mode has now entered the school. The *pedagog* has some overall responsibility for children's emotional welfare, balancing the 'academic' responsibilities of the teacher.[9] A third reason is to introduce more practical and aesthetic work into school, for all children, whether they attend the *fritidshem* or not, and this also is the specialism of the *pedagog*.

The effect is that the Swedish school is changing its curriculum by incorporating a quite different range of educational values. It is aiming at a more child-centred approach. At the same time the *fritidshem* and the *pedagog* are losing something of their earlier autonomy, and come under school management. The argument about 'child-centred' versus 'traditional' education in Sweden has been raised vividly by the contrasting value systems presented by the classroom and by the *fritidshem*, and a solution has been attempted by compartmentalizing each in the persons of the two professionals involved. As Johansson put it (1991, p. 66) 'By . . . setting the boundaries for their own sphere of competence, and mirroring it in another group's, they will achieve greater clarity in the perception of their own professional competence.'

There has been little research, as yet, on any educational or other effects of this integration on the children. One study (Hansen, 1994) shows, however, that children distinguish between the *pedagog* and the teacher: for example they talk about learning the 3 Rs when they talk about teachers, but talk more about social skills and attitudes in relation to the *pedagogs*. Other studies look at the professional relationship between teacher and *pedagog* and there is some indication that from a situation in which the teacher was seen as the leader of the team, the strengths of the *pedagog* and their training are being increasingly recognized (personal communication Björn Flisiñg, Gothenburg University).

An overall effect is that time which was once time spent privately by children, and which then became time which children spent in their 'free-time homes', has now to some extent been taken over by the school. The school has also taken over some of the ethos of the *fritidshem*, and staff who were once clearly distinct from the school are now working within it. In all these ways the school is increasing its role in the lives of children and parents.

School-age childcare in Germany

> Box 12.2 Work, school and school-age services in Germany
>
> - There is a large difference in mothers' employment rates between West Germany – where 50 per cent of women with a child under fifteen were
>
> *Continued*

employed, 41 per cent full-time – and East Germany – where 72 per cent were employed, 81 per cent full-time (1993).
- The difference between school holidays for children and average annual leave for employed adults is nine weeks.[10]
- Education is compulsory from the age of six. However, in West Germany about 75 per cent of children aged three to six years attend *Kindergarten*, and in East Germany almost all do so.
- School opening times vary. In some *Länder* (states) schools operate five half days a week, others alternate between five and six half days. Classes are held between 08.00 am and 12.30 pm, but the children's hours of attendance may vary from day to day.
- Germany's sixteen states are each broadly responsible for developing and implementing their own policy towards children. Although the first day shelter for school children – a *Hort* – was established in 1896 (Rolle and Kesberg, 1989), there was no substantial development until the social reconstruction after the Second World War together, in East Germany, with the increased employment of women. In West Germany further growth was linked to female employment and the changing expectations of women during the late 1980s.
- In West Germany most provision is in *Horte*. In 1990 there were places for 5 per cent of primary school children aged six to ten years, mostly in cities, with places available for 15 per cent to 29 per cent of children. Just over half the *Horte* (52 per cent) are managed by local authorities, the rest by private organizations, with public funding. These have usually been located outside school. A new development is for *Schulekinderhauser*, or school children's houses, on school premises with their own accommodation.
- In the former East Germany, central government funded *Schulhorten* – school shelters – in which children were usually looked after in their classroom by a teacher. Since the reunification of Germany, *Horte* have ceased to be part of the school system and now come under local authority youth services – although they are often organized in school buildings. In 1990, there were places for 88 per cent of primary school children (aged six to ten), in 1993 for between 35 per cent and 60 per cent (dependent on the state in which they lived).
- Most of the staff (57 per cent), have the qualification of *ErzieherIn* – perhaps up-bringer (female) is the closest translation – which is also a qualification for working in nurseries. It requires a three to five years, post-sixteen training.[11]
- *Horte* are mostly managed by local authorities, with the increased involvement recently of voluntary organizations (Miedaner and Bruner, 1991; Miedaner and Permien, 1992; Statistisches Bundesamt, 1992).

Perhaps the most significant development in Germany is that in Eastern Germany women are leaving employment and childcare services are declining. There is also, in Eastern Germany, a decline in the part of the school and of teachers in children's out-of-school lives, in that teachers no longer look after children after school and supervise their homework. What follows concentrates on current relationships between school and school-age childcare in Germany, after reunification.

Until the Swedish developments described earlier, Germany and Sweden were somewhat alike, especially in that the school day was rather short and irregular. Also, in Germany, as in Sweden, there is a relationship between school-age childcare services and the school. However, while the Swedish system brings the activities of the *fritidshem* into the school, and of the school into the *fritidshem*, in Germany the traffic is one way. Here the operation of the school penetrates the childcare service with school-generated activities, specifically homework, finding their place in the *Hort*.

Homework is a central feature of the German education system, where all children have to do homework, every day, from the time they enter school at age six. First children are taught in class during the relatively short school day. Then they have to practise, learn by heart and work through further examples at home. In Western Germany especially, this has been a serious responsibility for both child and parent – in practice, the mother, who becomes directly responsible for children's progress at school (Enders-Dragässer, 1991). This, together with being with children until they go to school in the morning – and the starting time may vary from day to day – and being available at the (again irregular) end of the short school day, means that much of mothers' time has been taken up by duties imposed by the school and connived by the rest of society. These have been powerful constraints, tying mothers to house and childcare, reinforcing their role of housewife and maintaining their inequality with men. Enders-Dragässer characterizes this as women carrying out unpaid and unrecognized educational work, to their own social disadvantage. The possibility of a short and irregular school day – with the economic advantages this offers to the state – is made possible by mothers responding to the school-timetable and by their taking on hours of unpaid teaching. Enders-Dragässer also notes that mothers' supervision of homework is a means of maintaining social disadvantage between children, in that more highly educated mothers, mothers for whom German is their first language and mothers who have themselves been educated in the German system, can carry out educational responsibilities with greater ease.

However, the burden of teaching homework is alleviated when children attend a *Hort*, so that mothers may more readily take part in employment. The *Horte* not only smooths out the irregularities of the school day, but the supervision of homework plays a significant part in the timetable as it does in *Schulekinderhauser*. When children finish school, they go to the *Hort* and do their homework, supervised and assisted by staff for whom this is an important part of their duties. These almost entirely female workers are not professional teachers – but then neither are the children's mothers, who would otherwise have carried out the task.

In some *Schulekinderhauser* the headteacher has time allocated each week to co-ordinate the approach to homework in school and in school-aged childcare. *Schulekinderhaus* staff also attend staff meetings at the school and there is some joint staff training. This co-operation is encouraged by the Ministries of Education and of Welfare of the *Land*, and supported by the corresponding local authority departments.

The programme is not totally devoted to homework, however. Meals are served and, when their studies are finished, children may go out to play, take part in art and craft activities, play with construction toys or go on outings.

School-age childcare in France

Box 12.3 Work, school and school-age services in France

- National background. This is another country with a relatively high level of employment. In 1993, 62 per cent of women with a child under fifteen years were employed and 69 per cent of employed mothers worked full-time. Yet again, there are big differences between school holidays and average annual leave for employed adults. On average this is eleven weeks.[12]
- Some experience of being with other children is seen as normal and desirable for all children from their first year. Many go to nursery school before they are three, with over 95 per cent of children aged three to six years attending. Compulsory education starts at six.
- The school operates on Monday, Tuesday, Thursday and Friday, with a whole or half-day free on Wednesday, and school attendance on Saturday morning until 11.30 am, although Saturday opening is diminishing. Hours are regular and long, with lessons from 8.30 am to 11.30 am and 13.30 pm to 16.30 pm, except for the many schools which are taking part in the recent developments described below.
- Many schools have offered childcare or homework supervision before and after school. However, France has recently developed a policy towards children and young people, which takes into account their need for care in their parents' absence, but places this within a much broader context. Childcare is not the central policy concern; legislation is framed in broadly educative terms, providing for cultural activities, recreation and sport and recognizing the child as a member and citizen of the local community. Nevertheless, the legislation also acknowledges the parental problems involved in managing the family timetable and explicitly states that the services provide childcare (*l'accueil*).[13] The main funding minis-

Continued

> tries are the *Ministère de la jeunesse et des sports* and the *Ministère de la culture et de l'éducation*. Policy is implemented by contracts[14] between central government and local partnerships consisting mainly of voluntary organizations and local authorities.
> - There is an extensive network of services with two forms of organization: *services périscolaires* (the responsibility of the school) and *services extrascolaires*. (This is not the place to deal with *services extrascolaires*, save to say that they are widespread and independent of the school, although often using school premises, for example during holidays and on Wednesday afternoons, and providing residential opportunities during the holidays.) The policy has been in development since 1985, and is now known as *l'aménagement des rythmes de vie de l'enfants et du jeune* – 'looking after the life rhythms of the child and the young person'. The *services périscolaires*, like the Swedish model, are integrated with the school rather than co-ordinated with it, as in Germany.

French policy is for the school to manage both formal educational curriculum *and* extra-curricular activities and to draw on local resources in order to provide these. A special characteristic of the French system is that, in so doing, school authorities are urged to keep in mind children's *daily physical and psychological rhythms*. The annexe to a government circular explains and gives advice about this (*Ministère de l'éducation national de la jeunesse et des sports*, 1988). For example, it says that in the early afternoon children are lethargic, so that intellectual activities or intense physical effort is not appropriate at this time. Instead, children should be able to relax and choose what they want to do, leaving more demanding activities to later in the day. Schools are permitted to arrange their hours and activities, curricular and extra-curricular, accordingly. This revives a theme which goes back to the beginning of compulsory education when, in some European countries, there was debate as to the optimum length and placement of school hours for children's wellbeing (Meijvogel, 1991). It also builds on French experiments in the 1950s and 60s.

So, during the early afternoon, in order to cater for children's altered physiological and psychological state, schools may incorporate extra-curricular sport, creative activities and free play, and bring in non-teaching staff. They may also take children out to local facilities and places of interest. Later in the afternoon children return, hopefully refreshed and ready for more formal class activities, which are now extended beyond the previous end of the formal school day. When these are over children are cared for, and have recreation until their parents collect them.

The policy has had a rapid effect. By 1990/91, 2579 schools had reorganized the lunch break, double the number for 1989/90. Similar numbers rearranged the teaching time at the beginning of the afternoon. In the same year 1485 schools had integrated into their timetable the childcare service originally provided separately for the period before school began (in 1989/90, no schools had done this). This expansion continues (Leseve-Nicolle, 1994, p. 51).

Adults taking part in *services périscolaires* include volunteer parents, sports staff, artists and class teachers. There are also general non-teaching staff, the *animateurs* (animators – people who stimulate activities). Unlike in Sweden or Germany, the *animateurs* are not yet professionalized and are officially described as occasional workers or volunteers. Nevertheless, some are employed for substantial hours and, professionalized or not, there is a short training for *animateurs*, the *BAFA*.[15]

An evaluation of the French policy found positive outcomes for the children in terms of improved behaviour, greater tolerance in their dealings with others, an improvement in the general climate of the school, less violence and greater participation and concentration in class (Leseve-Nicolle, 1994, p. 51). It also found positive results for the school and its relationships, and its openness to the local community. At the same time there were some negative findings: difficulties in developing school timetables, the tendency to merely add on activities without a real consideration for managing the time available and, sometimes, little consultation or information being passed between local organizations and the school (Leseve-Nicolle, 1994, p. 52).

The French model represents something of a revolution in the organization of the school and its curriculum. Care services and leisure-time activities are assimilated by the school, under its direction, without the intervention of another profession – as with the *pedagog* in the Swedish situation. The orientation of the school to the community is changed and the school takes a responsibility for introducing the child directly into civil life and the opportunities it can offer. In all this the domain of the school is much enlarged, more so than in the Swedish integrated day, and more than in the German *Schulekinderhaus* – both of which, nevertheless, augment the role of the school.

Discussion

The background to this chapter is that, as in other industrially and technologically developed regions, school, parental employment and family responsibilities have been out of kilter – and they continue to be so in those countries where childcare services are undeveloped. An important factor in the development of childcare services is the increased participation of women in the workforce, whether this arises from concerns about female equality and/or from the need to make use of women's labour and skills. Women are less available to facilitate their children's schooling by delivering them to and collecting them from school – or school transport – each day; there is less possibility for them to tailor their day to the vagaries of the school timetable, supervise homework and be in attendance during the long school holidays. To the extent that they participate in the labour market, their availability for childcare is reduced to the same level as that of the child's employed father. Other agencies or individuals must, therefore, undertake some of the complexities involved in looking after school-age children, unless the child is to be at risk, both educationally and in other ways.

After more than a century of universal education it is becoming recognized that the school contributes to parents' childcare problems. At the same time, by strategies such as regularizing its timetable and/or incorporating an element of childcare, the school is capable of delivering a variety of solutions. The three case studies strikingly show the effect of different social contexts in shaping childcare policies which involve the school. The more salient differences informing and deriving from these contexts include social policy towards children, the history of the school and its curriculum, the status of women and changes in the construction of motherhood.

A developing relationship between the school and school-age childcare is a policy trend which is apparent elsewhere, for example in Austria, Denmark and Norway. In Belgium, too, there is much after-school supervision, mostly the initiatives of individual schools and not pedagogically developed – which has been criticized in some quarters (Humblet and Mahoux, 1994; Peeters, 1995).

The school does not play a part in childcare provision throughout the European Union, however. There are the new school-age childcare centres in Flanders, set up under a short-term government initiative, whose policy is precisely to maintain distance from the school curriculum. Here staff, drawn from unemployed women who have had a short training, are explicitly discouraged from including homework in their activities. This is largely because of the value placed on free play and creative activities in these centres. This contrasts strongly with the German example, where homework supervision is a key function. It also provides a contrast with Sweden in that two different curricula – academic education as against creativity and self-realization – are, in different ways, compartmentalized. In Flanders the two curricula are delivered by separate institutions and in Sweden by different personnel within the same institution.

There is also the case of Portugal, where many centres set themselves the task of supporting children's education, but without any formal liaison with the school. And there are Member States like the UK, where school-derived activities – at least at the time of writing – play little part in school-age childcare centres. (UK policy and practice is discussed and described at length in Petrie, 1994, and Petrie and Poland, 1995.)[16]

Yet even where there is no explicit educational or welfare policy on the relationship between school and school-age childcare, a relationship always exists. This is because childcare services are subordinate to the school, if only because they must accommodate to the school timetable and calendar. In fact they mirror the traditional subordination of mothers to the school. Childcare is subordinate to the school in any public funding received and often professionally, in that staff have little or no training compared with the professional teacher and are less well paid. Sweden and Denmark provide a contrast to this, but nevertheless the education and training of the *pedagog*, although professional, is somewhat shorter than that of the teacher and not all workers in the *fritidshem* are required to hold a professional qualification. These are services which partially replace the care work performed by mothers and, in differing degrees from one country to the next, share some of the low status accorded to motherhood. It is arguable that in those countries where women have greater equality (such as Sweden and Denmark), the people who take over some of their traditional work are also accorded a higher status.

Given the subordination of childcare services, in the case study countries – France, Germany and Sweden – where there *is* formal educational policy linking schooling and childcare, there are nevertheless marked differences in the theories and value bases from which policies derive. In Sweden, there is certainly – but not only – a pragmatic basis for the transfer of out-of-school services to the school, and their integration with it. With the aim of school-age childcare for all who need it, building it into the dominant and universal public institution – the school – makes economic and educational sense. This is especially so as Swedish school-age childcare services already have educational goals and are robust and professionalized, with a twenty-year history. They also draw strength from preschool care services, in that they are part of an overall childcare policy and, importantly, their staff share a similar professional ethos with nursery staff. This is based on a shared, if specialized, education and training. The development of these professions and the services, where they work, means that for almost a generation, Swedish parents and therefore policy-makers have been exposed to a set of educational values which differ markedly from those of the school and which may inform their beliefs about children and their appropriate education. Perhaps a different way of looking at the recently developed Swedish policy is in terms of the school colonizing the *fritidshem*. The very success of the new services, and their ways of working with children, have made them an attractive educational acquisition. The values underlying integration are more than financial opportunism. There is also an appeal to what has become a powerful child-centred theory of education, resulting in an expansion of the school curriculum to provide for the 'whole child', with expressive, affective and interpersonal needs. Importing the values and the practice of the *fritidshem* into the school allows this curriculum to be included in the school. It is also true that, because the *fritidshem* and its staff have been brought into the school, and because the hours of compulsory schooling are now longer, the school plays a greater part in organizing the daily life of children. It has become a more powerful, if changed, social institution.

In France, too, there has been a re-evaluation of the school and its function for children, parents and the community. Here there has always been a long school day and care services have been an adjunct to the school on a non-professionalized basis. Now there is a reinvention of the school and its place in the community. The starting point is two different sets of theories and values. The first set is political and incorporates *citizenship* – with all its historic and modern resonance – and *decentralization*, a current aim of French government. The integration which is aimed at here is on a much grander scale than in Sweden. In France the desired integration is of the child with the community, an integration mediated by the school, as one local partner in the child's education and upbringing. The child's citizenship is brought to the foreground in that she or he is located as a member of the local community, with the rights and duties, potential and actual, which this location implies. The policy must also be seen within the context of decentralization, which places the locus for decision-making within the local community, rather than with central government. The provision and management of resources for the enlargement of the school's function and curriculum both spring from these values: it is public policy to provide central government money for local partnerships which facilitate the child's use of local resources and their entry into civic life.

The second set of values underlying the French policy draws on *psychological and physiological* theory and is child-centred. The intention is to reorganize the elements of care, play, formal education and cultural activities throughout the school day, with a view to serving the child's 'biological rhythms'. As in Sweden, the school is envisaged as playing a larger part in the lives of children than it did previously. It provides – or will eventually provide – for more of children's perceived needs and have more control over the organization of their time. In a quite different way, the French school has also obtained new resources, a different orientation towards its task and an enlargement of it.

The case of Germany provides a care service which again is clearly subordinate to the school in that it serves its academic ends, and takes over the function of the parent (mother) directly, including her duty to supervise homework. The intention is that children whose mothers cannot themselves provide childcare and homework supervision, because they are at work, will not suffer as a result. There is also the need, in East Germany, to replace the teacher as homework supervisor.

The German policy is thus less revolutionary and less theoretically based than either the French or Swedish models, in that it substitutes, pragmatically, one caregiver/educator for another. The co-ordination that is developing between school and childcare is in the interest of efficiency, so that the children's educational welfare is best served, with an approximation to the model it replaces. But as well as taking over certain general responsibilities for children's safety and physical welfare, in supervising homework the *Horte* and the *Schulekinderhauser* also undertake the traditionally maternal responsibilities *which have derived, specifically, from the school*. In so doing they illuminate the complex relationship between the school and parental responsibilities, and how this relationship differs between countries. Schools have something of a care role, as well as an educational role. They may deliver services for children's welfare, such as school meals (universally in Sweden) or medical services (as in the UK) which relate more closely to physical health than to education. But, while offering educational and other resources, the school also presents the parent with additional duties. Parents have to manage their children's schooling, including homework supervision. In Germany, most obviously in the *Schulekinderhaus*, there has been some withdrawal of responsibility for homework, from the parent and back to the school. There are questions to be asked about the outcomes of this policy, which concern children's progress at school, and whether the new services will remove or maintain disadvantage between them. For example, are there differences between the attainment of children doing homework in childcare services which are closely co-ordinated with the school, those doing homework in services with less co-ordination and those doing homework supervised by mothers – with all the social and educational differences to be found in this group? Whatever the outcome for children, the provision of services has implications for the equality of women in German society. Where services are available they make maternal employment a more feasible option and this, in turn, relates to women's status in society – although the relationship between equality and female employment may be complicated by other social factors. The withdrawal of services in East Germany (and in other former members of the communist bloc) returns some women, and children with them, to the private domain of the home. Nevertheless, many mothers in Eastern Germany are still employed, full-time, and many children attend childcare services.

In conclusion, the end of the twentieth century in Europe sees a multiplicity of policy options with regard to school-age childcare. Among these are the reinvention of the school to incorporate new subject areas and a concern for the whole child. There is also the development of new services to complement the school and its curriculum. Time will tell if any of these becomes a dominant model. The case studies showed examples of countries where the school has a developing and growing role in children's lives. Elsewhere, where this is less the case, children are nevertheless spending time in facilities for group care and recreation which children of a previous generation spent at home or out and about with their contemporaries. Their mothers escape some of the constraints of the home and the stereotypical activities of housework by entering the more public arena of employment. Children, meanwhile, are both less domestically controlled and at the same time less 'free' within the public space of the neighbourhood. Within the European Union and elsewhere, there is a perceivable shift in adults' organization of children's time and of their use of space. Social control is increasingly mediated by school-age childcare services, whether within the institution of the school or otherwise. I hope that this chapter has indicated some of this shift and its different manifestations at national and regional levels within Europe. School-age childcare presents a rich field for comparing policy options in their different local contexts and for demonstrating the impact of policies on the social status of children.

Notes

1 The main exceptions are Luxembourg, Ireland, The Netherlands and the UK. These countries provide little publicly funded provision for three-year-olds and the last three countries provide for most four-year-olds in primary school (admitting them before compulsory school age).
2 For some parents, public holidays and weekends also present a problem. Children are out of school at these times, but parents in employment such as health work, retail trade, transport or tourism may not be free.
3 The exception to entitlement is the UK, where leave is seen as a matter to be agreed between individual employers and their workers.
4 The greatest difference – fourteen weeks – is between the annual leave of Irish parents and the school holidays of their secondary school children. Most usually the gap is between ten and eleven and a half weeks (Spain, Greece and Ireland for primary school children, and Portugal, France, Belgium and Luxembourg for all children). Five countries (Greece for secondary schools, Germany, the UK, Sweden and Austria) have an eight to nine and a half weeks' difference. Three countries have differences of six and a half to seven weeks (Denmark, The Netherlands, Italy).
5 In addition to annual leave, each parent is entitled to eighteen months Child Care Leave, full-time or part-time, to be taken before a child is eight years old. During these years, parents also have the right to work 75 per cent working hours (without compensation), and the right to 60–120 days leave per year per family (paid at 80–90 per cent of earnings) if a child, or the child's normal carer, is ill. Parents of four to twelve year olds may take two days per year to visit a school or childcare centre.
6 At ten years, young people may go to free-time clubs, suitable to their growing independence, immediately after school and in the holidays. The hours before school are less of a problem for these young people who can look after themselves and get themselves to school.
7 The main emphasis in the Danish *pedagog* training is on theory, including developmental psychology, and pedagogics, with methodology and practical training in arts, crafts and physical education also included. The training is co-ordinated with teacher-training and training for work in preschool centres.
8 In a somewhat similar approach, the teacher and the *pedagog* work together in the year of preschool education for six-year-olds.
9 A similar compartmentalizing of function exists in the British secondary school, with teachers who have special responsibility for 'pastoral care'.
10 Each parent is entitled to ten days paid leave per year to care for a sick child if they have one child under twelve and twenty-five days if they have two or more children; single parents are entitled to twenty or fifty days leave.
11 The curriculum includes pedagogy, psychology, sociology, sports instruction, the arts and music. There is a year's practice placement. Other staff

have trained as a *SozialpädagogIn* – literally a social educator (again female) – which requires a three to four years, post-nineteen training, and also includes a year's practice placement. Still others have a non-specific qualification, such as teaching or nursing, which is seen as appropriate for the job.
12 Each worker is entitled to three days leave per year to care for a sick child under sixteen years (increased to five days for parents with three or more children).
13 '... *la mise en place d'un ensemble varié de dispositifs visants, notamment, à rechercher les solutions les meilleures aux problèmes de transports, à améliorer la sécurité des enfants, à leur faciliter l'accès des équipments sportifs et culturels, à diversifier les conditions d'accueil en dehors du temps scolaire, en fonction des contraintes d'emploi du temps des familles, dans la journée, dans la semaine, pendants les congés, etc. ....*' (Ministère de l'éducation national de la jeunesse et des sports *et al.*, 1989).
14 E.g. *contrat d'aménagement du temps de l'enfant; contrat ville-enfant; contrat ville-enfant-jeune.*
15 BAFA is required for the majority of staff working in the *services extrascolaires*. It comprises an initial eight-day course providing an overview of child development, team work, the law, child protection, safety and hygiene, practical and pedagogic skills and providing for children from different backgrounds, and for those with disability. Training continues over thirty months. Fourteen days are spent in a placement, and a further six to eight days are given to deepening the candidate's general understanding and enhancing specialist skills.
16 However, a very few schools may include childcare or homework supervision in their activities, and school premises may be used by other organizations for childcare services.

References

Berechnungen der Bundesvereinigung der Deutschen Arbeitgeberverbände auf der Grundlage von Informationen der ausländischen Schwesterorganisationen, Stand 1, November 1993.
DIRECTORATE OF EDUCATION, CULTURE AND SPORT (1993) *School Holidays in the Member States of the Council for Cultural Cooperation*, Strasbourg, Conucil for Cultural Cooperation.
ENDERS-DRAGÄSSER, UTA (1991) 'Childcare: Love, work and exploitation', in PETRIE, PAT, MEIJVOGEL, RIA and ENDERS-DRAGÄSSER, UTA (Eds) *Women Studies International Forum (Special Edition)*, **14**, 6.
EURYDICE (1993) *Organisation of School Time in the Member States of the European Community*, Brussels, Commission of the European Community.

HANSEN, M. (1994) The child and teacher in two co-operative teaching traditions', paper presented at Fourth Annual Conference of the EECERA on the Quality of Early Childhood Education, Göteborg, Sweden.
HARMER LANGDREN, S. (1991) 'School-age childcare in Sweden with special reference to the integrated school day in Lund', in *ENSAC, Second European Conference on School-Age Childcare, School-age Childcare Services: Organisation, Content and Staffing, Different National Experiences*, Gothenburg, Department of Education and Educational Research, University of Gothenburg, November 1990.
HUMBLET, PERRINE and MAHOUX, CÉCILE (1994) *Les activités extra-scolaires: garde ou accueil?* Commission Communautaire Française, Brussels.
JOHANSSON, INGE (1991) 'Staff and professionality', in *ENSAC, Second European Conference on School-Age Children, School-age childcare services: Organisation, Content and Staffing, Different National Experiences*, Gothenburg, Department of Education and Educational Research, University of Gothenburg, November 1990.
LESEVE-NICOLLE, CATHERINE (1994) 'L'accueil et le temps libre de jeunes enfants', in *Journée de la Famille, 22 Septembre 1994, Actes du Colloque*, L'aménagement des rythmes de vie de l'enfant et du jeune.
MEIJVOGEL, MARIA C. (1991) *Geen kruimels tussen de boeken: Schooltijden, overblijven en de ontwikkeling van buitenschoolse opvang in Nederland*, Groningen: PhD published thesis.
MEIJVOGEL, R. and PETRIE, P. (1996) *School-age childcare in the European Union: A survey*, London, Commission of the European Union.
MIEDANER, L. and BRUNER, C. (1991) *Der Hort in Zahlen, Misere eines Bildungs und Betereuungsangebot für Schulkinder*, München, DJI Arbeitspapier 4-027.
MIEDANER, L. and PERMIEN, H. (1992) 'Betreuungssituation und Nachmittagsgestaltung von Mädchen und Jungen zur Weiterentwicklung famlienergänzender Angebote', in DJI (Ed.) *Was tun Kinder am Nachtmittag?*, München, DJI, pp. 171–215.
Ministère de l'Éducation National de la Jeunesse et des Sports (1988) *Annexe de Prof. Hubery Montagner*, lettre du 2 Août 1988.
PEETERS, J. (1995) 'School-age childcare in Flanders', in *ENSAC Fifth International Congress, Ghent, 1994: Empowering the Parents*, Ghent, VBJK & KZ.
PETRIE, PAT (1994) *Play and Care, Out-of-school*, London, HMSO.
PETRIE, P. and POLAND, G. (1995) *After School and in the Holidays: A Survey of Provision*, London, Thomas Coram Research Unit, Institute of Education, University of London.
ROLLE, JÜRGEN and KESBERG, EDITH (1989) *Materialienband zur Hortgeschichte*, Köln, Sozialpädagogisches Institut.
SOCIALSTYRELSEN (1992) *Svarta Malin*, Stockholm, Socialstyrelsen.
STATISTISCHES BUNDESAMT (December 1990, Stand: September 1992) *Statistik der jugendhilfe Teil III Einrichtungen und tätige Personen. Verfügbare*

Plätze in Horten in Einrchtungen mit altersgemischte Gruppen am 31, Wiesbaden, Statistisches Bundesamt.

THE SWEDISH INSTITUE (1994) *Child Care in Sweden*, Stockholm, The Swedish Institute.

TREVELYAN, JANET (1919) *Evening Play Centres for Children*, London, Methuen.

Chapter 13

Early Childhood Services in Europe: Qualities and Quality

Peter Moss

In 1986, while Barbara Tizard was Director of the Thomas Coram Research Unit, I was asked by the European Commission to co-ordinate a group of experts (one from each of the then twelve Member States). This Childcare Network was to work on the subject of 'childcare services' for employed parents, and was established by the Commission as part of its programme to promote equal opportunities between women and men in the labour market. Over the years its remit broadened. This was partly because the members of the Network took the view that the care needs of working parents should not be considered, or indeed provided for, in isolation from the other needs of young children and their parents; we decided to look at the full range of services providing care, education and recreation to young children and their families. But it was also because the Commission extended our brief to cover the whole area of 'reconciling' employment with the care and upbringing of children. The Childcare Network was renamed the Network on Childcare and Other Measures to Reconcile Employment and Family Responsibilities of Women and Men. It took on a number of new areas like leave arrangements for workers with children and measures to support the increased participation by men in the care and upbringing of children.

However, in this chapter I concentrate on our original interest – services providing care, education and recreation for young children and their families – which I shall label 'early childhood services' as a form of short-hand. In this case, 'young children' means children under compulsory school age, although the Network extended its work to children up to the age of ten years and has recently published a review of services providing care and recreation for school age children (Meijvogel and Petrie, 1996). The chapter begins by providing a brief overview of these services in the fifteen Member States, drawing on the Network's third and most recent review of services in the European Union (EU) (EC Childcare Network, 1996a), considers some of the features of UK services that are unusual from a wider European perspective and concludes, more reflectively, by considering two issues that working in Europe has brought to the fore for me: the concept of early childhood services and the concept of quality in these services.

Early Childhood Services in Europe

Early childhood services in the EU

The actual age range covered by early childhood services is determined by two pieces of policy. At the upper end, the age of compulsory schooling mainly determines when children move into the primary school system. In all but three EU Member States, compulsory schooling begins at six or (in the Nordic countries) seven. At the lower end, the age at which children begin to receive non-parental care is affected in a number of countries by the workings of parental leave, leave which is equally available to mothers and fathers and which is intended to give parents the opportunity to spend more time caring for a young child (in contrast to maternity leave, a legal entitlement in all Member States, which is for mothers and intended as a health and welfare measure to protect women in late pregnancy and mothers and their infants in the immediate aftermath of childbirth).

Parental leave is generally available in all but three Member States as a legal entitlement (except in the case of Belgium it is based on collective agreements). In practice, parental leave varies considerably between countries – in length, payment, flexibility and whether it is an individual or family right (see Figure 13.1 for the availability of parental leave, as well as paternity leave and leave for family reasons (i.e. to care for sick children), and for the combined length of maternity and parental leave and benefit payment to parents taking leave). It also varies considerably in its impact. In some countries, such as Spain, Portugal, Greece and France, take-up is minimal, but in others, notably the Nordic countries and Germany and Austria, it is widely used, usually by mothers. For example, in Austria 80 per cent of children under two have a parent taking leave and only 3 per cent attend a publicly funded service; while in Sweden, the age at which children start in services has gradually increased over the last twenty years as leave policy has developed, and the numbers under twelve months in nurseries have fallen from 3000 to just 155 (for a fuller discussion of leave arrangements and their operation, see EC Childcare Network, 1994; OECD, 1995).

In between parental leave and compulsory school age, there has been a postwar expansion in early childhood services, offering young children widening opportunities or, viewed from a different perspective, subjecting them to growing institutionalization. The availability of publicly funded services[1] in all Member States, except Luxembourg, is shown in Figure 13.2, with a more detailed account presented in Table 13.1 in the Appendix. The picture is rather different for children under and over three. Most Member States now offer three or four years provision for children from three through until they start school at six or seven. Such universal coverage is already on offer in Belgium, France and Italy, and an explicit aim of policy in Finland, Sweden, Denmark, Germany and Spain. Provision is made in centre-based services – nursery schools or kindergartens mainly, but also some age-integrated centres combining under and over threes. This may be supplemented by services (centre-based or family daycare) providing care and recreation outside school hours;

243

Peter Moss

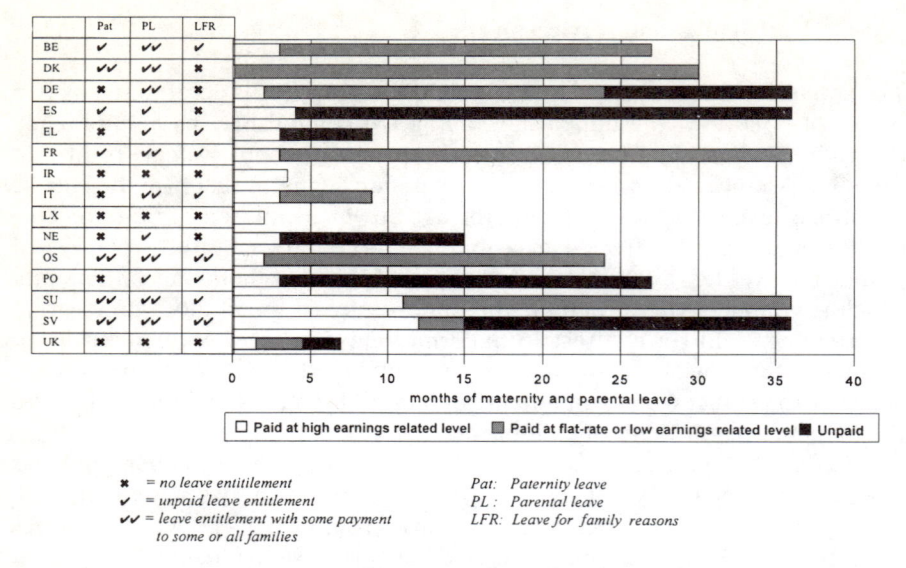

Figure 13.1 *Statutory leave for workers with children*

these services are most widespread in Belgium and France (and not needed in the Nordic countries, where centres are open on a full-time, year-round basis).

Overall, therefore, provision for children over three years is high, growing and mainly publicly funded. The situation is more variable for children under three. In most cases levels of publicly funded provision are relatively low, below 10 per cent and often below 5 per cent. Most arrangements for children under three involve privately funded services (mainly family daycare, but also nannies and private nurseries) or else informal care, through social networks. Indeed, the most widespread provision for children under three outside the publicly funded system is made by relatives, in particular grandmothers. Yet despite the importance of this group, they are invisible in statistics and usually unsupported by public authorities. It seems likely that over time, their availability will not keep up with increasing parental demand and may actually fall, especially as employment levels increase among older women. It is also not clear how far relatives are used as a matter of choice, rather than simply as a matter of necessity, but it seems likely that at least some parents would opt for more formal provision if it was available.

Early Childhood Services in Europe

The main exceptions – countries which offer publicly funded services for over 20 per cent of children under three – are Belgium and France and the three Nordic members of the EU, each of which has made a legal or political commitment to provide publicly funded services for all children from twelve months up to at least school age (the assumption is that children under twelve months will be at home with parents taking leave). In these Nordic countries, with high levels of female employment and well-developed public services, relatively little use is made of either privately funded services or informal arrangements. For example, in Sweden in 1994, 63 per cent of children aged between three months and seven years received some form of non-parental care, the proportion increasing from just 3 per cent of children under twelve months (a consequence of parental leave), to 42 per cent of one year-olds, then 60–75 per cent of children aged two and over. Over 80 per cent of children receiving non-parental care were in services provided by local authorities, with the remaining small minority split between attendance at private services and informal, unpaid care.

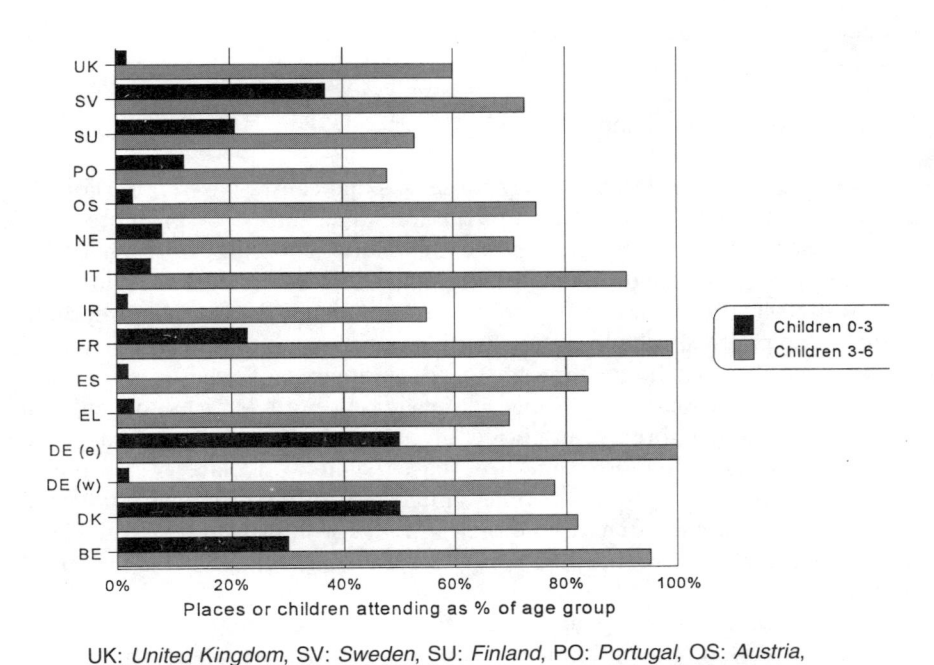

UK: *United Kingdom*, SV: *Sweden*, SU: *Finland*, PO: *Portugal*, OS: *Austria*, NE: *The Netherlands*, IT: *Italy*, IR: *Ireland*, FR: *France*, ES: *Spain*, EL: *Greece*, DE (e): *East Germany*, DE (w): *West Germany*, DK: *Denmark*, BE: *Belgium*

Figure 13.2 *Levels of publicly funded services for young children: 1991–94*

Provision for children under three is also more varied than for older children. Apart from the role of private and informal carers, there are four main types of publicly funded provision. First, centres providing only for children under three are found in most countries. Second, age-integrated centres, taking children under three and from three to compulsory school-age and sometimes older, are a common form of provision in a number of countries, including Sweden, Finland, Denmark, Ireland, the Netherlands and the UK; but they are also found to a lesser extent in most other countries. Third, organized family daycare is important in a number of countries, notably the Nordic countries (in Denmark, nearly two-thirds of children under three in publicly funded provision are in organized family daycare), France and Belgium. Organized family daycare is a service provided by individual carers in their own homes who are recruited, paid and supported by public authorities or publicly funded private organizations. Family daycare, whether organized or private, is, however, almost unknown in Greece, Italy and Spain – indeed, the languages of these countries have no words for family daycare, organized or not (for a more detailed account of family daycare in the EU, see Karlsson, 1995). Finally, in Belgium and France, two-year-olds are admitted to the system of nursery schooling. The large number of two-year-olds in the education system is one reason for the relatively high coverage rates for publicly funded services in Belgium and France.

Three critical issues

Whereas there is an emerging policy consensus that centre-based provision for children over three is desirable for children themselves, to promote their development and prepare them for compulsory schooling, no such policy consensus exists for children under three years. Indeed, at least four different policy approaches are discernible. In several countries, the explicit policy aim is to enable parents to have choice between employment and caring for children under three at home through the development of measures that will support either option. Thus France is developing both services for children under three and a three-year period of parental leave. Finland has gone even further; every child under three has a right to a place in a publicly funded service while at the same time families are entitled to receive financial support to care for their children either at home or in private services. These countries therefore combine long periods of leave and relatively high levels of services.

In the UK, the policy aim is also choice – that parents should choose whether to work or stay at home. But unlike France and Finland, that choice is viewed as a purely private matter, with the state having no direct interest in the reconciliation of employment and family responsibilities. Public policy therefore is to remain neutral as between employment or caring for children at home, and to express this neutrality by providing no general measures to support either option. Hence the UK has a situation shared only by Ireland of no entitlement to parental leave and no access for employed parents to the limited supply of publicly funded services. Employed parents who need care for their children must make private arrangements, either informally through relatives and friends, or formally, by buying services within an expanding and largely unsubsidized private market.

In Denmark and Sweden, the policy is that parents should take a period of leave when children are under twelve to fifteen months, after which their participation in the labour market is assumed and supported through the provision of early childhood services and other means. New Swedish legislation requires local authorities to provide services for children up to the age of twelve years; while the Danish government has made a political commitment to provide places for children up to school age by 1996. However, in both countries, this entitlement or commitment applies only to children over twelve months, since younger children are assumed to be at home with parents on leave. In these cases, there is a combination of paid leave of moderate length, followed by the provision of extensive publicly funded services to which employed parents have a right of access – although not necessarily parents who are not employed.

A fourth aim of policy is to encourage a parent, invariably the mother, to remain at home until children reach the age of three. In this case, there is a long period of leave combined with low levels of publicly funded provision. This pattern can be seen in the former West Germany and in Austria, where more than 80 per cent of children under two have a parent on leave. An interesting contrast can be made between West and East Germany. Before reunification, East Germany had a very similar policy to Sweden and Denmark, with a one-year paid parental leave followed by nearly universal access to publicly funded services. Since reunification, the former leave arrangement has been superseded by the West German policy of three years leave, partly low paid and partly unpaid, which encourages women to stay at home. Levels of service provision have fallen, especially for children under three, in part in response to a large drop in the birth rate but also in response to the reduced demand for services due to falling employment and rising costs to parents using services. Levels of provision in the East, however, still remain among the highest in the EU, and far ahead of those in West Germany, especially for children under three.

Each policy option raises many questions, in terms of child and family welfare, equal opportunities and so on. For example, what conditions are needed to ensure real choice for mothers and fathers? What are the implications for children of encouraging private market solutions in societies with large and growing economic inequalities between families? Can equality of opportunity on the labour market be achieved if policies, in effect, encourage mothers to take long periods of time out of the labour market and do not actively promote the equal sharing of family responsibilities between mothers and fathers? Do policies that expect both parents to be employed put undue pressure on some families and some parents, who would prefer one parent to be at home? And what happens when, as in Sweden in recent years, the labour market cannot provide sufficient jobs for parents and unemployment grows?

A second issue concerns the relationship between the services for children under and over three. In the Nordic countries, all services for children under school-age are part of an integrated, coherent and increasingly comprehensive system. This system provides a single framework that encompasses services for children under and over three; as a result, these services share common legislation, administrative responsibility, funding, opening hours, staffing and so on. One consequence is that in all Nordic countries many children are in age-integrated centres, which accommodate children from a few months up to school-age.

The Nordic system is integrated at national level within the welfare system, separate from the education system. Services for young children have also been the responsibility of welfare departments in local authorities, separate from schools. However, an important development has been occurring at local authority level in Sweden since 1993: in most local authorities, responsibility for services for children under school-age and for services providing care and recreation for children of school-age and for schools is now integrated within one department.

Spain is also seeking to develop an integrated and coherent system of services for children under and over three. Unlike the Nordic countries, this is based on the integration – at national, regional and local levels – of all services for children from nought to six within the education system, following a major reform of the whole Spanish education system in 1990 which defined nought to six as the first stage of that system. The implementation of this reform, and the development of a genuinely coherent system, still has some way to go; but for many countries in Europe, the Spanish experience will be very important because of this education-based approach (for more detailed accounts of the Danish and Spanish systems, see Moss and Penn, 1996).

Elsewhere in the EU, there is a split between services for children under and over three. In most cases, services for children under three are in the welfare system, while all or most of those for children over three are in the education system – although as already noted, in Belgium and France two-year-olds may find themselves in nursery schools or in services in the welfare system. In Austria and Germany, all services for children under school-age are in the welfare system, but in practice the system for under and over threes is far from being integrated and coherent; in particular, there is an ambivalence about providing services for children under three, reflected in very low levels of provision (excepting East Germany), while provision for children over three is generally accepted. In Germany, for example, there will be a legal right of access to services from 1996 – but for children from three to six.

Early Childhood Services in Europe

This split means that services for most children under three operate within a different framework to services for most children over three. To take three examples, parents contribute to the costs of publicly funded services for children under three in the welfare system – but services for children in the education system are free of charge. Services in the welfare system are usually open all day and all year – but services in the education system follow school hours and school terms. Finally, services in the welfare system have higher staffing levels – but lower levels of staff training and pay than services in the education system.

The final issue concerns the relationship between parents, employers and the state in the provision of care and education for children under three. Within the EU, there is no consensus among Member States about the respective responsibilities of these three parties. The Nordic countries have taken the view that the responsibility for services is primarily to be shared between the state and parents. All three Nordic Member States have moved to accepting that parents have a right of access to publicly funded services, but in all cases parents contribute towards the cost on the basis of income and family circumstances (parents pay on average around 15 per cent of costs in Finland and Sweden and around 20 per cent in Denmark). The state also takes responsibility for providing a framework of basic leave entitlements. The employers' role is to support and supplement leave, but not to provide or subsidize services, except through general taxation.

In France, the same relationship holds for leave arrangements. But the provision of services for children under three, with the exception of nursery education, recognizes a clear role for employers. All employers contribute to regional funds which finance cash benefits to parents. But these 'family allowance funds' (*Caisses d'Allocations Familiales*) also provide subsidies to existing services, as well as stimulating new services through agreements made with local authorities under which the funds pay part of the cost of new services (*contrats enfance*). Overall, these funds and parents each contribute about a quarter of the costs of publicly funded services for children under three, while the remaining half comes from local and regional authorities.

The Netherlands also seeks to involve employers in the provision of services but on a very different basis. Under a special funding programme introduced by the government in 1990 and due to finish at the end of 1996, central government funds contribute to the cost of new places, but at a low level, less than half. The remaining costs are paid partly by parents and partly by either local authorities or individual employers. There is a strong emphasis on individual employers funding places for members of their workforce, and employer support for services is mentioned in an increasing number of collective agreements. Central government funding is therefore used as an inducement to encourage individual employers to subsidize places in services for their employees.

Peter Moss

The distinction between the French and Dutch approach is interesting. In France all employers are required to contribute, and their money goes into a general fund which is used to support a wide range of services, not only for children with employed parents. When employers contribute, they are not buying a place for members of their workforce and the use of services is not tied to a parent's job. In short, employers are contributing to the development of a wide range of services for children and families. In the Netherlands, by contrast, employers only contribute financially if they choose to because they consider it to be in their interests; if they decide to contribute, then employers subsidize places specifically for their own employees and which are therefore tied to a parent's job. Whereas in France, employers are supporting family policy, the Dutch policy is mainly driven by labour-market considerations, with employers being encouraged to fund services which are viewed primarily as a means to encourage an adequate labour supply.

Finally, in Germany, or at least West Germany, Ireland and the UK, the state plays a minimal role in providing services for children under three, and does so mostly for a small minority of children considered to be particularly disadvantaged or at high risk. The assumption is that parents are responsible for making their own private care arrangements, unless they have an employer prepared to offer some assistance. Employers are neither required to contribute to the costs of services, nor are there inducements for them to do so; if they choose to fund places for their employees, as some do, then the costs are usually shared between themselves and their employees. The main distinction is that the German state has accepted responsibility for parental leave, which is a legal entitlement, whereas in Ireland and the UK, any leave depends on the policies of individual employers.

The UK in a European perspective

In many respects, looked at from a wider European perspective, the position of the UK is distinctive and rather unusual. Some of the components that make up that position have already been mentioned. The UK is one of only three Member States that provides no general entitlement to parental leave (the others are Ireland and Luxembourg). The UK and Ireland are the only countries which do not accept parental employment as a criterion for admission to publicly funded services in the welfare system. Underlying both policies, there is a strong political ideology that the management of employment and family life is essentially a private matter, to be resolved through the exercise of parental choice and parental measures without public intervention and support. This policy position is associated (although what is cause and what effect is hard to determine) by unusual parental employment patterns: fathers work the longest hours in Europe, most employed mothers have part-time jobs (the proportion is only higher in the Netherlands) and many part-time employed mothers work very short hours (the average hours worked by part-time employed mothers are the shortest in the EU except for the Netherlands) (for more information on parental employment in the EU, see EC Childcare Network, 1996a).

But there are other distinctive features. The UK is one of only three countries which starts compulsory schooling as early as five. The others are Luxembourg (where the age is four) and the Netherlands. Compared to most of Europe, the UK has very limited provision of nursery schooling; this form of provision is not generally available, and when available mostly offers part-time attendance for three terms; the UK is the only European country to operate a mainly part-time, shift system of nursery schooling as a deliberate matter of policy. Even the recent government commitment to provide a part-time 'preschool' place for all four-year-olds in 1997 will leave the UK far behind what has already been attained in most European countries. Like the only two other Member States with limited or no nursery schooling (Ireland and the Netherlands), the UK has partly filled the gap through the development of playgroups (another very part-time service) and the admission of large numbers of children to primary school before compulsory school-age. Early compulsory school-age, even earlier admission to primary school and the part-time nature of most 'pre-primary' provision have combined to ensure that nursery schooling is in effect a short preparation for primary school, rather than evolving as a distinct and substantial stage of the education system. Consequently, many UK children experience a period of considerable discontinuity between the age of three and five, moving through playgroup, nursery class and reception class, while their Continental counterparts are experiencing the relative continuity of a three-year spell in nursery school or kindergarten.

The UK is not, however, entirely distinct. It shares the divided approach to early childhood services found in a number of other Member States, with a split between 'daycare' or 'childcare' services located in the welfare system, and 'nursery schooling' and 'early admission to reception class' located in education. The welfare system exclusively covers children under three while children over three are covered by both systems. Recent education legislation and the Children Act 1989 accept and reinforce this split.

Concepts of services and quality

In the early 1970s, I went to work at Thomas Coram Research Unit when it was established at the London University Institute of Education. It was then that I was introduced to early childhood services both by my own new parenthood, but also by the Unit's first director, Professor Jack Tizard. His concept of early childhood services influenced me greatly. He was appalled by the state of services in the UK, which apart from being insufficient in number and grossly underresourced, were fragmented and inflexible, unable at various levels to meet the needs of children or families. His vision was of local communities served by 'children's centres', each centre accessible and affordable to all families in its catchment area with children from birth to primary school age. Rather than offering a fixed menu of services, each centre should be flexible and responsive to what parents wanted, a community institution that was multifunctional, capable of meeting and integrating core and interrelated needs such as care, education, support and health, but also able to respond to other needs – even as mundane as launderettes, at a time when many families did not have washing machines.

After this initial work at Thomas Coram, other issues claimed my attention. Working in Europe has helped me to rediscover and appreciate the importance of having an explicit concept about the nature of services and the relevance and far-sightedness of Jack Tizard's particular concept. The European influence here is selective. Many European services and service systems remain fixed in a narrow, inflexible and unifunctional model, reflected in the language used to discuss services: 'childcare for working parents' or 'daycare for children in need' or 'nursery education for three- and four-year-olds'. However, there are examples, at the level of individual services or of service systems, of attempts to develop both an integrated and multifunctional approach, as for example described in this account of services in Northern Italy:

> The 1971 law that passed responsibility for *asili nido* [nurseries for children under three] to local and regional governments defines the main aims of these services as providing care for children to support families and women's employment. However, the local authorities which manage most *asili nido* have increasingly regarded them also as centres for the education and socialization of children, the development of their potential and wellbeing and the promotion of a children's culture, as well as offering a preventive service for children 'at risk' or otherwise disadvantaged. The most recently developed services – *nuove tipologie/servizi integrativi* – are intended to offer opportunities for socialization, education and play for children, especially those who do not already attend other services. They are particularly concerned with the needs of non-employed parents and other carers (who may also include grandparents caring for grandchildren) and parents who want care for their children but not for a full day... They provide parents, in particular mothers, and children, often the only child in the family, with the possibility of escape from loneliness and isolation. (EC Childcare Network, 1996a, p. 73)

In such examples, it is possible to see being put into practice, in the same way as the 'children's centres' envisaged by Jack Tizard, a concept of early childhood services as multifunctional community institutions of cultural, economic and social significance, and as such capable of responding to the needs and circumstances of local children and families. This is in clear contrast to other concepts of services, which are in many respects still dominant in many parts of Europe: the service as a means of delivering to children and families a predetermined and restricted programme or intervention (a treatment model); or the service selling a product to a consumer (a business model).

The concept of service is also relevant to the concept of quality in early childhood services. Here again, a little personal history may be in order. My disciplinary background is neither in psychology nor education. I studied history at university, then trained as a social worker. My introduction to children's services was through work with children with learning disabilities and involvement in the movement to remove these children from care in large institutions: what were then called in the UK 'subnormality hospitals' (Jack Tizard was a leading pioneer for this movement). That movement in the UK, which also included adult men and women with learning difficulties, was influenced from an early stage by work initiated in the USA which emphasized the values-based nature of services, in particular how models of services reflected views about the nature and value of people with learning disabilities, and linked assessments of quality to an explicit and coherent values base.

This background disposed me from the start to view discussions about quality in any type of service as, in the first place, discussions about values and beliefs, and strongly influenced by the concepts held about the users of services. Defining quality is in essence a political process in the sense that it involves values and interests, power and negotiation. This approach has provided a sound basis for the work on quality in early childhood services undertaken since 1990 by the Network (EC Childcare Network, 1990; Balaguer, Mestres and Penn, 1991; EC Childcare Network 1996b). Rather than a search for *quality universals*, the work has started from the assumption that there are *quality perspectives*, that convergence of these perspectives should be sought but that complete convergence is neither necessary nor even desirable.

This approach to quality has developed both through the work of the Childcare Network and parallel work with researchers from six countries which resulted in an edited book, *Valuing Quality in Early Childhood Services* (Moss and Pence, 1994). The book develops the concept of quality in early childhood services (or in fact in any service) as in essence a relative and constructed concept, not an objective reality, and as a dynamic concept, with perspectives and definitions evolving over time. In short, there may be many different understandings of what quality means, because definitions of quality are rooted in the values, beliefs, needs and interests of a variety of groups with an interest or stake in early childhood services – including children, parents, the workforce and other specialist experts, local communities, employers and the wider society.

This concept of quality implies that the process of defining quality – *how* quality is defined and *by whom* – is critically important. Discussion, description and evaluation of quality has tended to be dominated by experts from government, certain professions and academic research. It has involved the exercise of power based on claims of academic or professional expertise and knowledge – although these experts may be motivated by benign concerns and are often unaware that they are exercising power or, indeed, that they are also operating on the basis of values, beliefs and interests. This 'exclusionary approach' often involves an assumption, usually implicit, that quality is an objective reality, a sort of Holy Grail to be discovered and brought back by a select order of suitably qualified and technically equipped specialists.

This 'exclusionary approach' can be contrasted with an 'inclusionary approach':

> a new paradigm for defining quality based on participation by a broad range of stakeholders, and recognition of values, beliefs and interests underpinning definitions. Within this alternative paradigm, the roles, processes and principles typically found within the exclusionary paradigm are transformed: limited participation is replaced by broad access to the process of definition; power concentration gives way to power distribution; few voices make way for many; an assumption of rational objectivity is challenged by recognition of the essential subjectivity of the process and the role of values, beliefs and interests; the search for quality universals becomes the exchange of quality perspectives leading to definitions specific to a particular spatial and temporal context and capable of evolving through a dynamic and continuous process. (Pence and Moss, 1994, pp. 172–3)

A concept similar to this 'inclusionary approach' has been described by Swedish researchers Gunilla Dahlberg and Gunnar Åsén (1994, p. 166), but it is referred to by them as an 'associative model' for defining objectives:

> This model is based on an idea, a vision, of combining the professional and the political model [of goal setting] with an idea of civic participation and democracy. Fundamental to the associative model is that institutions for early childhood education and care are viewed as institutions bearing cultural and social values... Accordingly, how quality in early childhood education and care is defined and evaluated will be a concern not only for politicians, experts, administrators and professionals, but will also be a matter for the broader citizenry... It becomes important to create forums or arenas for discussion and reflection where people can engage as citizens with devotion and vision... and within these arenas a lively dialogue could take place, in which early childhood education and care are placed within a larger societal context.

There are several reasons for arguing that the adoption of an 'inclusionary approach' or 'associative model' is important for the future of early childhood services. The first concerns the issue of legitimacy for these services, and has been developed by Dahlberg and Åsén (1994). At a time when public services are under attack, if early childhood services are to be protected and, in future, develop, they must make their work and practice highly visible and engage as wide a range of stakeholders as possible in debate about that work and practice. An inclusionary or associative approach, therefore, is an important means of increasing an understanding of services and the importance attached to them and of developing a wider sense of identification and ownership with their objectives and practice.

The second reason is because the approach values and supports plurality. This can be seen as an end in itself. Concluding an anthropological study of conditions contributing to the social ecology of childhood, Weisner (1989) argues that 'in a democratic society, the nurturance and understanding of diversity rather than the production of conformity should remain a fundamental social value'. Yet there are strong forces working for the adoption of standard concepts and standard measures, creating a process of ideological and intellectual colonization leading to the global distribution of one kind of 'common frame of reference' and a world of uniformity (Woodhead, 1995). There is a possibility that the USA will establish hegemony in the area of quality in early childhood services in the same way it has already done in other cultural, technological and academic areas, and despite the fact that early childhood services in the USA are neither comparable to services in many other countries nor viewed, even by many American experts themselves, as adequate.

Alan Pence has used an environmental analogy to argue the importance of valuing and supporting diversity and plurality in the context of childrearing and early childhood services. He likens the variety of childrearing practices which currently exist in different cultures and subcultures to endangered species which must be preserved, since they contain the genes for new and challenging ways of thinking, learning and being which we may one day need as conventional Western ideas fail us (Pence, 1995). This belief in the importance and mutual benefit derived from diversity has informed the development of an innovative, cross-cultural curriculum model which Pence calls the 'generative curriculum'. In this model, professional Euro–Western ideas about learning processes are matched against specific local conditions and ideas – Pence gives the example of his university department working with First Nation people in Canada – and discussed and developed in as open and inclusive a way as possible with community elders, parents, workers and other stakeholders in early childhood services (Pence and McCallum, 1994).

The last reason why the concept of quality adopted is so important relates to the concept of services. The inclusionary approach fits best with the concept of early childhood services as community institutions or resources, responsive to the needs, interests and perspectives of their local communities and playing a major role not only at individual and family level but also in supporting community cohesion and development. In many respects our societies are becoming increasingly diverse. Local services need to match this diversity, being attuned to the particular needs and circumstances of families that use them and of their local communities, and also able to respond to change. An associative model or inclusionary approach to quality is consistent with services which seek to be relevant and responsive, rather then prescriptive, and provides a means for translating a commitment to responsiveness and relevance into practice.

In this chapter, I have discussed some of the qualities that characterize early childhood services in the European Union and different concepts of these services. I have also outlined different concepts of quality. The conceptualization of services and quality has implications not only for the services themselves, but also for research. For if the concept is adopted of early childhood services as multifunctional community resources, addressing the needs of a wider range of stakeholders, then not only do many existing services have to transform themselves, but new, broader and more multidisciplinary approaches to research will need to be adopted. Similarly, research on quality will need to change:

> The self-contained, scientifically controlled model of Western positivist empirical study is restricted in its ability to perceive and understand social and cultural assumptions, values and mores outside its practitioners' own traditions and orientations. Such research is problematic not so much for its generation of wrong answers, as for limitations in its posing of questions. The current literature on quality care is problematic both in its assumptions of what constitutes desirable developmental universals, and in its restricted understanding of diverse environments, social change and cultural diversity... [There needs to be] movement away from the ever finer measurement of micro-system environmental variables to an awareness and appreciation of quality care perspectives as held by an expanded reference group. (Pence and McCallum, 1994, p. 121)

This transition in research on quality in early childhood services, to operating within an 'inclusionary approach', will have major implications. Sociology, anthropology, political science and other disciplines will have a major contribution to make alongside developmental psychology; researchers will have to recognize their own position as stakeholders in services, with particular interests, needs and perspectives; and research itself will have to focus more on the process of defining quality and working in partnership with services and communities themselves in that process and the subsequent process of implementing definitions.

Note

1 'Publicly funded' services are wholly or mainly subsidised from public sources but are not necessarily publicly managed; they may be managed by private organizations. The proportion of publicly funded services that are privately managed varies between countries and is more common among services in the welfare system than in the education system.

References

BALAGUER, I., MESTRES, J. and PENN, H. (1991) *Quality in Services for Young Children: A Discussion Paper*, Brussels, European Commission Equal Opportunities Unit.
DAHLBERG, G. and ÅSÉN, G. (1994) 'Evaluation and regulation: A question of empowerment', in MOSS, P. and PENCE, A. (Eds) *Valuing Quality in Early Childhood Services: New Approaches to Defining Quality*, London, Paul Chapman Publishing.
EC CHILDCARE NETWORK (1990) *Quality in Childcare Services – Seminar Report*, Brussels, European Commission Equal Opportunities Unit.
EC CHILDCARE NETWORK (1994) *Leave Arrangements for Workers with Children*, Brussels, European Commission Equal Opportunities Unit.
EC CHILDCARE NETWORK (1996a) *Review of Services for Young Children in the European Union*, Brussels, European Commission Equal Opportunities Unit.
EC CHILDCARE NETWORK (1996b) *Quality Targets in Services for Young Children*, Brussels, European Commission Equal Opportunities Unit.
KARLSSON, M. (1995) *Family Day Care in Europe*, Brussels, European Commission Equal Opportunities Unit.
MEIJVOGEL, R. and PETRIE, P. (1996) *School-age Childcare in the European Union*, Brussels, European Commission Equal Opportunities Unit.
MOSS, P. and PENCE, A. (Eds) (1994) *Valuing Quality in Early Childhood Services: New Approaches to Defining Quality*, London, Paul Chapman Publishing.
MOSS, P. and PENN, H. (1996) *Transforming Nursery Education*, London, Paul Chapman Publishing.
OECD (ORGANIZATION FOR ECONOMIC CO-OPERATION AND DEVELOPMENT) (1995) *Employment Outlook, July 1995*, Paris, OECD.
PENCE, A. (1995) 'Cross-cultural partnerships in training', paper given at Institute of Education Early Years Seminar Series, University of London, July 1995.
PENCE, A. and MCCALLUM, M. (1994) 'Developing cross-cultural partnerships: implications for child care quality research and practice', in MOSS, P. and PENCE, A. (Eds) *Valuing Quality in Early Childhood Services: New Approaches to Defining Quality*, London, Paul Chapman Publishing.

PENCE, A. and MOSS, P. (1994) 'Towards an inclusionary approach in defining quality', in MOSS, P. and PENCE, A. (Eds) *Valuing Quality in Early Childhood Services: New Approaches to Defining Quality*, London, Paul Chapman Publishing.

WEISNER, T. (1989) 'Cultural and universal aspects of social support for children: Evidence from the Abuluyia of Kenya', in BELLE, D. (Ed.) *Children's Social Networks and Social Support*, New York, Wiley.

WOODHEAD, M. (1995) *In search of the rainbow: Pathways to quality in large scale programmes for young disadvantaged children*, The Hague, Bernard van Leer Foundation.

Appendix

Table 13.1 Provision of publicly funded early childhood services in Member States

	A	B	C	D	Children 0–3	Children 3–6
Belgium	27	**	6	1993	30%	95%+
Denmark	30	**	7	1994	48%	82%
Germany	36	*	6	1990	2% (W)	78% (W)
					50% (E)	100% (E)
Greece	9	**	6	1993	#3%	#70% (a)
Spain	36	*	6	1993	?2%	84%
France	36	**	6	1993	23%	99%
Ireland	3		6	1993	2%	55%
Italy	9		6	1991	6%	91%
N'lands	15	**	5	1993	#8% (a)	#71% (a)
Austria	24		6	1994	3%	75%
Portugal	27		6	1993	12%	48%
Finland	36		7	1994	21%	53%
Sweden	36		7	1994	33%	72%
UK	7	*	5	1993	2%	#60% (a)

Key

Column A gives the length of maternity leave + parental leave in months available per family after the birth of each child.

Column B indicates whether subsidies are available to parents (in addition to subsidies paid direct to services) to cover part of their costs for using services for young children. * = subsidy available to lower income parents only; ** = subsidy available to some/all parents, irrespective of income.

Column C shows the age at which compulsory schooling begins.

Column D shows to what year the figures in the next three columns refer.

(a) Figure includes some children in compulsory schooling (i.e. where compulsory schooling begins before six).

? approximate figure.

important qualification, see *Note on Table 13.1 and Figure 13.2*.

Appendix

Note on Table 13.1 and Figure 13.2

The age of compulsory schooling is relevant because it affects the figures given for services for children aged three to six years. As well as services in the welfare system, these services include pre-primary schooling; early admission to primary school; and children attending compulsory schooling (in the case of countries where compulsory schooling begins before six).

Countries (or even different systems within the same country) vary in whether they collect data on 'places available' or 'children attending'. Figure 13.1 and Table 13.2 reflect this mix of data. They give information on:

places available for Belgium and France (0–3, except for two-year-olds in pre-primary schooling); Germany, Italy (0–3), The Netherlands, Portugal and UK;

and information on:

children attending for Belgium and France (two-year-olds in pre-primary schooling and 3–6), Denmark, Greece, Spain, Ireland, Italy (3–6), Austria, Finland and Sweden.

The two measures will not differ significantly when all or nearly all 'places available' are used full-time and if there are few or no vacancies. However, in some services in some countries a significant number of places are used on a part-time basis and, in effect, shared by two children; in these cases, data on 'children attending' will significantly over-state the 'places available' and the volume of services supplied. The difference between 'places available' and 'children attending' is significant in services in the welfare system in Ireland, the Netherlands and the UK and in pre-primary schooling in the UK. In these cases, estimated 'place available' data rather than 'children attending' data have been used in Figure 13.2 and Table 13.1 where available (i.e. for the UK and the Netherlands).

Two final qualifications need to be made about Figure 13.2 and Table 13.1. The first concerns information on services in the welfare system for Greece, the Netherlands and the UK. These countries do not produce statistics for children aged 0–3 and 3–6; in Greece, statistics are for children aged $0-2^{1}/_{2}-5^{1}/_{2}$ years, in the Netherlands for children aged 0–4 years and in the UK for children aged 0–5 years. In these cases, estimates have been made for children aged 0–3 and 3–6 years.

The second qualification concerns the definition of 'publicly-funded'. In nearly all cases, this means that more than half of the total costs of a service are paid from public sources, and usually between 75% and 100%. The main exception to this is the Netherlands, where public funding usually covers less than half the costs of services in the welfare system. The Netherlands figure for publicly-funded provision also excludes playgroups (peuterspeelzalen). Although most places in this form of provision receive some public funds, average hours of opening and attendance are so much shorter than for other services that it would be potentially misleading to include information on them either for 'children attending' or 'places available'.

List of Contributors

Dr Tessa Blackstone
Master of Birkbeck College
University of London
Malet Street
London WC1E 7HX

Professor Alan Clarke
Visiting Professor
University of Hertforshire
College Lane
Hatfield
Hertforshire AL109AB

Professor Ann Clarke
University of Hertfordshire
College Lane
Hatfield
Hertfordshire AL109AB

Professor Judy Dunn
Institute of Psychiatry
113 Denmark Hill
London SE5 8AF

Professor Philip Graham
Developmental Psychiatry Section
Department of Psychiatry
University of Cambridge
Douglas House
18b Trumpington Road
Cambridge CB2 2AH

Dr Jill Hodges
Department of Psychological Medicine

List of Contributors

The Hospital for Sick Children
Great Ormond Street
London WC1N 3JH

Professor Martin Hughes
School of Education
University of Exeter
St Luke's
Exeter EX1 2LU

Jo Mortimore
Institute of Education
University of London
20 Bedford Way
London WC1H 0AL

Professor Peter Mortimore
Institute of Education
University of London
20 Bedford Way
London WC1H 0AL

Peter Moss
Thomas Coram Research Unit
Institute of Education, University of London
27/28 Woburn Square
London WC1H 0AA

Charlie Owen
Thomas Coram Research Unit
Institute of Education, University of London
27/28 Woburn Square
London WC1N 0AA

Dr Pat Petrie
Thomas Coram Research Unit
Institute of Education, University of London
27/28 Woburn Square
London WC1H 0AA

Dr Ann Phoenix
Department of Psychology
Birkbeck College
University of London

List of Contributors

Malet Street
London WC1E 7HX

Ian Plewis
Thomas Coram Research Unit
Institute of Education, University of London
27/28 Woburn Square
London WC1H 0AA

Professor Martin Richards
Centre for Family Research
University of Cambridge
Free School Lane
Cambridge CB2 3RF

Sir Michael Rutter
Professor of Psychiatry
Institute of Psychiatry
University of London
De Crespigny Park
London SE5 8AF

Professor William Yule
Institute of Psychiatry
University of London
De Crespigny Park
London SE5 8AF

Index

Abbot, D. 110
Acock, A. C. 189, 202
Adam Smith Institute 207
ADI 37
adolescent development following institutional care 71–5
adoption
　and adolescent development 71–5
　and attachment 68–9, 76–7
　and childhood development 69–71
　late 53
　transracial 111, 126–8
affective disorder associated with childhood behaviour and personality 51
African-Caribbean pupils and educational inequality 136–47
age, effects on sequelae of brain lesions 32–3
Aicardi, J. 42
Ainsworth, M. D. S. 51, 59, 63, 66, 67, 77
Alansky, J. A. 52, 60
Alibhai-Brown, Y. 117, 133
Amato, P. R. 189, 190, 193, 194, 195, 201
Ames, E. W. 77
Andersen, J. C. 61
Angelman syndrome 36
Angold, A. 37, 41
Appleton, M. 86, 92
Arasteh, J. D. 189, 203
Åsén, G. 254, 255, 257

associate staff 152
Astington, J. W. 82, 92
attachment
　disorganized/disoriented 64
　and family placement 68–9
　insecure-avoidant 63, 64, 66, 75
　insecure-resistant 63–4
　and institutional care 65–9, 73–5, 76–7
　intergenerational transmission of behaviour 52
　and nursery environment 65–7
　predictive failures 51–3
　secure 63, 66
attention deficit disorder 172, 176
autism 33–4, 36, 39–40, 172, 174
Autism Diagnostic Interview 37
Autism Diagnostic Observation Schedule 37

Baddeley, A. D. 40, 41
Baert, A. E. 51, 61
Baghurst, P. 175, 182
Bagley, C. 126, 133
Bailey, A. 33, 34, 36, 40, 41, 43, 44, 182
Bainham, A. 188, 201
Bakwin, H. 31, 41
Bakwin, R. M. M. 31, 41
Balaguer, I. 253, 257
Bandura, A. 48, 57, 59
Barbara, A. 114, 133
Barber, B. L. 195, 202
Barden, R. C. 87, 93–4

264

Baron-Cohen, S. 43
Bartak, L. 173, 183
Bartsch, K. 83, 92
Beardsall, L. 82, 86, 93
Bebbington, A. 111, 133
Beckwith, R. 87, 92
Beeghly, M. 83, 92
behavioural phenotypes 34–7, 39
behavioural science, uncertainties in 47
Bellissimo, A. 192, 204
Bellugi, U. 37, 41, 43
Beloff, H. 24, 25
Bem, D. J. 50, 60
Benoit, D. 52, 59
Bhrolchain, M. N. 189, 190, 202
Blatchford, P. 8, 99, 110, 145, 147, 148
Blehar, M. 77
Block, J. 49, 59
Bloom, L. 87, 92
Blum, L. 91, 92
Bolton, P. 34, 35, 36, 38, 41, 45, 183
Booth, A. 193, 194, 201
Bornstein, M. H. 56, 59
Bowlby, J. 51, 57, 59, 64, 67, 72, 73, 75, 77
Brah, A. 112, 133
brain
  lesion 31, 32–3
  plasticity 33
Bramble, D. 176, 181
Bretherton, I. 66, 77, 83, 92, 93
Broadfoot, P. 110
Broman, S. H. 35, 40, 41
Brown, G. 173, 181
Brown, G. W. 175, 181, 183
Brown, J. R. 83, 84, 86, 87, 88, 90, 91, 92, 93
Brown, W. T. 42
Bruner, C. 229, 240
Bruner, J. S. 85, 92
Burchell, B. 97, 98, 105, 110
Burgoyne, J. 189, 198, 202
Burke, J. 8, 99, 110, 147, 148

Burns, S. 189, 197, 206
Busch, C. 55, 62
Butterworth, G. 86, 92

Callanan, M. A. 85, 92–3
Cameron, K. 170, 181
Campbell, R. 108, 109
Canavan, A. G. M. 33, 42
CAPA 37
Carey, S. 33, 46
Carlson, E. A. 63, 74, 77, 79
Carnie, J. 54, 62
Carr, J. 57, 59
Carriger, M. S. 56, 61
Carter, M. C. 77
Caspi, A. 50, 60, 61
Cassidy, J. 66, 78
causal language 83
CECIL research 139–47
census data
  ethnic group 118–19
  mixed couples 119–20
  mixed-parentage 120–1
Central Advisory Committee for Education 109
Centre for Policy Studies 207
cerebral palsy 34
Chadwick, O. 30, 31, 32, 33, 41, 44, 45
chance and development 57–8
Changes in the Classroom Experience of Children in Inner London 139–47
Chappell, R. 189, 190, 202
Chase-Lansdale, P. 190, 202
Cherlin, A. J. 190, 202, 205
Chess, S. 50, 52, 60, 172, 181
Child and Adolescent Psychiatric Assessment 37
child mental health
  changes in clinical practice 169–71
  classification of disorders 175
  evidence-based clinical practice 176–8
  and family relationships 172–3

Index

genetic factors 172
and life events 173
research 170
 aetiological 171–4
 clinical trials 176
 contribution to clinical
  assessment 174–5
 impact on public policy 178–80
 school effects 173
child sexual abuse, predictive
 failure 53–4
childcare services
 preschool 97–8, 242–57, 259–60
 school-age 220–39
Children Act 1989 188, 197–8
Children's Rights Office 188, 202
Chisholm, K. 68, 70, 77
Choice and Diversity 102
city technology college staffing
 innovations 151–67
City Technology Trust 151, 167
Clark, J. 195, 202
Clarke, A. D. B. 49, 50, 53, 54, 55, 58, 60
Clarke, A. M. 48, 49, 50, 53, 54, 55, 58, 60
Clarke, K. 196, 202
Clingempeel, W. G. 189, 192, 203
Cockett, M. 192, 202
cognitive psychology 174
cohabitation 200
Cohen, I. L. 37, 42, 45
Coleman, M. 193, 203
Collins, P. H. 112, 130, 133
Commission on British Business and
 Public Policy 215
Commission on Social Justice 212–13, 219
conduct disorder 174
 aetiology 172–3
 association with childhood
  behaviour and personality 51
constancy model 48
conversation *see* family conversation
Cooper, R. 62

Cornford, J. 218
Costello, E. J. 37, 41
Cox, A. 41, 175, 181
Cox, M. 189, 203
Cox, R. 189, 203
Craig, G. 196, 202
Creps, C. 88, 93
Crittenden, P. M. 66, 67, 77
Croll, P. 110
Crowson, M. 41
CTC staffing innovations 151–67
cumulative advantage/disadvantage 144–5

Dahlberg, G. 254, 255, 257
David, M. E. 96, 109
Davis, G. 198, 202
Demo, D. E. 189, 202
Dennis, D. W. 64, 77
Department for Education 102, 109
Department of Education and
 Science 102, 109, 151, 167, 171, 181
Desforges, C. 104, 106, 109
development
 and institutional care 65–77
 predictions of 48–9, 56–9
 predictive failures 49–56
 unpredictability 48
developmental transformation 72
Diamond, I. 189, 190, 202
Dias, K. 42
DiLavore, P. C. 37, 42
Dillon, P. A. 191, 202
Directorate of Education, Culture
 and Sport 239
disadvantage 58
discourse *see* family conversation
divorce 197–201
 childcare arrangements 187–8
 and conduct disorder 172–3
 current legislation 185
 economic factors 195–6
 grounds 187
 and parental relationships 193–4

266

processes affecting children 190–3
rates 186–7
research and social policy 193–7
and wellbeing of children 189–90
Dobash, R. E. 203
Dobash, R. P. 54, 62
Docking, J. W. 96, 109
domestic life, trend to privatization 186–8
Donelan-McCall, N. 90, 92
Douglas, G. 185, 188, 201, 202
Douglas, J. W. B. 178, 181
Down syndrome 34
Downey, D. B. 194, 202
Dunn, J. 50, 61, 82, 83, 84, 86, 87, 88, 89, 90, 91, 92, 93, 94, 95
Duyvesteyn, M. G. 52, 62
Dykens, E. M. 35, 42
Dyson, M. 189, 205

Early Years Trainers Anti-racist Network 133
EC Childcare Network 242, 251, 252, 253, 254, 257
Ecob, R. 147
education
 following Education Reform Act 1988 103–9
 market forces in 102
 role of parents in 96–7, 101
Education Reform Act 1988 101–3, 137–9, 151
 research on parents following implementation 103–9
educational achievement 99–100
educational inequality 136–47
Egeland, B. 179, 181
Eggebeen, D. J. 194, 202
Eisenberg, A. R. 87, 93
Eisenberg, J. M. 177, 182
Elander, J. 30, 42
Elder, G. H. 50, 60
Elliott, B. J. 189, 190, 193, 195, 202, 203
Ellis, N. R. 35, 42

Emery, R. E. 189, 191, 192, 198, 202, 203
Eminson, M. 29, 45
Enders-Dragässer, U. 230, 239
epilepsy 30–2
epileptic personality 29–30
Erickson, M. F. 179, 181
Esser, G. 51, 56, 60, 61
European Network for School-age Childcare 220
European Union, early childcare services 243–50, 259–60
Eurydice 223, 239
Evans, L. 109
Everett, C. A. 195, 203
evidence-based medicine in child mental health 176–8
Eysenck, M. W. 174, 181

Fabes, R.A. 91, 93
false belief paradigm 82–3
family conversation 81–2, 98–9
 emotional and pragmatic context 87–8
 and gender 91
 patterns over time 86
 reflective 88
 significance of partner 89–90
 and social class 90–1
 and social understanding 82–5
Family Law Bill 185, 187, 198
family placement
 and adolescent development 71–5
 and attachment 68–9, 76–7
 and childhood development 69–71
family relationships and child mental health 172–3
Farquhar, C. 8, 99, 110, 147, 148
Fassam, M. 179, 182
Feingold, D. 211, 218
Felleman, E. S. 87, 93–4
Ferguson, D. M. 58, 60
Ferri, E. 194, 203
Field, J. 204

Index

Fincham, F. D. 190, 203
Fine, D. R. 187, 203
Fine, M. A. 187, 203
Fivush, R. 91, 93
Fleeting, M. 61
Flint, J. 35, 39, 42
Fonagy, P. 52, 60, 62, 66, 77, 176, 184
Foucault, M. 116, 133
Fox, N. A. 52, 60
Fox, N. E. 74, 79
fragile X anomaly 34, 35, 37, 39
France
  school-age childcare 231–3
  see also European Union
Freeman, B. J. 64, 78
Freeman, N. H. 93
Freud, A. 74, 77
friends as conversational partners 90
Frith, U. 174, 181
Fryer, P. 114, 116, 133

Ganong, L. H. 193, 203
Gardner, J. 46
Garnham, A. 196, 203
Garvey, C. 85, 93
Garwood, F. 200, 203
Gatzanis, S. R. M. 61
gender
  and family conversation 91
  interaction with race and educational inequality 136–47
generative curriculum 255
Germany
  school-age childcare 228–31
  see also European Union
Gillespie, G. 196, 203
Gillis, J. R. 186, 203
Gleick, J. 47, 60
Glendinning, L. 196, 202
Glyn, A. 213, 218
Gold, D. R. 55, 62
Goldfarb, W. 68, 73, 75, 77, 78

Goldsmith, H. H. 52, 60
Goldstein, H. 146, 147
Goode, S. 41, 43
Goode, W. J. 186, 189, 203
Goodman, R. 32, 33, 42, 172, 181
Goodson, I. 166, 167
Goodwin, M. S. 80
Goodyer, I. 173, 181
Gordon, R. G. 170, 181
Gottesman, I. 41, 43, 182
Gottman, J. M. 195, 204
Grafman, J. 35, 40, 41
Graham, P. 30, 32, 44, 171, 173, 174, 175, 176, 179, 181, 182, 183
Grant, J. 41, 43
Greco, P. 177, 182
Griffiths, A. 96, 109
Grossman, K. 66, 78
Grossman, K. E. 66, 78
Grych, J. H. 190, 203

Haber, J. D. 195, 206
Hagberg, G. 36, 42
Hagerman, R. J. 35, 37, 42, 43
Hakimi-Minesh, Y. 64, 78
Hall, C. I. 126, 133
Hall, S. 112, 114, 133
Hamilton, D. 96, 109
Hansen, M. 228, 240
Hargreaves, A. 166, 167
Harkness, H. R. 61
Harmer, L. S. 227, 240
Harrington, R. 41, 183
Harris, J. C. 36, 42
Harris, R. 32, 43
Harris, T. 173, 181
Haskey, J. 122, 133
Hatcher, R. 127, 134
head injury 31
Heemsbergen, J. 43
Henriques, F. 113, 114, 133
Herbison, G. P. 61
Hermann, B. P. 32, 42
Hersov, L. 169, 182
Hesse, E. 64, 78

268

Hetherington, E. M. 189, 192, 203
Hewison, J. 100, 109, 110, 179, 182
Hewitt, P. 211, 218
Heywood, C. A. 33, 42
Higgitt, A. 60
Higgott, R. 218
Hodges, J. 67, 69, 70, 71, 75, 78, 79, 175, 182
Hodges, K. 175, 182
Hoggett, B. 188, 198, 203
Holbrook, D. 175, 181
Holden, C. 104, 106, 109
Holdgrafen, M. 43
Holmes, R. 127, 128, 133
home as learning environment 98–9
Honig, A. S. 15, 25
Horwood, L. J. 58, 60
Howlin, P. 33, 45
HPRT deficiency 35
Hughes, M. 3, 8, 81, 84, 91, 94, 96, 98, 103, 104, 105, 106, 109, 110
Humblet, P. 234, 240
hybridity 114–15
hyperkinetic disorder 172, 176
hypodescent 112
hypoxanthine phosphoribosyltransferase deficiency 35

identity and race 126–8
Ihinger-Tallman, M. 192, 194, 203
ILEA Junior School Project 137
infant information-processing 56
Infant School Project 136–7
inhibition 50
innovation in CTC staffing 151–67
Institute of Economic Affairs 207
Institute of Public Policy Research 207–18
institutional care
 and adolescent development 71–5
 and attachment 65–9, 73–5, 76–7
 and childhood development 69–71
intelligence 54–6

IPPR 207–18
IQ 54–6
Isaacs, E. 46

Jackson, E. 195, 203
James, A. L. 196, 199, 204
James, S. 216, 218
Jenkins, E. C. 42
Jenkins, J. 179, 182
Jernigan, T. L. 37, 41
Johansson, I. 228, 240
Johnson, A. M. 187, 204
Jordan, H. 43
Joseph, A. 65, 68, 79
Juffer, F. 52, 62

Kagan, J. 49–50, 57, 60
Kaler, S. R. 64, 78
Kalter, N. 189, 204
Kalverboer, A. F. 31, 42
Kanner, L. 36, 43, 177, 182
Kaplan, C. A. 174, 182
Kaplan, N. 66, 78
Karlsson, M. 246, 257
Karmiloff-Smith, A. 37, 43
Katz, L. F. 195, 204
Kaufman, K. R. 32, 43
Kazdin, A. 172, 182
Keane, M. T. 174, 181
Keep, E. 218
Keith, B. 189, 190, 201
Kerr, M. 50, 61
Kesberg, E. 229, 240
Kiernan, K. E. 187, 189, 190, 194, 202, 204
Kimmerley, N. L. 52, 60
Kirton, D. 126, 133
Klackenberg-Larsson, I. 61
Klima, E. 43
Knight, J. 171, 182
Knights, E. 196, 203
Kolvin, I. 58, 61
Kuebli, J. 91, 93
Kuh, D. 189, 204
Kyriakdou, C. 93

Index

Labour Force Survey 118, 122–5
Ladd, G. W. 89, 94
LaFreniere, P. J. 74, 75, 78
Lally, J. R. 15, 25
Lambert, W. W. 61
Landsdown, G. 197, 204
language, causal 83
Lanyardo, M. 175, 182
Lappen, J. 46
Laucht, M. 56, 61
Laurence, K. M. 55, 62
Le Couteur, A. 34, 37, 40, 41, 43, 172, 182, 183
Leekham, S. R. 89, 94
Lenhart, L. 174, 182
Lesch-Nyhan syndrome 35, 39
Leseve-Nicolle, C. 233, 240
Levin, B. 108, 110
Levitt, E. E. 170, 182
Lewis, C. 89, 93
Lewis, D. 147
Lewis, M. 57, 61
Liddle, C. 58, 61
Lieberman, A. F. 63, 78
life events and child mental health 173
Lipton, R. C. 68, 79
Lochman, J. E. 174, 182
Lord, C. 37, 42, 43
Lord Chancellor's Department 185, 204
Lynskey, M. 58, 60

McCall, R. E. 56, 61
McCallum, M. 255, 256, 257
McCarthy, P. 191, 192, 205
McCartney, K. 48, 61
McCormick, S. E. 93
Macdonald, H. 41, 183
MacDonald, K. 70, 78
McFarlane, A. H. 192, 204
Macfarlane, J. W. 49, 61
McFie, J. 32, 43
Maclay, D. T. 170, 182
Maclean, M. 189, 195, 196, 203, 204

McLennan, J. 43
McRoy, R. 126, 133
Madge, N. 179, 182
Mahoux, C. 234, 240
Main, M. 64, 66, 78
Mangione, P. L. 15, 25
Manheimer, H. 80
Maridaki-Kossotaki, K. 93
marriage, interracial 112, 113
  census data 119–20
  opposition to 115–17
Marsh, C. 132, 133
Martin, F. 171, 182
Martin, J. 152, 168
Martin, J. L. 61
Masters, J. C. 87, 93–4
maternal deprivation 64, 72
maternal employment 222–3
maternal sensitivity 66
Matrimonial Causes Act 1857 186, 187
Matthew effect 144–5
Maughan, B. 75, 79, 183
Mawhood, L. 33, 43, 45
Mazzocco, M. M. 37, 43
Medical Research Council 38, 43
Mednick, S. A. 51, 61
Meijvogel, M. C. 232, 240
Meijvogel, R. 220, 222, 240, 242, 257
Mendlewicz, J. 31, 42
mental retardation
  and behavioural phenotypes 34–7
  future research needs 37–41
Merttens, R. 96, 110
Mestres, J. 153, 257
Miedaner, L. 229, 240
Miles, J. 111, 133
Miliband, D. 213, 214, 218
Miller, C. 87, 94
Miller, F. J. W. 61
Milowe, I. D. 80
minimal cerebral/brain dysfunction 31

Ministère de l'Éducation National de la Jeunesse et des Sports 232, 239, 240
Minogue, M. 4, 7
miscegenation 113, 114, 115
Misch, P. 62
Mistina, D. 193, 203
Mitchell, A. 189, 191, 197, 205
mixed-parentage 111, 125–32
  and age 122–3
  construction as problematic 111–17
  demographic trends 117–25
  and family structure 124–5
  objections to 115–17
  terminology 113–14
Moffitt, T. E. 55, 61
Mohdehi, J. 64, 78
Monck, E. 72, 79
Monk, E. 62
Montague, A. 117, 133
Morison, S. J. 77
Morison, V. 62
Morrison, D. R. 190, 205
Morrow, V. 196, 205
Mortimore, J. 97, 98, 105, 110, 152, 167, 168
Mortimore, P. 137, 147, 152, 167, 168, 173, 183
Moss, P. 248, 253, 254, 257, 258
mothers as conversational partners 89
Mullen, P. E. 53, 61
multigene disorders 40
multilevel modelling 146
Munn, P. 83, 93
Murch, M. 185, 188, 198, 201, 202

Nash, P. 96, 103, 105, 110
National Child Development Study, development of adopted and illegitimate children 75
National Curriculum 103
  and educational inequality 136–47
Neill, S. 109

Network on Childcare and Other Measures to Reconcile Employment and Family Responsibilities of Women and Men 242
neurofibromatosis 34, 39
neurological disorder, psychiatric risk associated 30–2
Newcombe, F. 32, 43
Newton, P. E. 83, 84, 94
NFER 147
non-attachment 63
Norman, G. R. 192, 204
Norment, L. 113, 134
nurseries and attachment 65–7
Nyhan, W. L. 35, 43

O'Brien, G. 35, 36, 43
OECD 243, 257
Oguntoye, K. 134
Oliver, C. 35, 43
Olweus, D. 173, 179, 183
one drop rule 112, 128–9
OPCS/GRO(S) 132, 134
Opitz, M. 114, 134
Oppenheim, C. 195, 205
Ormrod, R. 189, 198, 202
Osborn, M. 110
Ouston, J. 183
Owen, C. 116, 118, 134

Paccia, J. 46
Packwood, A. 109
Pancake, V. R. 74, 79
parental choice 102, 103–4
parental leave 243, 244
parenting plan 199
parents
  development of relationship with schools 106–7
  and Education Reform Act 102–3
  effect on children's educational achievements 99–100
  effect of conflict on children 190, 192, 195

involvement in nursery education 97–8
relationships and divorce 193–4
research regarding following the Education Reform Act 103–9
role in children's education 96–7, 101, 107–9
teacher responsiveness to views 104–6
Parent's Charter, The 102
Park, R. E. 117, 134
Parke, R. D. 89, 94
Parker, D. 114, 130, 134
Parker, K. C. H. 52, 59
Pawl, J. H. 63, 78
Peeters, J. 234, 240
Pence, A. 253, 254, 255, 256, 257, 258
Penn, H. 248, 253, 257
Pennington, B. F. 37, 43
Pepinster, C. 217, 219
Permien, H. 229, 240
Perner, J. 82, 89, 94
Perry, A. 185, 188, 201, 202
personality development, predictive failures 49–51
personality disorder 51
Petrie, P. 220, 222, 234, 240, 242, 257
Phillips, R. 186, 205
Phillips, W. 33, 34, 36, 40, 41
Phinney, J. 126, 134
Phoenix, A. 4, 8, 111, 126, 127, 130, 134
Piaget, J. 89, 94
Pickles, A. 41, 43, 44, 75, 79
Pilling, D. 58, 61
Piper, C. 185, 205
Plewis, I. 8, 99, 108, 110, 137, 140, 141, 145, 147, 148
Plomin, R. 38, 45, 50, 61
Plowden Report 97
Pocock, S. 178, 183
Poland, G. 234, 240
Pollard, A. 108, 110

Powell, B. 194, 202
Prader-Willi syndrome 35–6, 39
predictions 48–9, 56–9
 and attachment 51–3
 and childhood sexual abuse 53–4
 of intelligence 54–6
 of personality development 49–51
Prendergast, M. 41
Provence, S. 68, 79
psychiatric risk associated with neuro-epileptic disorders 30–2
psychodynamic therapy 170
Pugh, G. 198, 206

quality in early childhood services 253–6
Quinton, D. 58, 61

race
 and educational inequality 136–47
 and identity 126–8
 and polarization 111–15
Rachman, S. R. 171, 183
Raffe, D. 218
Ramos, O. 42
Ratcliffe, S. G. 37, 44
reading difficulty in neuro-epileptic disorder 30
Reddy, V. 83, 85, 86, 92, 94
Rees, J. 67, 68, 79
Reibstein, J. 187, 205
Reilly, S. L. 40, 45
research in child mental health 169–80
Rett, A. 36, 44
Rett syndrome 36
Rett Syndrome Diagnostic Criteria Working Group 36, 44
Reuter, E. B. 112, 134
Rezac, S. J. 193, 194, 201
Rhoades, H. 196, 205
Richards, M. P. M. 185, 186, 187, 189, 190, 193, 194, 195, 196, 198, 200, 202, 203, 205, 206

Richman, N. 173, 183
Richmond, A. H. 116, 134
Riffel, A. 108, 110
Rios, P. 41, 43
risk taking in CTC staffing 154
Robb, S. 46
Robertson, S. 43
Robins, L. 171, 183
Roche, J. 188, 205
Rodgers, B. 51, 61, 189, 205
Rogoff, B. 85, 94
Rolle, J. 229, 240
Romans, S. E. 61
Root, M. P. P. 119, 122, 125, 129, 134
Rose, D. 62
Rosenthal, D. 126, 134
Ruffman, T. 89, 94
Rutter, M. 30, 31, 33, 34, 36, 37, 38, 39, 40, 41, 42, 43, 44, 45, 52, 57, 58, 61, 72, 76, 79, 171, 172, 173, 174, 175, 179, 180, 181, 182, 183, 184, 189, 205

Sammons, P. 137, 147, 148
Scarr, S. 48, 61
Schacher, R. 32, 44
Schafer, W. D. 52, 60
Schaffer, D. 31, 32, 43, 44
Schmidt, M. 56, 61
Schmidt, M. H. 51, 60
Schneider, G. E. 33, 45
Schofield, W. N. 100, 110
Scholnik, E. K. 83, 85, 94
school
  influence on child mental health 173
  influence on childcare services 223–4
school-age childcare services 220–39
Schopler, E. 43
Scott, D. McL. 61
Searson, S. M. 174, 182
Seidel, U. P. 30, 45
Seidenberg, M. 32, 42

sexual abuse, predictive failure 53–4
Shaffer, D. 41, 45, 175, 184
Shatz, M. 84, 94
Sheldrick, C. 179, 184
Shulman, S. 74, 79
shyness 50–1
siblings as conversational partners 89–90
Sigman, M. D. 56, 59
Sillitoe, K. 118, 134
Silva, P. A. 61
Silverman, W. 45
Simonoff, E. 35, 36, 38, 41, 44, 45, 183
Simpson, B. 191, 192, 194, 205
Sing, C. F. 40, 45
single gene disorders 39–40
Skuse, D. 53, 62
Slater, A. 56, 62
Slater, E. J. 195, 206
Slomkowski, C. M. 82, 84, 93, 94
Small, J. 113, 114, 134
Smith, C. 198, 206
Smith, D. 180, 184
Smith, M. 178, 179, 182, 183
Snidman, N. 50, 60
Social Affairs Unit 207
social class and family conversation 90–1
social understanding
  association with early experience 86
  development 85
  and family conversation 82–5
  significance of conversational partners in development 89–90
Socialstyrelsen 226, 240
Spangler, G. 78
Spickard, P. R. 112, 115, 134
Spitz, R. A. 64, 79
Sroufe, L. A. 63, 72, 74, 75, 76, 77, 78, 79, 80, 179, 181
staffing innovations in CTCs 151–67
Statistisches Bundesamt 229, 240

273

Index

Stattin, H. 61
Steele, H. and M. 52, 60, 62, 66, 77
Stein, N. 87, 94
Stevenson, J. 172, 173, 181, 182
Stoll, L. 147
Stone, D. 218
Stone, F. 172, 184
Stone, M. H. 60, 62
Stonequist, E. V. 117, 134
Strange Situation test 51
Strayer, J. 91, 94
Sturge, C. 175, 184
Sudhalter, V. 37, 42, 45
Suess, D. 78
Sunday school 221
Sweden
   school-age childcare 225–8
   see also European Union
Swedish Institute 225, 241
Sweeting, H. 190, 206

Target, M. 60, 176, 184
Tashakkori, A. 64, 78
Tasker, F. L. 193, 206
Taylor, D. C. 29, 45
Taylor, E. 31, 46
teachers
   professionalism 98
   responsiveness to parents' views 104–6
   staffing innovations in CTCs 151–67
temperament 52
Tesla, C. 93
Tew, B. J. 55, 62
theory of mind tasks in childhood 82, 84
Thomas, A. 50, 52, 60, 172, 181
Thomas, H. 152, 168
Thomas, P. 6, 8
Thompson, A. E. 174, 182
Thompson, J. 41
Tizard, B. 3, 8, 29, 30, 31, 36, 40, 45, 53, 62, 63, 65, 67, 68, 69, 70, 71, 73, 78, 79, 81, 84, 91, 94, 97, 98, 99, 100, 101, 105, 110, 111, 126, 127, 130, 134, 136, 138, 145, 147, 148
Tizard, J. 45, 63, 65, 68, 79, 109, 110, 170, 173, 179, 182, 183
Trevelyan, J. 222, 241
Tripp, J. 192, 202
Troyna, B. 127, 134
Tsai, S. 144, 148
tuberous sclerosis 34, 39–40
Tulving, E. 40, 45
Turk, J. 35, 45

Udwin, O. 37, 45
UN Convention on the Rights of the Child 185–6, 188, 200
Uncertainty Principle 47
United Kingdom
   early childcare services 250–1
   see also European Union
Unzer, L. 78
Utting, D. 187, 206

van der Werf, S. 46
Van IJzendoorn, M. H. 52, 62
van Praag, H. M. 31, 42
Vargha-Khadem, F. 33, 46
Vass, J. 96, 110
Veltman, M. 108, 110, 140, 141, 145, 148
Vietze, P. M. 42
Visram, R. 114, 126, 134
Vizard, E. 62
Vygotsky, L. S. 85, 94

Wadsworth, J. 204
Wadsworth, M. E. J. 189, 204
Walberg, H. J. 144, 148
Walker, J. 191, 192, 205
Wall, S. 77
Walzak, Y. 189, 197, 206
Wang, P. P. 37, 41
Warwick, H. 190, 203
Wasoff, F. 203
Waterhouse, L. 54, 62

Waters, E. 74, 77, 80
Wechsler Intelligence Scale for
    Children – Revised 55
Wechsler Pre-school and Primary
    Scale of Intelligence 55
Weisner, T. 255, 258
Weiss, C. 4, 6, 8
Weiss, R. S. 189, 206
Wellings, R. 204
Wellman, H. M. 82, 83, 92, 94
West, P. 190, 206
White, L. 194, 196, 206
White, P. H. 118, 134
Whitmore, K. 30, 45, 179, 184
Wicks, M. 187, 204
Wikeley, F. 96, 103, 105, 110
Williams syndrome 37
Wilson, A. 116, 135
Wilson, J. 46
Wilson, M. S. 93
Wilson, R. S. 48, 62
Wing, C. S. 83, 85, 94

Wippman, J. 74, 80
WISC-R 55
Witting, B. 51, 59
Woerner, W. 51, 60
Wolf, D. 94
Wolf-Schein, E. G. 45
Wolff, P. H. 37, 46
Woodhead, M. 255, 258
Woodhouse, G. 146, 148
Woods, B. T. 33, 46
WPPSI 55

Yarrow, L. J. 73, 80
Young, L. 133
Young, R. J. C. 112, 114, 135
Youngblade, L. 83, 84, 93, 95
Yule, W. 30, 31, 32, 35, 36, 37, 39,
    42, 43, 44, 45, 46, 55, 62, 171,
    175, 179, 183
Yuzda, E. 41

Zack, N. 114, 135